Off the
Beaten Path®

washington

Help Us Keep This Guide Up to Date

Every effort has been made by the author and editors to make this guide as accurate and useful as possible. However, many changes can occur after a guide is published—establishments close, phone numbers change, hiking trails are rerouted, facilities come under new management, etc.

We would love to hear from you concerning your experiences with this guide and how you feel it could be improved and be kept up to date. While we may not be able to respond to all comments and suggestions, we'll take them to heart, and we'll make certain to share them with the author. Please send your comments and suggestions to the following address:

The Globe Pequot Press
Reader Response/Editorial Department
P.O. Box 480
Guilford, CT 06437

Or you may e-mail us at: editorial@GlobePequot.com

Thanks for your input, and happy travels!

INSIDERS'GUIDE®

OFF THE BEATEN PATH® SERIES

Off the Beaten Path®

SEVENTH EDITION

washington

A GUIDE TO UNIQUE PLACES

MYRNA OAKLEY

INSIDERS'GUIDE®

GUILFORD, CONNECTICUT
AN IMPRINT OF THE GLOBE PEQUOT PRESS

The prices, rates, and hours listed in this guidebook
were confirmed at press time. We recommend,
however, that you call establishments to obtain
current information before traveling.

To buy books in quantity for corporate use
or incentives, call **(800) 962–0973**
or e-mail **premiums@GlobePequot.com.**

INSIDERS' GUIDE®

Copyright © 1993, 1996, 1999, 2001, 2003, 2005, 2007 Morris Book Publishing, LLC

Text design by Linda Loiewski
Maps by Equator Graphics © Morris Book Publishing, LLC
Illustrations by Carole Drong
Spot photography throughout © Miles Ertman/Masterfile

ISSN: 1540-8442
ISBN-13: 978-0-7627-4216-5
ISBN-10: 0-7627-4216-X

Manufactured in the United States of America
Seventh Edition/First Printing

To David and Sandra,

our family hosts at Hood Canal

with its great views of the water, the tides, and of morning sunrises.

To friends and family far and wide who enjoy

discovering and rediscovering the nooks and crannies

of the Pacific Northwest.

To all those friendly and welcoming innkeepers who, throughout the years,

always keep the lights on for travelers.

And, especially, to Suzanne Kort and Todd Litman,

who traveled the state's byways in the early 1990s

to develop the first edition of *Washington Off the Beaten Path.*

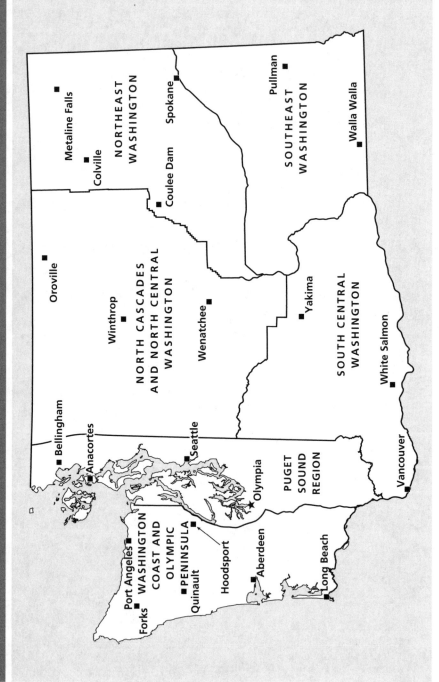

Contents

Acknowledgments

Oceans of thanks to dozens of folks who offered helpful information to update their sections of the state—restaurant, cafe, bakery, and coffee shop owners; museums and historic sites staff and volunteers; shopkeepers and innkeepers; staff and volunteers at visitor information centers throughout the state; and regional history gurus for information on train depot and historic hotel renovations, on ghost towns, and on rails-to-trails projects.

A special note of thanks to:

- Staff members at Fort Clatsop National Memorial (www.nps.gov/focl) in Astoria for providing information sources on the Lewis & Clark Bicentennial.
- Michael Miller of Lion's Paw Inn Bed & Breakfast and Susie Goldsmith and Bill Verner of Boreas Bed & Breakfast Inn for updates on the Ilwaco, Seaview, and Long Beach areas.
- Louann Yager of the Port Angeles Visitor Center and Diane Schostack of the Forks Visitor Center for updates on the northern Olympic Peninsula.
- Gig Harbor innkeeper Meri Fountain of Fountains Bed & Breakfast for updates on the Gig Harbor–Fox Island areas.
- Tacoma innkeeper Cheryl Teifke of DeVoe Mansion Bed & Breakfast for updates on Tacoma-area museums, inns, and eateries.
- Innkeeper Donna McAllister of Schnauzer Crossing Bed & Breakfast for helpful updates on Bellingham attractions and eateries; and Margaret Davidson Frey of Anacortes for updates on shops, eateries, and lodgings. Judy Atherton of Skagit General Store for updating the historic Newhalem and Ross Lake areas of the North Cascades and Curran Cosgrove of the Washington Department of Fish and Wildlife for help with information and maps on the Great Washington State Birding Trail Cascades loop.
- Leavenworth innkeepers Monty and Karen Turner of the Run of the River Bed & Breakfast for updating their Central Cascades area.
- Innkeeper Mary Pittis of Iron Horse Inn Bed & Breakfast, Cle Elum; innkeeper Marcia Williams of Wren's Nest Bed & Breakfast, Ellensburg; and Shari Dover of Yakima, for updates on attractions and eateries in their areas.
- Doris Martin of the Kettle Falls Visitor Information Center for help with updating eateries in the far northeast corner of the state.

- Leslee Miller of Premier Alpacas Ranch and Guest House in Uniontown; Janet Barstow of Ray Chatters Printing Museum in Palouse; and Ann McCann of the Dayton Visitor Information Center for their helpful updates on the far southeast corner of the state.
- And an extra special note of thanks to the dedicated copy editors, editors, and staff at Globe Pequot who have the mind-boggling task of overseeing the revisions for all fifty states for the Off the Beaten Path series.

Introduction

Washington is a generous state, offering adventures for many types of travelers. You'll find dense evergreen forests, fertile farmlands, dynamic cities, and foggy islands as well as secluded windblown beaches, waterside walks, small-town cafes and coffee shops, and tiny hamlets, particularly in the far southeast and far northeast corners. There are many well-known tourist destinations, but the real fun begins when you explore off the beaten path.

Because of my interest in cozy bed-and-breakfast inns and great public gardens along with a longtime interest in historic downtown and neighborhood renovations, historic building renovations, rails-to-trails projects, and live local theater, readers will find these subjects expanded in this, the seventh edition of *Washington Off the Beaten Path*.

Using This Guide to Plan Great Trips

As you choose months and dates for your trips, plan around the Pacific Northwest's four distinct seasons: The busiest times for most destinations west of the Cascade Mountains, particularly around Puget Sound waters and the San Juan Islands, will be during July and August. Major freeways and all ferries will carry more traffic; waiting lines at ferry terminals also will be longer. If you want less traffic and fewer crowds, plan to travel midweek or travel early spring, April through June, and early autumn, September through October. Autumn in the Northwest is sunny and warm, with fall colors especially fine in October.

If you enjoy snow and winter sports, plan treks to the Cascade Mountain regions from late November through February. Be prepared with a sturdy vehicle, all-weather tires, extra-warm clothing, emergency kits, and plenty of snacks and beverages. To start your research you'll find helpful telephone numbers and Web sites in the Skiing Washington sidebar in the "Mountain Passes, Valleys, and Canyons" section of the North Cascades and North Central Washington chapter.

The eastern half of the Evergreen State offers crisp, cold winters and hot, dry summers. Travel early spring and fall for some of the best weather east of the Cascade Mountains. Eastern Washington also offers fewer crowds, quieter byways, and many pleasant, undiscovered destinations. You'll encounter friendly locals who are glad to help travelers with directions. *Note:* Plan for long distances between services in the eastern regions—gas up often and load up on picnic foods, snacks, beverages, and ice for the cooler.

To help plan your accommodations, within each chapter you will find lodging suggestions including cozy bed-and-breakfast inns, with telephone numbers and, usually, a Web site as well. Nearly all establishments these days are smoke free and do not allow pets. Leashed pets are usually allowed at state campgrounds and RV parks. See Places to Stay at the end of each chapter for selected RV parks and larger motor inns. Call ahead to ask specific questions and to make lodging reservations. See Places to Eat at the end of each chapter for cafes, coffee shops, and casual restaurants in selected towns and cities. You will also find eateries mentioned within each chapter.

A FEW MORE IDEAS AND SUGGESTIONS

I suggest that you maintain a flexible schedule as much as possible when traveling through the Evergreen State. Allow plenty of time and leave room for interesting happenings and conversation with local folks.

Also, even with the best research, you may find a place or attraction closed or discover that hours or telephone numbers have changed. If this occurs, stop at the nearest visitor information center, where the staff and volunteers can offer current information and suggestions. Often these centers are open weekends during summer months. Additionally, local folks are usually willing to offer travelers information, ideas, and directions.

If you're traveling with youngsters, encourage them to write notes to new folks they meet on your travels and to collect information on historic sights,

A Word about . . .

Pets: Except for state campgrounds and RV parks, where leashed pets are usually allowed, assume that most places do not allow pets on the premises.

Eateries: Hours tend to range from longer in the summer to shorter in the winter, especially in the San Juan Islands and the farther off the beaten path you travel from the larger cities. If in doubt, stop at visitor information centers to check on the local eateries.

Web sites: Generally, assume that information you obtain from travel-related Web sites is not necessarily current unless you see a paragraph or sentence that clearly states frequent updates. Outdated information can languish on these sites for years. If you're unsure, e-mail the Web master with specific questions.

Crossing the U.S.–Canadian border: Expect tighter security at all customs crossings across the northern border of Washington State, and take proof of U.S. citizenship such as a voter's registration card. Carrying only a driver's license is not sufficient. No firearms are allowed into Canada. For pets, have proof of recent rabies vaccination.

attractions, geology and natural history, and whatever else tickles their fancies. In this way you can help the kids become savvy travelers who appreciate making new friends and who care for preserving towns and cities as well as respecting the great outdoors.

TRAVEL STYLES AND INTERESTS

You say you and your family are rugged outdoors types? You like four-season recreation info? Go to the chapter on North Cascades and North Central Washington. For assistance with serious backcountry and wilderness trip planning, contact the Outdoor Recreation Information Center in the REI flagship store in Seattle (206–470–4060).

Or perhaps you and your family are water-loving types. You like salt water, surf sounds, and watching the incoming and outgoing tides. Go to the chapters on Washington Coast and Olympic Peninsula and on Puget Sound and the Islands.

If you have a hankerin' to pull on the Levi's, cowboy or cowgirl boots, and a wide-brimmed hat or you want to see a rodeo or ride a horse, browse Northeast Washington, Southeast Washington, and the Okanogan Valley region in the North Cascades and North Central Washington chapter.

What if you want to explore the routes taken by the Lewis and Clark expedition and check on activities following the bicentennial from 2002 through 2006? Go to the chapters on the Washington Coast and Olympic Peninsula, South Central Washington, and Southeast Washington.

A FINAL WORD

May your travels in the Pacific Northwest be filled with great adventures, much serendipity, many new vistas, and new friends from the diverse cultures that live and work in this vast region of waters, islands, mountains, rolling farmlands, deep gorges, and high deserts. Please let us know of new places you find that you'd like to recommend for the next edition of *Washington Off the Beaten Path*.

Fast Facts about Washington

- **Population:** 6.2 million
- **Area:** 65,625 square miles
- **Capital:** Olympia, located in Thurston County south of Seattle and at the southernmost tip of Puget Sound
- **Number of counties:** thirty-nine
- **County names, from west to east:** Wahkiakum, Pacific, Grays Harbor,

Jefferson, Clallam, Mason, Thurston, Lewis, Cowlitz, Clark, Skamania, Pierce, King, Kitsap, Snohomish, Island, San Juan, Skagit, Whatcom, Okanogan, Chelan, Kittitas, Yakima, Klickitat, Benton, Grant, Douglas, Ferry, Lincoln, Adams, Franklin, Walla Walla, Columbia, Asotin, Garfield, Whitman, Spokane, Stevens, Pend Oreille

- **Highest point:** Mount Rainier (14,411 feet), located southeast of Tacoma
- **Largest county:** Okanogan
- **Least populated county:** Ferry (under 8,000)
- **Major body of water:** Puget Sound, which carves deep into the northwest section of the state from the Strait of Juan de Fuca south to Olympia
- **Major rivers:** Columbia River/Lake Roosevelt Reservoir east of the Cascade Mountain Range; Snake River, which flows west from the Idaho border and empties into the Columbia River at Pasco–Kennewick
- **Largest natural lake:** Lake Chelan, which extends some 55 miles into mountain wilderness areas from Chelan to Stehekin in the North Cascades
- **Nickname**: Evergreen State
- **State animal:** Roosevelt elk
- **State bird:** goldfinch
- **State fish:** steelhead trout
- **State flower:** coastal rhododendron
- **State gem/rock:** petrified wood
- **State tree:** western hemlock

Washington Coast and Olympic Peninsula

Washington's Pacific Ocean coastline stretches from the Strait of Juan de Fuca in the north to the mouth of the Columbia River in the south. It's a region of contrasts. The Olympic Peninsula's ocean shoreline is rugged, with steep cliffs and rocky formations sculpted by wave and wind. Farther south are gentle, sandy beaches lined with summer cottages and tourist communities. Grays Harbor and Willapa Bay break up the coastline and create extensive inland wetlands that are important wildlife habitats. The Olympic Peninsula rain forest has the highest annual rainfall on the continental United States, yet the Dungeness Valley on the Strait of Juan de Fuca—near the community of Sequim—has the lowest precipitation on the coast north of California and Oregon.

The snow-covered peaks of the Olympic Mountains provide a stunning backdrop to beaches, forests, and valleys in the region.

Most of the coastal area is thickly forested and includes some of the world's largest living trees. Many local families have been loggers, fishermen, or mill workers for three or four generations. In the coastal and inland areas of the Olympic Peninsula are several small Indian reservations including the Makah, the Jamestown S'Klallam, the Lower Elwah, the

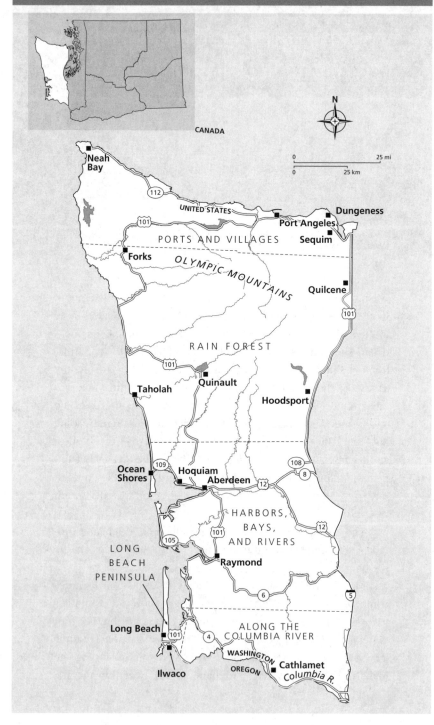

WASHINGTON COAST AND OLYMPIC PENINSULA

CANADA

N

0 _____ 25 mi
0 _____ 25 km

Neah Bay

112

UNITED STATES

101

Dungeness

Port Angeles

PORTS AND VILLAGES

Sequim

Forks

OLYMPIC MOUNTAINS

Quilcene

101

RAIN FOREST

101

Taholah

Quinault

Hoodsport

109

108

8

Ocean Shores

Hoquiam

Aberdeen

12

HARBORS, BAYS, AND RIVERS

101

12

LONG BEACH PENINSULA

105

Raymond

6

5

ALONG THE COLUMBIA RIVER

Long Beach

101

4

WASHINGTON

OREGON

Cathlamet

Columbia R.

Ilwaco

Quileute, the Hoh, the Quinault, the Shoalwater, and the Skokomish. Travelers can visit local historical museums, walk secluded beaches, learn about the region's unique natural environment, or enjoy busy beachside tourist areas. Outdoor activities include hiking, bicycling, fishing, birding, and beachcombing. Bring along rain gear and good walking shoes or boots so that you and the kids can take advantage of the many trails and beaches that are accessible most of the year.

WASHINGTON COAST'S TOP HITS

Aberdeen Museum of History
Aberdeen

Arthur D. Feiro Marine Laboratory
Port Angeles

Boreas Bed & Breakfast Inn
Long Beach

Dennis Company
Raymond

Dungeness National Wildlife Refuge
Sequim

Grays Harbor Historical Seaport
Grays Harbor

**Groveland Cottage
Bed and Breakfast Inn**
Sequim

**Hoh River Visitor Center
and Nature Trail**
Forks

**Hood Canal Oysterfest &
Seafood Festival**
Shelton

Hurricane Ridge
Port Angeles

Ilwaco Heritage Museum
Ilwaco

Klipsan Beach Cottages
Ocean Park

Lake Quinault Resort
North Shore, Lake Quinault

Leadbetter Point State Park
Oysterville

Lewis and Clark Interpretive Center
Ilwaco

**Lewis and Clark National Wildlife
Refuge**
Skamokawa

Lion's Paw Inn Bed & Breakfast
Seaview

Lake Crescent Resort
Lake Crescent

Makah Museum
Neah Bay

Pacific County Historical Museum
South Bend

Puget Island
Cathlamet

Tokeland Hotel & Restaurant
Tokeland

Westport Maritime Museum
Westport

Willapa Bay Interpretive Center
Nahcotta

World Kite Museum and Hall of Fame
Long Beach

Ports and Villages

Fifteen miles west and north of Olympia on U.S. Highway 101, as you access the *Hood Canal* area, on the far northern horizon those craggy *Olympic Mountains* will come into view, unless obscured by clouds. You reach first the lumber town of *Shelton,* dominated by a lumber mill that sprawls along the waterfront. You can view the whole complex from the hilltop viewpoint adjacent to the huge sawmill wheel that stands as a monument to the lumber industry and a welcome to visitors who approach town from the south. A good place to start your exploration is at the Shelton Visitor Information Center, located in an old caboose on Railroad Avenue in front of the U.S. Post Office. Nearby, you can order a juicy hamburger or fresh seafood at *Big E's* (324 West Railroad Avenue; 360–426–2186). For quick snacks and great coffee and espresso in

Lavender Town U.S.A.

Sequim's rich soil and low rainfall along with warm temperatures have spawned a new agricultural industry. Waves of lavender plants from pale violet to deep purple grow on farms large and small in the Dungeness Valley. To see and sniff hundreds of varieties such as Provence, Grosso, and Munstead, plan to attend the annual *Lavender Festival* the third weekend of July. Enjoy a host of activities that includes farm tours, a street fair, great food, art shows, and music fests. See www.lavender festival.com for details, then come and enjoy visiting lavender farms and meeting their friendly owners. Find lavender plants for your gardens and stock up on lavender soaps, bath oils, and lotions for your senses.

Cedarbrook Herb & Lavender Farm
(360) 683–7733
www.lavenderfarms.com/cedarbrook

The Cutting Garden
and Farmhouse Gallery
(360) 681–3099
www.cuttinggarden.com

Jardin du Soleil Lavender
(360) 582–1185
www.jardindusoleil.com

Lost Mountain Lavender and
The Cottage Gifts
(360) 681–2782
www.lostmountainlavender.com

Olympic Lavender Farm
(360) 683–4475
www.olympiclavender.com

Purple Haze Lavender Farm
(360) 683–1714
www.purplehazelavender.com

Willow Lavender Farm and
The Weary Gardener
handmade body and soap products
(360) 452–7342
www.thewearygardener.com

FAVORITE ATTRACTIONS

Mouth of the Columbia River
(Fort Canby State Park, near Ilwaco)

Hurricane Ridge
Olympic National Park

Hoh Rain Forest
Olympic National Park

Makah Museum
Neah Bay

Shelton, check out **Urraco Coffee Roaster Company** at 628 South Cota Street (360–462–5282) and **Riverside Espresso** at 332 South First Street (360–426–3300).

At the corner of Railroad Avenue and Fifth Street, the **Mason County Historical Society Museum** (360–426–1020) offers exhibits of the region's logging and frontier past. Located in a library building constructed in 1914, the museum features family photographs, pioneer tools and artifacts, and a nineteenth-century schoolroom. The museum is open from noon to 5:00 P.M. Thursday through Sunday from June through September, and Thursday through Saturday from October through May. Stroll down Railroad Avenue and Cota Street to get a feel for the town and its eclectic antiques and secondhand shops.

From Shelton continue north on US 101 along the salty tidal waters of Hood Canal, passing through waterside communities such as Hoodsport, Lilliwaup, Brinnon, and Quilcene on your way to Port Townsend, Sequim, and Port Angeles in the northeasternmost section of the Olympic Peninsula.

A scenic spot that may entice you to stay overnight to explore the Hood Canal area is the **Glen Ayr Canal Resort** (360–877–9522) located about 4 miles north of Hoodsport at 25381 North US 101. Call the Johnson family and ask about the comfy motel rooms, suites, and RV sites with wide views of the tidal waters. Or, continue north on winding US 101 for 1½ miles and check out waterside RV sites at **Rest-a-While RV Park** (360–877–9474; www.restawhile .com). You can also order great-tasting seafood at **The Honey Bee Snack Shack,** open weekends on the park grounds. Or, continue north another 10 miles to Eldon and hunker down at the **Hungry Bear Restaurant**, a longtime favorite of the locals.

The towering peaks of the Olympic Mountains shelter the northernmost Dungeness Valley from the copious rainfall of the rest of the region, making it the "banana belt" of the Northwest coast.

The town of **Sequim** (www.cityofsequim.com) is the commercial center of the valley and a good base from which to explore this scenic region. For an overnight stay on a secluded hilltop, call the **Greywolf Inn Bed-and-**

Breakfast (395 Keeler Road; 360–683–5889), which offers hospitality in a rural setting outside town.

For those who would like to be closer to the water, check out *Juan de Fuca Cottages* (182 Marine Drive; 360–683–4433; www.juandefuca.com), where there are six cozy cottages with kitchens and wide-angle views of the strait. You could also call *Dungeness Bay Motel* (140 Marine Drive; 888–683–3013; www.dungenessbay.com) and ask about their five comfy units with great water views.

Just west of the Sequim city limits at the end of Hendrickson Road is the *Dungeness River Railroad Bridge Park,* a scenic spot with nature trails to the river. On another excursion take Taylor Cut-off Road south from US 101 toward the mountains to reach *Lost Mountain Winery* at 3174 Lost Mountain Road. The small facility currently produces approximately 1,000 cases per year of hearty Italian-style reds, several of which have won local awards. The winery is open daily from 11:00 A.M. to 5:00 P.M. in summer and by appointment the rest of the year. Call the winery at (360) 683–5229, or visit Web sites www .lostmountain.com and www.northsoundwineries.com.

You'll find a delightful place to eat lunch at *Petals Garden Cafe* at *Cedarbrook Herb & Lavender Farm* (1345 South Sequim Avenue; 360–683–4541). The twelve-acre farm planted in aromatic herbs and native plants is open year-round except for January and February. You can purchase fresh flowers, lavender plants, dried herbs, herb vinegars, dried flower bouquets and wreaths, garlic ropes, and herb sachets. Lavender lovers can stop at *Purple Haze Lavender Farm* (180 Bell Bottom Lane; 360–683–1714) to inspect a colorful display garden, collect a bouquet from the U-pick field of lavender plants, and browse a nice selection of lavender products during the summer season. Open Thursday through Sunday, 10:00 A.M. to 4:00 P.M.

To explore the historic community of *Dungeness,* head north from US 101 on Sequim–Dungeness Way in downtown Sequim. Dungeness is old by Washington State standards, named in 1792 by British explorer Captain George Vancouver.

Charles Seal established the Dungeness Trading Company in the 1890s and built a large country farmhouse with the proceeds. Simone Nichols has renovated Seal's home into *Groveland Cottage Bed and Breakfast Inn* (4861 Sequim–Dungeness Way; 360–683–3565; www.northolympic.com/groveland). Guests sleep in cozy rooms on the second floor and wake up to views of the Olympic Mountains and the inn's gardens. A delicious breakfast is served in the dining room on the main floor.

In the town of Dungeness, you'll see the historic *Dungeness Schoolhouse,* built in 1892 and used to educate local children until 1955, as well as several turn-of-the-century homes amid fields, creeks, and wetlands. Sequim–Dungeness Way ends near Cline Spit and at the ever-popular ***Three Crabs Restaurant*** (360–683–4264), known for its lunch and dinner seafood specialties, such as Dungeness cracked crab, smoked salmon, oysters supreme, almond red snapper, and halibut. In the downtown Sequim area, try ***Oak Table Cafe*** at 292 West Bell Avenue (360–683–2179) for waist-bulging breakfasts; ***Cafe Cafe Coffee House*** at 755 West Washington Street (360–681–3132) for homemade soups, salads, fruit smoothies, awesome espresso, and desserts; ***The Buzz Coffee Shop*** at 128 North Sequim Avenue (360–683–2503); and Petals Garden Cafe for tasty gourmet lunches in a garden setting.

Golf buffs can call ahead to plan a round of nine or eighteen holes at ***Dungeness Golf & Country Club,*** located at 1965 Woodcock Road, Sequim (360–683–6344). From several fairways and greens, you can also enjoy views of the Olympic Mountains to the south.

A fun place to visit near Dungeness is the ***Olympic Game Farm*** at 1423 Ward Road (360–683–4295 or 800–778–4295; www.olygamefarm.com). Guided walking tours in summer or drive-through tours year-round will put you in the company of four-legged stars. Walt Disney Studios has employed farm residents, including grizzlies and wolves, in more than eighty wildlife productions. Many animals you'll see there, from Siberian tigers and African lions to North American timber wolves and bison, are on the endangered species list. Snacks are available for you as well as for the animals. The game farm opens daily at 9:00 A.M.

The ***Dungeness National Wildlife Refuge,*** located west of the game farm, offers an exhilarating immersion in an uncaged wilderness. Spring and fall are the best times to visit, when thousands of waterbirds make their annual migrations. From the parking lot you can take an easy ¼-mile hike to a viewpoint overlooking ***Dungeness Spit,*** one of the nation's largest natural sand hooks. To explore the spit, hardy and well-equipped hikers can follow the 5½-mile trail through the forest and down the beach. On the west side, you'll experience the roar of incoming waves; on the east, the quiet of a sheltered bay. Keep an eye out for playful harbor seals bobbing about as they fish and frolic offshore. The last half mile of the spit, beyond the ***New Dungeness Lighthouse,*** is closed to the public to ensure protection of the harbor seal adults and pups that reside there. The lighthouse, built in 1857 and automated in 1937, is the oldest one north of the Columbia River. The entrance fee to the refuge is $3.00 per family. For more information about hiking out on the Dungeness Spit and touring the lighthouse, call (360) 457–8451, or visit www.new dungenesslighthouse.com.

The best way to go through the Dungeness Valley between Sequim and Port Angeles is on the ***Old Olympic Highway.*** This pleasant, less-traveled route through green farmlands offers great views of the mountains rising to the south. Those yearning for luxurious lodgings and a gourmet breakfast in the midst of all this natural beauty could arrange to stay at **Domaine Madeleine Bed & Breakfast Inn** (146 Wildflower Lane, Port Angeles; 360–457–4174; www.domainemadeleine.com), a contemporary home situated on a bluff above the Strait of Juan de Fuca. Three of the four guest rooms have whirlpool tubs for two, and guests can wander five acres of grounds and gardens or cozy up in the living room near the huge basalt fireplace. The inn is about 5½ miles west of Sequim, a mile off the Old Olympic Highway.

For a different perspective, turn south on Deer Park Road (3 miles east of Port Angeles) for a winding 19-mile climb over the forest-covered slopes of Blue Mountain to **Deer Park** in Olympic National Park. Here you'll find an alpine campground and ranger station (open in summer only) and the trailhead to scenic hikes overlooking the Dungeness Valley, Port Angeles, and the Strait of Juan de Fuca.

Port Angeles (www.portangeles.net), the largest city on the Olympic Peninsula, is dominated by its busy waterfront. This deepwater harbor is a port of call for international shipping, a center of ocean fishing, a major Coast Guard station, and terminus for Black Ball's *Coho* ferry, which makes daily trips to Victoria, British Columbia, Canada. The City Pier, 1 block east of the ferry terminal, is a good starting point for your explorations. There you'll find a small park, a viewing tower, a berth for the 210-foot Coast Guard cutter *Active,* a public marine laboratory, and plenty of nearby restaurants and shops. The **Arthur D. Feiro Marine Laboratory** (360–417–6254), located on the City Pier, is the place to see and even touch the remarkable sea creatures that live on Washington's coast. You and the kids can watch the graceful movements of an octopus, stroke a stuffed sea lion, and handle a variety of living marine animals in the touch-tanks. Friendly volunteers answer questions and tell visitors about the Northwest region's marine ecology. The laboratory is open for a small admission fee from 10:00 A.M. to 8:00 P.M. daily, mid-June to Labor Day, and from noon to 4:00 P.M. on weekends the rest of the year.

To explore along the lively Port Angeles waterfront, pick up a walking-tour brochure at the visitor center (located next to the City Pier). The Waterfront Trail, which follows the harbor shore east along Hollywood Beach, is ideal for walking or bicycling. You can also bicycle west to **Ediz Hook,** the natural sand spit that forms the Port Angeles harbor. Bikes are available for rent at **Sound Bikes and Kayaks** (120 East Front Street; 360–457–1240; www.sound bikeskayaks.com). Not into biking today? Well, pop into **Captain T's,** located at 124 West Railroad Avenue (360–452–6549) for railroad-related T-shirts; or **Pacific Rim Hobby Shop,** 138 West Railroad Avenue (360–457–0794), for more railroad souvenirs. Then, for good eats in Port Angeles, try *Elizabeth & Co. Coffeehouse and Bakery* at 106 East First Street (360–452–5222) and, just across the street, a local breakfast favorite, *First Street Haven Cafe. Itty Bitty Buzz Coffee Shop* at 110 East First Street (360–565–8080) and *Olympic Bagel Company* at 802 East First Street (360–452–9100) offer awesome espresso and freshly baked gourmet bagels.

If you enjoy watching the waterfront activities, you could call *Ocean Crest Bed & Breakfast* (402 South M Street; 877–413–2169; www.northolympic.com/ oceancrest), a large, comfortable home that offers panoramic views of the harbor, the strait, and Vancouver Island beyond. Romantics might enjoy the old-world ambience of ca. 1910 *Tudor Inn Bed & Breakfast* (360–452–3138; www.tudorinn.com), located a few blocks from the ferry terminal. The innkeeper is happy to help guests plan day trips and other recreational activities. Visitors can also contact the innkeepers at *Five SeaSuns Bed & Breakfast,* located at 1006 South Lincoln Street (360–452–8248; www.seasuns.com). Guests find sumptuous accommodations and grounds that feature a pond, an elegant pergola for outdoor sitting, and beds and planters overflowing with colorful flowers.

While in the Sequim–Port Angeles area, consider an evening with live local theater. To see what's currently playing, from Broadway musicals to comedy and drama, contact the *Port Angeles Light Opera Association* (360–457–5630), *Port Angeles Community Playhouse* (360–452–6651), and *Olympic Theatre Arts* in Sequim (360–683–7326; www.olympictheatrearts.org). Don't miss the chance to meet these enthusiastic local performers—it's great fun.

Before continuing west from Port Angeles toward the far reaches of the Olympic Peninsula or east to Hood Canal, Port Townsend, or on to the Seattle metropolitan area, you and your travel mates can explore another adventurous option. Park your vehicle at the ferry dock on Railroad Avenue and hop aboard the **Victoria Express *Ferry*** (800–633–1589 or 360–472–8088; www.victoria express.com) that runs from Port Angeles across the Strait of Juan de Fuca to Victoria, British Columbia. The provincial capital, deliciously British in flavor, nestles at the southern tip of Vancouver Island, Canada.

Hurricane Ridge, accessible by an 18-mile paved road from Port Angeles, offers not only panoramic views of the Strait of Juan de Fuca and its Canadian islands to the north but also the alpine meadows and glacier-covered peaks of the Olympic Mountains to the south. During the summer park rangers lead walks and answer visitors' questions. The Hurricane Ridge Lodge, open 10:00 A.M. to 5:00 P.M. during summer and winter, includes a museum, deli, and gift shop. Restrooms are open year-round. Camping is available in the Heart o' the Hills campground, 5 miles from the lodge on the Hurricane Ridge Road. Campfire programs are given nightly in the campground amphitheater from

Quick Guide to Victoria, British Columbia, and Vancouver Island

Getting to Victoria from Port Angeles is easy. Park at the Port Angeles ferry terminal and either hop aboard the *Victoria Express* Ferry (800–633–1589; www.victoriaexpress .com) as a day foot passenger, or, if you want to take your vehicle and explore more of Vancouver Island, board The M.V. *Coho* ferry for its ninety-five-minute cruise across the Strait of Juan de Fuca (360–457–4491; www.ferrytovictoria.com).

Easy walking and seeing in Victoria's scenic Inner Harbour area: You can visit the ivy-covered Empress Hotel; the stately Parliament buildings and landscaped grounds, which sparkle with thousands of lights after dark; and the Provincial Museum (don't miss it). You can also view the boat activity from sitting areas along the Inner Harbour walkways and sample a plethora of cafes, coffeehouses, boutiques, and tea houses.

Visitor information: Contact Victoria Travel Info-Centre (250–953–2003) and Tourism British Columbia (800–435–5622; www.hellobc.com).

Other places to explore near Victoria: Don't miss the Butchart Gardens north of Victoria (plan summer visits during midweek to avoid the crowds). Also within short driving distance are Brentwood Bay and Saanich Inlet (try Seahorses Café near Mill Bay ferry landing); Sooke (good hiking, eateries, and shops); and Port Alberni (fishing and forestry village).

North to the seaside community of Sidney: For eats on the waterfront at Port Sidney Marina, try Rum Runner Pub (250–656–5643); Boondocks Café & Pub on First Street (250–656–4088); and Fish on Fifth Café on Fifth Street (250–656–4022).

For overnight lodging check Best Western Emerald Isle Inn (800–315–3377) and Miraloma Inn on the Cove (877–956–6622).

From Sidney you can visit the San Juan Islands via international ferry sailing on Washington State Ferries (www.wsdot.wa.gov/ferries). Check with Friday Harbor Visitor Information (360–378–5240; www.sanjuanisland.org and www.guideto sanjuans.com).

U.S. and Canadian customs: Carry a minimum of two pieces of identification, including picture ID and voter's registration card, passport, or birth certificate. For pets, proof of rabies vaccination is necessary. Firearms are not allowed into Canada.

July 1 through Labor Day. For more information stop by the Olympic National Park Visitor Center in Port Angeles at 600 East Park Avenue (360–565–3130), open daily from 8:30 A.M. to 5:30 P.M. July 1 through September 30 and 9:00 A.M. to 4:00 P.M. the rest of the year. A helpful Web site is www.nps.gov/olym.

Nine miles west of Port Angeles, you can turn south on Olympic Hot Springs Road to explore the scenic *Elwha River Valley.* Although the lower portion of the river is now dammed, there is still much to see. Stop at the Elwha Ranger Station for information on hiking trails and the Olympic Hot Springs, or take a raft trip down the scenic Elwha River. Contact **Olympic Raft and Kayak** (123 Lake Aldwell Road; 360–452–1443). Ask about rafting trips on the Elwha River and sea kayaking on Lake Aldwell. Also see www.raftandkayak .com for other seasonal trips.

Continuing west of Port Angeles, you can either follow US 101 inland or take Highway 112 along the coastline. If you opt for the inland route, you'll find **Lake Crescent** set in the surrounding forests. The lake is 10 miles long and more than a mile wide. Much of the area around the lake is preserved as part of the Olympic National Park. A right turn onto East Beach Road at Lake Crescent's eastern edge takes you along a scenic, winding lakeside road to **Log Cabin Resort** (3183 East Beach Road; 360–928–3325). Established in 1895 on the lake's isolated north shore, the "sunny side of the lake," the resort, with its unpretentious cabins, RV sites, general store, and restaurant, provides a secluded, friendly atmosphere. Be sure to stop by the Soda Jerk Cafe for an espresso or a thick milkshake. Guests can rent rowboats or canoes to enjoy fishing or relaxing on the lake. You can hike among giant old-growth cedars and firs or rent mountain bikes to explore forest trails. Lace up the hiking boots, grab the jackets, pack bottles of water, and head out on the 4-mile Spruce Division Railroad Trail, originally a railroad grade built during World War I to help extract spruce logs for airplane production. The trek is a great way to experience the lake's north shore.

A visitor information center is located on the lake's south shore, just off US 101, in a log cabin built in 1905 by Olympic forest ranger Chris Morgenroth. From the cabin a ¾-mile trail follows a level, gravel path through the forest that ends with an uphill climb to 90-foot **Marymere Falls,** offering visitors a pleasant excursion through the rain forest. **Lake Crescent Lodge** (416 Lake Crescent Road; 360–928–3211; www.lakecrescentlodge.com), just west of the visitor center, is a classic old resort that has changed little since it was built on the lakeshore in 1916. While staying here in 1937, President Franklin Roosevelt decided to create Olympic National Park in order to preserve this area's beauty for future generations. Visitors enjoy lodge rooms or cottages, boating, fishing, and nature hikes, in addition to lounging under the shade of a lakeside tree. In the resort's restaurant you can watch the sunset over the lake while savoring a fine dinner.

The **Olympic Park Institute,** located nearby at the historic **Rosemary Inn,** offers programs for children and adults on subjects ranging from creative writing to natural history and environmental ethics. The rustic resort, established on Lake Crescent in 1914, is considered an outstanding example of the Craftsman era of American architecture. For a calendar of upcoming classes,

Lake Crescent Lodge sunroom

contact the Olympic Park Institute, 111 Barnes Point Road (800–775–3720 or 360–928–3720; www.olympicparkinstitute.org).

You'll find forested campgrounds, boat rentals, and groceries at Fairholm on the western edge of Lake Crescent. Farther west on US 101, a 12-mile drive north on Sol Duc Road takes you to **Sol Duc Hot Springs Resort** (360–327–3583; www.northolympic.com/solduc). *Sol Duc* means "sparkling water" in the Quileute language. Visitors have been flocking to the healthful mineral waters at Sol Duc since a magnificent spa was first built at the site in 1912 (which, sadly, burned in 1916). The resort, open mid-April through the end of September, offers three large outdoor hot mineral pools, a freshwater heated swimming pool and poolside deli, a restaurant, massage therapy, a gift shop, groceries, RV hookups, and cabins. Camping, hiking trails, and naturalist programs are available at the **Sol Duc Campground** located nearby.

Take the Highway 112 turnoff at the junction west of Port Angeles if you and your travel mates hanker for more close-up views of the Olympic Peninsula's rugged northern coastline. Ten miles west of Port Angeles, turn on Camp Hayden Road to reach **Salt Creek Recreation Area,** a marine sanctuary with tidal pools full of waving sea anemones, gooseneck barnacles, coal-black mussels, and colorful starfish, as well as kelp beds and rocky islands offshore. Also nearby is Clallam County park and campground, which offers campsites, showers, and beach area. Continuing west on Highway 112, you may see a gray whale spouting offshore or, perhaps, a pod of orcas or a California sea lion swimming by. Watch for crowds of harbor seals relaxing on the small off-shore islands.

Continue west to **Neah Bay** or take the turnoff on Hoko-Ozette Road, just past the fishing village of Sekiu on Clallam Bay, to **Lake Ozette.** The lake, which is the largest natural body of freshwater in Washington State, is a great place to enjoy a canoe or rowboat. By boat you can explore miles of wild shoreline and secluded campsites not accessible by land. The 10-mile loop trail around the lake to the ocean beach makes a long day hike, or you can pack in food, water, and gear and stay overnight at secluded coastal campsites. The ranger station at the lake can provide tide tables and other important information you need before heading out on these potentially dangerous beach trails. The park offers interpretive programs in the summer as well as a pleasant twenty-two-site campground at the lake's north end.

Or contact **Lost Resort Campground** (20860 Hoko-Ozette Road, Clallam Bay; 360–963–2899); it's about ¼ mile from the ranger station. For even more civilized accommodations, contact **Winters Summer Bed & Breakfast** overlooking the Strait of Juan de Fuca at 16651 Highway 112, Clallam Bay; (360) 963–2264; www.northolympic.com/winters. It's open March through September.

For an easy day hike from Ozette, walk along the 3-mile boardwalk over coastal wetlands to Cape Alava, the site of an ancient Makah Indian fishing village that was buried by a mud slide 500 years ago and recently excavated. The well-preserved contents of the village, exposed by tidal action in the 1970s, are housed at the **Makah Museum** (360–645–2711), which is part of the Makah Cultural and Research Center in Neah Bay, on the Makah Indian Reservation, located about 60 miles west of Port Angeles. Owned and operated by the Makah Tribe, the museum tells the story of people who lived a rigorous life hunting whales, seals, and fish. The museum craft shop and other shops in

Olympic National Park

Olympic National Park was designated as a World Heritage Site by UNESCO on October 27, 1981, and contains the largest and best example of virgin temperate rain forest in the western hemisphere, the largest intact stand of coniferous forest in the contiguous forty-eight states, and the largest wild herd of Roosevelt elk. The park contains more than 1,200 types of plants, more than 300 species of birds, and more than 70 species of mammals. At least 8 kinds of plants and 18 kinds of animals are found only on the Olympic Peninsula and nowhere else in the world, including the Olympic marmot, chipmunk, and snow mole; the Flett's violet, Piper's bellflower, and Olympic Mountain daisy; and the Beardslee and Crescenti trout. The park's Mount Olympus is the wettest place in the continental United States, averaging an annual rainfall of 200 inches (16.7 feet). For natural history workshops and field seminars, contact Olympic Park Institute at (800) 775–3720, www.olympicparkinstitute.org.

town display the work of Neah Bay's resident Makah artists. The museum, which charges a small entrance fee, is located on Bayview Avenue and is open daily from 10:00 A.M. to 5:00 P.M.

Neah Bay is also the site of the annual Makah Days celebration, held the last weekend in August, which features traditional salmon bakes along with dancing and singing and canoe races.

There are several motels and small RV parks in Neah Bay—try *Cape Motel & RV Park* (360–645–2250) and *Tyee Motel* (360–645–2223).

Follow signs to the Makah Air Force Station, west of Neah Bay, and take the right-hand fork to reach the renovated ¾-mile trail to *Cape Flattery,* the northwesternmost point in the contiguous United States. Along the trail are several observation decks, and you'll find two picnic tables at trail's end. This rocky point has great views of Tatoosh Island, a half-mile-long volcanic outcropping that was once a favorite Makah retreat and is now home to a century-old lighthouse and nesting seabirds. This is a good place to get a close-up view of gray whales, which are often sighted feeding in the area during their annual migrations up the coast from May through June. Blustery Cape Flattery is well known for its average of 215 days of precipitation a year—be sure to bring rain gear and sturdy, waterproof boots.

To reach the more primitive and scenic ocean beaches, take the south fork at the Air Force Station. *Hobuck* and *Sooes Beaches* are located on the outer coast a few miles south of Neah Bay. From Makah Bay south the beaches are primitive and untouched by tourism. *Note:* Pack hearty snacks and beverages before leaving Port Angeles. The *Makah National Fish Hatchery,* located on a dirt road just south of Sooes Beach, is open daily year-round and welcomes visitors to its salmon-spawning facilities. When you're ready to continue your peninsula journey, return east on Highway 112 and take the turnoff south on Burnt Mountain Road, located 6 miles south of Clallam Bay, back to US 101.

Samuel Morse, Indian Agent

At the turn of the last century, no white man saw or knew more than Samuel Morse did of the Makah Indian tribal members who lived at the far northern tip of Washington's Olympic Peninsula. Morse served as the U.S. government's Indian agent at Neah Bay from 1897 to 1903. He was called on to perform marriages, settle disputes, and represent the Makah people to the federal government. You can read about Morse's interesting adventures with the Makah people in *Winter Brothers,* written by western author Ivan Doig.

Rain Forest

Burnt Mountain Road connects to US 101 at Sappho. A mile farther west you can take Pavel Road 2 miles to the *Sol Duc Salmon Hatchery.* The hatchery has a small interpretive center with colorful dioramas illustrating the life cycle of the salmon and the challenges facing the fisheries industries. Just north of the community of Forks, La Push Road connects US 101 with *Rialto Beach, Mora Campground* (part of Olympic National Park), and the Quileute native community of *La Push.* A short distance from the beach is *Manitou Lodge* (813 Kilmer Road, Forks; 360–374–6295; www.manitoulodge.com). Visitors to this rain-forest hideaway can take advantage of its proximity to forests, rivers, and unspoiled beaches to enjoy a variety of outdoor activities. Or just hole up with a good novel and relax by the huge lodge fireplace. Breakfast is served in the lodge's pleasant dining room. To get to Manitou Lodge, follow La Push Road 8 miles west of US 101, turn right onto Mora Road, and then right again onto Kilmer Road after crossing the single-lane bridge over the Sol Duc River. To bed down closer to the ocean, try *La Push Ocean Park Resort,* (330 Ocean Drive; 360–374–5267 or 800–487–1267; www.ocean-park.org), a Quileute tribal enterprise. Guests enjoy ocean views and access to miles of sandy and rocky beaches ideal for beachcombing. Whale watching is a popular activity during the spring months.

Located on US 101, *Forks* is primarily a logging town. The *Forks Timber Museum* (360–374–9663), located south of town, offers a comprehensive introduction to the history, economy, and culture of logging. Historical photographs, old logging equipment, and dioramas give a glimpse of what life was like in old logging camps and pioneer homes and how simple tools and hard work were employed to fell, transport, and cut timber into commercial lumber. The old-fashioned Fourth of July celebration in Forks highlights traditional logging skill competitions. For more information contact the Forks Chamber of Commerce (360) 374–2531 or (800) 443–6757; www.forkswa.com.

For good eats along US 101 in Forks, and to meet loggers and local folks, try *Forks Coffee Shop Cafe* (360–374–6769) near the Forks Motel. There you'll see old Forks newspapers, a couple of stuffed elk heads, and you'll be served by friendly waitstaff. You could also stop by another local favorite, the coffee bar at the *Thriftway Grocery,* at the south end of Forks on US 101. The *Smokehouse Restaurant* (360–374–6258) offers excellent smoked salmon and fresh seafood, as well as freshly baked pies. Others suggest the *Golden Gate Chinese Restaurant* (360–374–5528), which serves Szechuan-style entrees.

For a pleasant place to stay in Forks, call Susan and Bill Brager at *Miller Tree Inn Bed & Breakfast* (360–374–6806; www.millertreeinn.com), a 1917 homestead on three parklike acres located at 654 East Division Street, 6 blocks east of the only stoplight in town. At *Misty Valley Inn Bed & Breakfast,* at 194894 US 101 North (360–374–9389; www.mistyvalleyinn.com), guests enjoy pastoral views and gourmet breakfasts. If you'd like a cozy self-contained cottage right in Forks, contact *Shady Nook Cottages* (360–374–5497; www.shadynook cottage.com). *Note:* Unless you are camping or driving a self-contained RV and to avoid being disappointed during July, August, and September, be sure to arrange your overnight accommodations well ahead of visiting the Forks–Neah Bay area. If all facilities are full, call the Forks Visitor Information Center (360–374–2531 or 800–443–6757) for assistance.

Accessed 10 miles south of Forks, Upper Hoh Road follows the Hoh River Valley 18 miles east into one of the thickest parts of the rain forest. At the end of the road is the Olympic National Park's *Hoh River Visitor Center and Nature Trail.* This area receives more than 120 inches of rain annually, creating a lush multilayered environment highlighted with every shade of green imaginable. Even a short excursion through the Hall of Mosses Trail or along the Spruce Nature Trail offers an opportunity to experience the grandeur of the old-growth hemlock forest that once covered much of western Washington. To reach more secluded parts of the forest, you can walk a few miles toward the Blue Glacier, or hardier folks well prepared with food, water, and gear can take longer hikes to backcountry campsites such as Olympus (9 miles from the visitor center) or Glacier Meadows (an additional 8 miles). Contact the Hoh River Visitor Center at (360) 374–6925.

Located 7 miles south of Upper Hoh Road near milepost 172 is the *Hoh Humm Ranch* (171763 US 101; 360–374–5337), a working farm owned by the Huelsdonk family and situated on the banks of the Hoh River along with llamas, deer, goats, and cattle, plus the resident ranch cats. Two ranch-house guest rooms share a bath, and a hearty farm breakfast is included. You and the kids can fish from the riverbank or just relax and enjoy the scenery.

Folksy Forks

Folks in Forks, on the far north section of the Olympic Peninsula, say their community is so far off the beaten path that the one stoplight in the center of town is the only one within 160 miles. "People still chitchat in grocery lines here, rather than talking on their cell phones," says one local resident.

Storm Watching 101

The best times to head to coastal areas for watching Pacific storms are mid-November to mid-February. When big winter storms are forecast, they can unleash walloping wave action, towers of foamy spray, and hours of howling winds. Joining the gaggle of intrepid stormwatchers is easy—just dress in warm sweaters, windbreakers, boots, hats, and gloves, then grab the cameras and head to safe places along the coastline to have a gander. Check these travel sources for current information on the safest perches from which to watch Washington's coastal storms:

Cape Disappointment State Park at Ilwaco
(360) 642–3078
www.parks.wa.gov

Forks Visitor Information Center
(360) 374–2531 or (800) 443–6757
www.forkswa.com

Long Beach Peninsula Visitors Bureau
(360) 642–2400 or (800) 451–2542
www.funbeach.com

Westport/Grayland Visitor Information Center
(800) 345–6223

Westport Maritime Museum and Lighthouse
(360) 268–0078

The **Rain Forest Hostel** (360–374–2270; www.rainforesthostel.com), located 23 miles south of Forks on US 101, offers basic accommodations at a minimal price; reservations are required. It's a popular base for young adult travelers exploring the Olympic Peninsula, so part of the fun is meeting visitors from around the world.

US 101 curves west to follow the cliffs above *Ruby* and *Kalaloch* (pronounced CLAY-lock) *Beaches,* offering magnificent views of the Pacific Ocean. It's a rugged coastline littered with sea stacks and rock pillars where waves leap, foam, and crash against rocks, driftwood, and offshore islands. At night you'll see flashes from the lighthouse, which has provided a warning to coastal mariners since it was built in 1891 on distant Destruction Island.

At Queets the highway turns inland to Lake Quinault. This is one of the densest part of the rain forest. To experience this lush and green place, with its giant cedar, hemlock, and spruce trees, you can stay at *Lochaerie Resort Cabins* (638 North Shore Road, Amanda Park; 360–288–2215; www.lochaerie.com), located 4 miles east of US 101 on the lake's north shore. The six rustic cabins have changed little since they were built on the cliffs above the lake in the 1920s and 1930s. Each cabin has a fireplace, kitchen, and views of the lake—everything needed for a romantic sojourn. Guests can explore the driftwood-covered beach or hike nearby on rain-forest trails. Additional information about day hikes can be obtained from the Quinault Ranger Station (360–288–2525) and from the Quinault River Ranger Station (360–288–2444). Good eateries nearby suggested by locals include *Salmon House Restaurant* at Rain Forest Resort Village (360–288–2535 or 800–255–6936; www.rainforestresort.com), the *Shake Mill Restaurant,* at 6080 Highway 101 in Amanda Park (360–288–2377), and the *Internet Coffee Cafe* (360–288–0571), also in Amanda Park. Rain Forest Resort Village also offers lake-view cabins.

On the south side of the lake 2 miles east of the highway on South Shore Road sits *Lake Quinault Lodge* (800–562–6672 or 360–288–2900; www.visit lakequinault.com), a ninety-two–room waterfront resort built in 1926. Guests can rent boats and canoes for exploring the lake, enjoy a game of badminton on the grass, soak in the swimming pool, and enjoy gourmet dining in the Roosevelt Room, the lodge's restaurant. For more rustic accommodations ask about the *Boathouse Annex,* built in 1923. Pets are allowed in the annex, which offers eight guest rooms. None of the resort's rooms has a TV or a telephone.

If you'd like to explore the Quinault Valley rain forest and scenic Lake Quinault from the sunny side of the lake and stay in a more intimate lodging, contact the folks at *Lake Quinault Resort,* located on North Shore Road (800–650–2362; www.lakequinault.com). In this quiet spot relax in your Adirondack chair amid a flotilla of flowers and savor views of the lake, which can be seen from all the guest rooms. This section of the Olympic Peninsula also can be reached from Olympia by heading west on U.S. Highway 12 to Aberdeen and then north on US 101 for about 40 miles to Quinault and Amanda Park.

Harbors, Bays, and Rivers

The twin port cities of Hoquiam and Aberdeen on Grays Harbor are hardworking communities where logging, fishing, and shipping are nearly everybody's business. On a hillside above residential Hoquiam on Chenault Street sits the splendid *Hoquiam's Castle Bed and Breakfast* (360–533–2005; www.hoquiamcastle.com), built in 1897 by lumber baron Robert Lytle and now listed on the State and National Registers of Historic Places. The restored twenty-room mansion is filled with opulent antiques, lovely cut-glass windows, a turn-of-the-century saloon, and five spacious guest rooms outfitted with antique furnishings and finery from the late 1800s.

For other comfortable overnight accommodations in the area, try the historic *Cooney Mansion Bed & Breakfast* (1705 Fifth Street, Cosmopolis; 360–533–0602); *Aberdeen Mansion Bed & Breakfast* (807 North M Street, Aberdeen; 360–533–7079; www.aberdeenmansionbb.com); *A Harbor View*

Hoquiam's Castle

Bed & Breakfast in Aberdeen (360–533–7996; www.aharborview.com); and ***Abel House Bed & Breakfast*** (117 Fleet Street South, Montesano; 360–249–6002; www.abelhouse.com).

Downtown Hoquiam has a waterfront park where you can watch work- and pleasure boats on the river. Or you and the kids can climb the viewing tower at the end of Twenty-eighth Street on Grays Harbor to see the ocean-going cargo ships. Continue west past Hoquiam to follow the coast north on Highway 109 past a number of small resort communities. Along the way you'll find windswept beaches, art galleries, antiques and gift shops, and resorts. For more information on places to stay, contact the Washington Coast Visitor Information Center, in Copalis Beach, (800) 286–4552 or (360) 289–4552.

A few miles east of Hoquiam, the ***Aberdeen Museum of History,*** located at 111 East Third Street (360–533–1976), includes an eclectic variety of curiosities and displays from Grays Harbor's past. You'll see yesteryear's logging and farming equipment, period clothing, and toys. Exhibits include a blacksmith's shop, a general store, and a one-room schoolhouse. The museum is managed by an enthusiastic corps of volunteers, and it is open Wednesday through Sunday from 11:00 A.M. to 4:00 P.M. during the summer and weekends from noon to 4:00 P.M. during the winter.

Grays Harbor was a major shipbuilding center during the days of sail, when locally milled lumber was in great demand for hulls, masts, and spars. Three- and four-masted schooners, wooden steamships, and tugboats were constructed along the bay, and they crowded the harbor's docks. At the ***Grays Harbor Historical Seaport*** (712 Hagara Street; 360–532–8611), you can absorb this marine history and tour a full-scale reproduction of the *Lady Washington,* one of the ships used by explorer Robert Gray to sail into the harbor in 1792. The replica was built in 1989 as part of the state's centennial celebration and now sails regularly along the coast. Log onto www.ladywashington.com for information about dockside tours, educational programs, adventure sail training, and the current sailing schedule for ports in Washington State and also in the neighboring state of Oregon. For additional information about the area, contact the Grays Harbor Visitor Information Center (360–532–1924; www.graysharbor.com and www.graysharbor.org).

Twenty miles west of Aberdeen just off Highway 105, you'll find the town of *Westport,* where maritime life abounds. At the bustling marina the fishing and charter boats prepare for offshore tours or return loaded with fish and crabs. During the summer, catch the passengers-only ferry from Westport across the mouth of Grays Harbor to the tourist community of *Ocean Shores.* Linger in Ocean Shores and explore this scenic north coast area, including Ocean City, Copalis Beach, Pacific Beach, Moclips, and at the far northern end of Highway 109, Taholah. You'll find friendly coffee shops, funky cafes, cozy bookstores, and warm places to hole up for the night. Among them check out *Gibson's Bed & Breakfast* (360–289–7960; www.thegibsonsbandb.com), where Norman and Sally Gibson offer a friendly welcome to their guests, including treats at the soda fountain, a plethora of musical museum pieces to inspect, and an art deco–style movie theater complete with popcorn and movies.

Back in Westport check out the Westport boardwalk, an ideal place to stroll and watch the waterfront activity, and there's a tower with stairs to climb for a bird's-eye view of Grays Harbor.

The colonial-revival structure located at 2201 Westhaven Drive was built in 1939 to house the Coast Guard's Lifeboat Station at Grays Harbor. The building now houses the *Westport Maritime Museum* (360–268–0078; www.west portwa.com/museum) and is open from 10:00 A.M. to 4:00 P.M. Memorial Day weekend to Labor Day. Tours of the *Grays Harbor Lighthouse,* located nearby at Point Chehalis, were halted after 9/11 but have been resumed. Or you can see the lighthouse from a roadside viewing platform. The 107-foot-tall structure is more than a hundred years old, and its automated light, at 123 feet above the water, ranks as the highest light on the Washington coast.

March through May is the time to catch sight of migrating gray whale families as they swim north past Westport from their breeding lagoons in Baja California to the krill-rich waters of the Bering Sea near Alaska. The gray whale population once again numbers in the thousands due to international protection. To find out about whale-watching cruises, Contact the Westport–Grayland Chamber of Commerce (800–345–6223 or 360–268–9422; www.westportgray land-chamber.org).

TOP ANNUAL EVENTS ON THE WASHINGTON COAST AND OLYMPIC PENINSULA

Whale Fest
Westport, March–May
(800) 345–6223

Crab Races, Crab Feed
& Crab Derby
Westport, April
(800) 345–6223

Rainfest
Forks, mid-April
(800) 443–6757

Country Music Jam
Ocean Shores, first weekend in May
(800) 762–3224

Lavender Festival
Sequim, mid-July
(360) 683–6197

International Kite Festival
Long Beach, mid-August
(800) 451–2542

Clallam County Fair
Port Angeles, mid-August
(360) 417–2551

Makah Days
Neah Bay, last weekend in August
(360) 645–2201

Cranberry Harvest Festival
Grayland, second weekend in October
(800) 473–6018

Bed and Breakfast Open House Tour
Long Beach Peninsula, first weekend
in December
(800) 451–2542; www.funbeach.com

Following the coast south on US 101, you'll have wide views of the Pacific Ocean before turning east at Willapa Bay. This long, shallow bay is rich with wildlife and shellfish. You can sample this bounty by following the turnoff at the Shoalwater Indian Reservation to the *Tokeland Hotel & Restaurant,* located at 100 Hotel Road in Tokeland (360) 267–7006. The hotel's dining room offers a panoramic view of Willapa Bay as well as hearty food. Established in 1889 as the Kindred Inn, this is the oldest operating hotel in Washington State, offering simple but satisfying accommodations.

Raymond, located just south of the junction of Highways 101 and 105, is a pleasant town on the Willapa River serving loggers, fishermen, and tourists. The old *Dennis Company* building at Blake and Fifth Streets offers a glimpse of the region's history in an 85-foot-long mural depicting shipping and logging activity in 1905. Pop into *Ugly Ed's* (360–942–2345), located behind Dennis Company, for incredible junk, antiques, and collectibles. Then visit the *North-west Carriage Museum,* at 314 Alder Street (360–942–4150), open Wednesday through Saturday, noon to 4:00 P.M., where you and your family can inspect some twenty horse-drawn carriages, buggies, and sleighs dating from the late 1800s. Then you can browse for goodies at the *Willapa Public Market.*

Another favorite Raymond spot, the *Daily Perk* at 265 Fifth Street (360–942–3757), offers great coffee drinks, and *Sweet Dreams Bakery* at 310 Commercial Street (360–942–4962), offers baked goods to die for. For good seafood and tasty clam chowder, try *Harbor Grill* on Robert Bush Drive in nearby South Bend.

Continuing west on US 101, you'll pass through the picturesque village of *South Bend,* located on the Willapa River where it empties into Willipa Bay and the Pacific Ocean. The town's shoreline is worth a leisurely stroll to view the rough wooden fishing docks, piles of discarded oyster shells, and busy crab-processing plants. Plan to stay overnight at *Russell House Bed & Breakfast* (902 East Water Street; 888–484–6907; www.russellhousebb.com), a ca. 1891 Victorian mansion that offers cozy rooms and wide-angle views of the Willapa River and South Bend. For active families try *Summerhouse,* located in Raymond (360–942– 2843), which has a comfy guest house and two full RV hookups for your traveling companions. The *Pacific County Historical Museum,* on the highway at 1008 West Robert Bush Drive in South Bend (360–875–5224; www.pacificcohistory.org), offers glimpses of the area's colorful past. The museum is open daily 11:00 A.M to 4:00 P.M. Walk up the hill behind downtown, past some of the town's stately old houses, for great views of the Willapa River and the forested hills that lie beyond. On the corner of Memorial and Cowlitz Streets, you can visit one of Washington's finest county courthouses. Open during business hours, this elegant 1910 building sports an impressive art-glass dome and historical scenes painted in the 1940s.

The highway follows Willapa Bay's southeastern shore past South Bend. You'll pass rich wetland scenery including beds of eelgrass, feasting grounds for migrating black brant geese. The estuary environment supports a mind-boggling array of life-forms, from mud-dwelling clams, shrimps, and oysters to the millions of marine birds that consume them. After crossing the Naselle River, you'll pass pristine Long Island, part of *Willapa National Wildlife Refuge* (360–484–3482) and accessible only by private boat. The island supports a coastal rain forest that includes a stand of old-growth cedars as well as deer, bear, elk, grouse, beaver, and a diverse songbird population. Stop by the refuge headquarters, which is east of the highway across from the island's south end, for more information.

Long Beach Peninsula

The Long Beach Peninsula is an inviting place to explore for day or weekend rambles. The roar of the surf is never far off, the air is washed clean by ocean winds, and there are activities galore. The larger beachside communities are popular tourist destinations, but you don't have to go far to find lesser-known treasures and quiet walking trails.

You can enjoy a public art treasure hunt by searching for the numerous historical murals that grace the exteriors of department stores, cafes, and public buildings in Ilwaco, Seaview, Long Beach, and Ocean Park. A free Muralogue guide is available from the Long Beach Peninsula Visitor Center (800–451–2542 or 360–642–2400; www.funbeach.com).

Ilwaco is a fishing community at the peninsula's south end. The town's harbor is a great place to browse. You'll see charter boats with folks aboard heading out to fish for salmon, sturgeon, bottom fish, or tuna. In the harbor area are canneries for fish and crab processing, fresh-fish markets, gift shops, and eateries. Stop by *Festivals Coffee Net* at 151 Howerton Way (360–642–2288) for freshly baked cinnamon rolls, scones, cookies, and specialty coffee drinks along with great views of the bustling marina. For gourmet eats served up with Northwest wines and microbrews, the locals suggest *Pauly's Bistro,* also near the Ilwaco marina at 235 Howerton Way (360–642–8447); open daily for lunch and Friday and Saturday for dinner.

Between 1889 and 1930 the Ilwaco Railroad and Navigation Company transported goods and people up and down the peninsula, first by coach along the beach, then by narrow-gauge railway from Ilwaco to Nahcotta. Be sure to stop by the *Ilwaco Heritage Museum,* housed in the old telephone utilities building at 115 Southeast Lake Street (360–642–3446). You and the kids can see a scale model of the 1890s narrow-gauge railway that ran along the beach between Ilwaco and the small town of Nahcotta about 12 miles north. Often referred to as the Clamshell Railway, it ran on a schedule governed by the incoming and outgoing tides. The old railway depot is on display in the museum's courtyard. The museum is open year-round from 9:00 A.M. to 5:00 P.M. Monday through Saturday and noon to 4:00 P.M. Sunday. You can spot the first outdoor mural produced on the peninsula, a 1920s railway scene, on the north side of the Doupe Brothers Hardware Store at Ilwaco's only traffic light.

Two and a half miles southwest of Ilwaco, off US 101, *Cape Disappointment State Park* (360–642–3078) offers beaches, forest trails, campsites, and two historic lighthouses. Although you can camp here without reserving your spot, the sites by the ocean and each of the sixty hookups must be reserved. Reservations are recommended in summer. Call Washington State Parks Campground reservations toll-free at (888) 226–7688, or visit www.parks.wa.gov.

Waikiki Beach, a sheltered cove well supplied with driftwood and smooth sand near the park entrance, is a great place to watch the Columbia River's busy shipping activities. For even more dramatic views, hike along the established trail to the North Head Lighthouse. Nearby, the *Lewis and Clark*

Interpretive Center (360–642–3029) offers views of the Columbia River between the north and south jetties. A stroll through the center takes you on Lewis and Clark's heroic journey from Camp Du Bois in Wood River, Illinois, to the Pacific Ocean. The party's mainly river routes took them through sections of the states of Illinois, Missouri, Kansas, Nebraska, Iowa, South Dakota, North Dakota, Montana, Idaho, Washington, and Oregon.

North on US 101 the small town of Seaview offers several more outdoor murals. If you are in the mood for a leisurely stroll, Seaview's meandering back roads offer pleasant views of quaint cottages, many established during the late nineteenth century as summer retreats. The *Shelburne Country Inn and Heron & Beaver Pub* (4415 Pacific Highway; 360–642–2442 and 360–642–4142) was built in 1896 and restored in the 1970s. Along with antiques, homemade quilts, and a bountiful herb garden, the inn features hearty country breakfasts and lunches and light dinners in the pub.

Lewis and Clark Corps of Discovery 200th Anniversary

On November 7, 1805, William Clark wrote in his journal: "Great joy in camp we are in view of the Ocian. . . ." For the record, the party was still some 20 miles from the Pacific Ocean, but they finally arrived at the mouth of the Columbia River on November 15 and set up Station Camp. Although Clark scouted up the Long Beach Peninsula some 9 miles for a possible winter headquarters site, the party backtracked upriver and, on the advice of Clatsop Indians about food sources, started crossing to the Oregon side of the river on November 26. By December 7 the whole party was hunkered down at the Fort Clatsop site, and they began building their winter quarters. The Fort Clatsop National Memorial is near Astoria, which was established as a trading site at the mouth of the Columbia River in 1811. Planning your Corps of Discovery travel itineraries is easy. Check these sites for Bicentennial events and activities, which range through 2006 and into 2007:

Fort Clatsop National Memorial
Living-history programs mid-June through Labor Day
92343 Fort Clatsop Road
Astoria, Oregon
503–861–2471
www.nps.gov/focl

Lewis-Clark Discovery Center
A multimedia site incorporating the entire route from east to west
www.lewis-clark.org

Lewis and Clark Trail Heritage Foundation
www.lewisandclark.org

Pacific County Friends of Lewis and Clark
www.lewisandclarkwa.com

Sneak Over to Astoria

Drive across the 4⁴⁄₁₀-mile-long Astoria–Megler Bridge that spans the wide mouth of the Columbia River as it surges into the Pacific Ocean, and in just minutes you reach the small town of Astoria. It started as a fur-trading post in 1811. Here's a quick list of what to see in the downtown area, where a long-awaited renaissance is on the move:

Stop by **Pier 39,** former home of the Bumblebee Tuna Cannery, now renovated and housing the trendy **Rogue Ale Public House** and **Coffee Girl Coffeehouse & Cafe.**

Snoop into the new **Cannery Pier Hotel,** which offers magnificent views of the Columbia River from its public rooms and guest rooms.

See the ca. 1920 **Liberty Theater,** recently renovated to its former vaudevillian splendor.

Pop across the street to ogle the renovated **Hotel Elliott,** its splendid finery, rooftop garden, Cigar Room, and Cellar Wine Bar.

Good eats: **Baked Alaska Restaurant** at No. 1 Twelfth Street Dock (503–325–7414); **Columbian Café** at 1114 Marine Drive (503–325–2233); and **Wet Dog Café** at 144 Eleventh Street (503–325–6975).

Helpful information about the area: Astoria/Warrenton Area Visitor Information (800–875–6807; www.oldoregon.com); Seaside Visitors Bureau (888–306–2326; www.seasideor.com).

Long Beach, the largest town on your way up the peninsula, has a wooden boardwalk stretching several blocks along the beach from South Tenth Street. The boardwalk provides easy access to the roaring surf, rustling dune grass, and the wide, sandy beach. Subtle lighting along the way makes the boardwalk ideal for a romantic evening stroll. From here you can also spot the array of multicolored kites that folks of all ages fly on the beach in late August during the ***Washington State International Kite Festival.***

Stop by the ***World Kite Museum and Hall of Fame*** at 303 Sid Snyder Drive (360–642–4020; www.worldkitemuseum.com) in Long Beach, which features displays from delicate butterfly and dragon kites to huge fighting kites and videos showing kites flying high on local beaches. The museum's impressive collection numbers more than 1,300 kites representing cultures around the world. You can visit daily from 11:00 A.M. to 5:00 P.M. in summer and on weekends in winter. Look in a small alley between Second Street and Third Street South and between Pacific Highway 103 and Boulevard Street to see if the kids can find ***Fish Alley Theater.*** Tell them it's close to ***Boo-Boo's Putt-Putt Golf.*** Great fun for the whole family, this outdoor theater space offers you local storytellers, clowns, jugglers, face painters, and musicians during the summer months.

Fun places to grab a bite to eat on the Long Beach Peninsula include *The Berry Patch* (1513 Bay Avenue in Ocean Park; 360–665–5551); *Sand Dollar Deli & Pizza* (401 South Pacific in Long Beach; 360–642–3432); *The Crab Pot* (1917 Pacific Highway; 360–642–8870); and *Cottage Bakery & Deli* at 118 Pacific Highway in Long Beach (360–642–4441).

Continuing north, travelers can find access to the beach at both the Loomis Lake and the Pacific Pines State Parks, where you walk on sandy paths lined with wild strawberry plants. The beaches are great spots for seaside picnics. In this quieter section of the peninsula, *Blackwood Beach Cottages* at 20711 Pacific Way in Ocean Park (888–376–6356; www.blackwoodbeachcottages.com) offers five cottages with ocean and sunset views and three woodland cottages, all with kitchens and such pleasant amenities as Seattle's Best Coffee, Fran's chocolates, Tazo teas, and fresh flowers. If you like being closer to the action, check out *Boardwalk Cottages* at 800 Ocean Beach Boulevard South in Long Beach (800–569–3804; www.boardwalkcottages.com) or the *Seaview Motel & Cottages* at 3728 Pacific Way in Seaview (360–642–2450). To bed down in the former digs of the lighthouse keepers, located just inland from North Head Lighthouse and Cape Disappointment State Park, inquire at (360) 642–3078. For information on other cottages, motels, and beachside RV parks, contact the Long Beach Peninsula Visitor Information Center (360) 642–2400; www.funbeach.com.

Romantics can contact innkeepers Susie Goldsmith and Bill Verner at *Boreas Bed & Breakfast Inn,* also close to the ocean at 607 North Boulevard in Long Beach (888–642–8069; www.boreasinn.com). Guests are invited to take turns using the whirlpool spa located a few steps from the inn and housed in an enclosed cedar-and-glass gazebo. Breakfast is a lively event, with guests gathering on the main level for such tasty treats as roasted Washington pears stuffed with pecans, dried cranberries, cinnamon, and brown sugar; peach kuchen baked in custard; a three-mushroom frittata sautéed with sherry; and fresh-roasted organic coffee. Other pleasant bed-and-breakfast inns on the Long Beach Peninsula include the ca. 1911 Craftsman-style bungalow *Lion's Paw Inn Bed & Breakfast,* located at 3310 Pacific Highway South in Seaview 98644 (800–972–1046; www.thelionspawinn.com); and the ca. 1929 *Moby Dick Hotel & Restaurant* at 25814 Sandridge Road in Nahcotta (360–665–4543).

Head east (right) from Ocean Park on Bay Avenue and then north (left) on Sandridge Road to the tiny town of *Nahcotta,* the center of the peninsula's oyster industry. Native oysters, a tribal staple for centuries, were wiped out by the 1920s through overharvesting, disease, and freezing weather. The introduction of Japanese oysters and new cultivation techniques have made this

Willapa Bay area one of the foremost oyster-growing places in the world. Pop over to **Oysterville Sea Farms** at First and Clark Streets in Oysterville (360–665–6585; www.oysterville.net), to see the oyster-shucking process and to shop for fresh oysters and cranberry goodies.

Nahcotta's **Ark Restaurant and Bakery** (3310 273rd Street; 360–665–4133) is famous for regional culinary delights. Located on the Nahcotta dock, it offers travelers water views and meals featuring Willapa Bay oysters, Washington wild blackberries, Columbia River salmon, and sturgeon. The restaurant is open daily for dinner at 5:00 P.M. and for Sunday brunch from 11:00 A.M. to 3:00 P.M. Call ahead for reservations.

Just beyond the Ark Restaurant, stop to visit the **Willapa Bay Interpretive Center** at 273rd Place. The center, open from 10:00 A.M. to 3:00 P.M. on weekends Memorial Day through Labor Day, replicates an oyster station house and inside shows the chronology of 150 years of oyster growing on the bay. You'll also see the walls covered with old photographs, memorabilia, oyster-harvesting tools, maps, and a 20-foot mural of Willapa Bay. From here continue north on Sandridge Road to visit **Oysterville,** which was established in 1854 to house those early workers and families. You can see the local church, a one-room schoolhouse, the general store, and early 1900s houses as you stroll through this quiet bayside village.

Three miles north of Oysterville on Stackpole Road, take the tree-lined road out to **Leadbetter Point State Park,** part of the Willapa National Wildlife Refuge and located at the far point of the 28-mile-long peninsula. A favorite place for bird-watchers, Leadbetter Point's tidal flats overflow with migrating shorebirds and geese in April and May.

Along the Columbia River

The little town of **Chinook** was one of the most prosperous communities in Washington during the 1880s, when fishing traps lined the river, catching tons of fish to be processed in waterfront canneries. The traps were banned in 1935, but the port of Chinook is still one of the major fishing centers on the Long Beach Peninsula. You can still see many old homes built in the late 1800s. Next door to the old Methodist church on the corner of US 101 and Hazel Street in Chinook is **Little Ocean Annie's** (360–777–8387), which offers tasty fish-and-chips and seafood to go.

Scenic Highway 4 winds eastward through forestlands along the Columbia River, past the communities of Naselle, Grays River, Skamokawa, and Cathlamet. Plan to stop at the **Columbia White-tailed Deer National Wildlife Refuge,** with its 4,757 acres of diked floodplain and islands covered with thick grass and woodland habitat for birds and land animals. There are trails for walking or bicycling around the refuge.

Travelers can also find comfy lodgings at **Skamokawa Inn Bed and Breakfast,** 1391 West Highway 4, Skamokawa (360–795–8300 or 888–920–2777; www.skamokawakayak.com). Their light and airy guest rooms are situated in the historic Skamokawa General Store building, constructed on a wide deck that extends about 40 feet over the north bank of the Columbia River. The river views are splendid from your lofty perch on the second floor. You're looking out onto one of the main sections of the **Lewis and Clark Columbia River Water Trail** (see www.coasttrails.org) and to the adjacent 40,000-plus acres of the **Lewis and Clark National Wildlife Refuge** (360–795–3915). Ask the innkeepers or the refuge rangers about kayak rentals, instruction, and guide services for paddles on these scenic water trails. For eateries in the Skamokawa area, try the **Duck Inn Restaurant** (360–795–3655) and **Duffy's Irish Pub** (360–465–2898), located a few miles west in Grays River.

The town of **Cathlamet** sits above the Columbia River, well situated for watching the parade of river traffic and enjoying views of the rural farmland of **Puget Island.** The 4-mile-long island is perfect for an easy bicycle ride, and from the south end you can board one of the Columbia River ferries to the Oregon side of the river. Puget Island innkeeper Winnie Lowsma welcomes birders and butterfly watchers to **Redfern Farm Bed & Breakfast** (277 Cross Dike Road; 360–849–4108). You'll find two second-floor guest rooms (each with a private bath), an outdoor spa, and a back deck overlooking the family garden and orchard. You could also call the friendly innkeepers at the **Bradley House of Cathlamet Bed & Breakfast** located at 61 Main Street in Cathlamet (360–795–3030; www.bradleyhousebb.com). You can bed down in comfort in this gracious 1907 Eastlake home built by an early lumber baron. For tasty

On the Coastal Trail with Lewis and Clark

Captain William Clark's journal entry, November 26, 1805, describes the area that now comprises the **Lewis and Clark National Wildlife Refuge** near Skamokawa and Cathlamet: "Great numbers of Swan Geese Brant Ducks & Gulls in this great bend which is Crouded with low Islands covered with weeds grass etc. and overflowed every flood tide." This wild and scenic area today remains very much like it was in 1805, when Clark penned these words in his journal.

lunches or high tea, pop into the La-Tea-Dah Tea Room & Gift Shop, on the main floor of the inn. For a special dinner the innkeepers suggest driving 24 miles into Longview to dine at ***Rutherglen Mansion Inn,*** located at 420 Rutherglen Road (360–425–5816). Dinners and Sunday brunches at the mansion are legendary and may include, among other enticing entrees and desserts, fresh cracked crab, oysters Rockefeller, Alaska halibut, steak Diane, and bananas Foster. For simpler dining fare take the Wahkiakum County Ferry from Cathlamet across to the Oregon side of the Columbia River and find good eating at the ***Berry Patch Restaurant*** (503–455–2250) in Westport. It's open Friday through Sunday from 7:00 A.M. to 7:00 P.M. and Monday through Thursday until 3:00 P.M. The ***Wahkiakum County Historical Museum*** at 65 River Street in Cathlamet offers artifacts of work and daily life from when the town was young. From the Oregon side of the Columbia River you can head east on U.S. Highway 30 into the Portland environs. Or you can continue east on Highway 4 to Longview and reconnect with Interstate 5 for trips north to Olympia, Tacoma, and Seattle or south to Vancouver and Portland.

Places to Stay on the Washington Coast

AMANDA PARK

Lake Quinault Resort
314 North Shore Road
(800) 650–2362

Lochaerie Resort Cabins
638 North Shore Road
(360) 288–2215

CATHLAMET

Bradley House
Bed & Breakfast
61 Main Street
(360) 795–3030

Skamokawa Inn
Bed & Breakfast
1391 West State
Route 4
(360) 795–8300

DUNGENESS

Groveland Cottage
Bed and Breakfast
4861 Sequim–
Dungeness Way
(800) 879–8859
or (360) 683–3565

FORKS

Kalaloch Lodge
157151 Highway 101
(360) 962–2271

Miller Tree Inn
Bed & Breakfast
654 East Division Street
(800) 943–6563

Shady Nook Cottages
81 Ash Avenue
(360) 374–5497

HOOD CANAL

Glen Ayr Canal RV Park
25381 North Highway 101
Hoodsport
(360) 877–9522

Rest-a-While RV Park
Highway 101
(360) 877–9474

LA PUSH

La Push Ocean Park
Resort
700 Main Street
(800) 487–1267

LONG BEACH

Boardwalk Cottages
800 Ocean Beach
Boulevard South
(800) 569–3804

Boreas Bed & Breakfast
607 North Boulevard
(360) 642–8069

OCEAN PARK

Oceanaire RV Park
25918 R Street
(360) 665–4027

PORT ANGELES

Lake Crescent Lodge
416 Lake Crescent Road
(360) 928–3211

**Sol Duc Hot Springs
Resort**
Sol Duc Road
(360) 327–3583

SEAVIEW

**Lion's Paw Inn
Bed & Breakfast**
3310 Pacific Highway South
(800) 972–1046

Seaview Motel & Cottages
3728 Pacific Way
(360) 642–2450

SEQUIM

Dungeness Bay Motel
140 Marine Drive
(888) 683–3013

Juan de Fuca Cottages
182 Marine Drive
(360) 683–4433

Red Caboose Getaway
24 Old Coyote Way
(360) 683–7350

TOKELAND

**Tokeland Hotel
& Restaurant**
100 Hotel Road
(360) 267–7006

WESTPORT

Chateau Hotel Westport
710 Hancock
(360) 268–9101

Islander Motel & RV Park
421 Neddie Rose Drive
(800) 322–1740

Places to Eat on the Washington Coast

ABERDEEN

Billy's Bar and Grill
322 East Heron Street
(360) 533–7144

Bridges Restaurant
112 North G Street
(360) 532–6563

SELECTED VISITOR INFORMATION CENTERS

Forks Visitor Information Center
(800) 443–6757
www.forkswa.com

Hood Canal Visitor Information
www.discoverhoodcanal.com

**Long Beach Peninsula
Visitors Bureau**
(800) 451–2542;
www.funbeach.com

**Port Angeles Visitor
Information Center**
(360) 452–2363;
www.portangeles.net

Sequim Visitor Information Center
(800) 737–8462;
www.visitsun.com

**Westport/Grayland Chamber
of Commerce**
(800) 345–6223 or (360) 268–9422

HELPFUL WEB SITES ON THE WASHINGTON COAST AND OLYMPIC PENINSULA

Grays Harbor County
www.co.grays-harbor.wa.us/info/
tourismGH

Hood Canal
www.discoverhoodcanal.com

Lewis and Clark Bicentennial
www.lewisandclarkwa.com

Long Beach Peninsula
www.funbeach.com

Olympic National Forest
www.fs.fed.us/r6/olympia

Olympic National Park
www.nps.gov/olym/

The Olympic Peninsula
www.olympicspeninsula.org

CHINOOK

Little Ocean Annie's
Highway 101
(360) 777–8387

DUNGENESS

Three Crabs Restaurant
11 Three Crabs Road
(360) 683–4264

FORKS

Forks Coffee Shop Cafe
Highway 101
(360) 374–6769

Kalaloch Lodge Restaurant
157151 Highway 101
(360) 962–2271

Smoke House Restaurant
193161 Highway 101
(360) 374–6258

HOODSPORT/ELDON

Hoodsport Coffee Company
24240 North Highway 101
Hoodsport

Hungry Bear Restaurant
36830 North Highway 101
Eldon
(360) 877–0400

HOQUIAM

Seventh Street Sweet Shop & Cafe
317 Seventh Street
(360) 532–4784

ILWACO

Festivals Coffee Net
151 Howerton Avenue
(360) 642–2288

Pauly's Bistro
235 Howerton Way
Ilwaco Marina
(360) 642–8447

LONG BEACH

Cottage Bakery & Deli
118 Pacific Highway
(360) 642–4441

NAHCOTTA

The Ark Restaurant and Bakery
273rd Street and
Sandridge Road
(360) 665–4133

OCEAN PARK

Full Circle Cafe
1024 Bay Avenue
(360) 665–5385

PORT ANGELES

Elizabeth & Company Coffeehouse and Bakery
106 East First Street
(360) 452–5222

First Street Haven Cafe
107 East First Street
(360) 457–0352

Olympic Bagel Company
802 East First Street
(360) 452–9100

RAYMOND

Sweet Dreams Bakery
310 Commercial Street
(360) 942–4962

SEAVIEW

Heron & Beaver Pub
4415 Pacific Highway
(360) 642–4142

Julie's Loose Caboose Diner
Pacific Highway and Forty-
sixth Street
(360) 642–2894

SEQUIM

The Buzz Coffee Shop
128 North Sequim Avenue
(360) 683–2503

Cedar Creek Cuisine
665 North Sequim Avenue
(360) 683–3983

Oak Table Cafe
292 West Bell Avenue
(360) 683–2179

Petals Garden Cafe
1345 South Sequim Avenue
(360) 683–4541

WESTPORT

Islander Restaurant
421 Neddie Rose Drive
(360) 268–9166

ALSO WORTH SEEING

The Cranberry Museum & Farm
Long Beach

Fort Clatsop
Lewis and Clark's winter headquarters,
Astoria, Oregon

Lewis and Clark Discovery Dunes Trail
Port of Ilwaco to Long Beach

Moclips
Highway 109, north of Ocean Shores

Victoria and Sidney
B.C., Canada, access from ferries at
Port Angeles

Puget Sound Region

You could spend a lifetime exploring the Puget Sound region and still have more to discover. Puget Sound's inland waterways, cut by huge glaciers, offer travelers hundreds of miles of shoreline and friendly waterfront communities as well as numerous islands. The region's moist maritime climate supports lush forests and farms. A dynamic economy based on natural resources, agriculture, and industry has attracted a diverse culture. Many families live on the sound's larger islands, such as Anderson, Vashon, Bainbridge, Whidbey, Fidalgo, Guemes, Lummi, Shaw, Lopez, Orcas, and San Juan. It's a way of life that's slower, less frantic. Checking ferry schedules, waiting in ferry lines, and riding the small county ferries or the enormous green and white Washington State ferries consume a good bit of time. But it's an activity that visitors also can enjoy because ferry rides come with fresh saltwater smells, dipping seagulls, busy shorebirds, and other happy travelers along with wide-angle views of distant mountains, the swirling waters, and the smaller islands. And, if we're very lucky, we get to see a pod of whales, particularly the striking black-and-white Orcas.

You can still find old-timers who'll tell stories of what life was like when logging, fishing, and homesteading were the region's primary occupations; when the "mosquito fleet" of

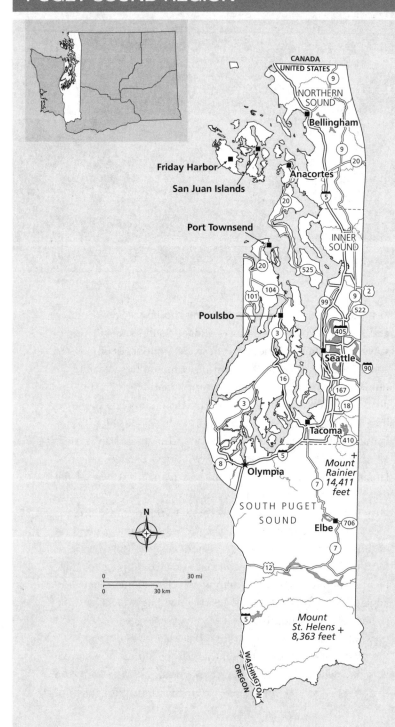

small steamships provided transportation between communities scattered along the extensive shoreline; when the rhythm of the tides was a dominant force in every resident's life, including the lives of Native peoples, many of whom live in tribal communities on small reservations scattered around Puget Sound and the Olympic Peninsula.

The cities of Olympia, Tacoma, Seattle, Bellevue, Edmonds, and Everett form an urban corridor along the east side of Puget Sound.

South Puget Sound

Mount Rainier is a dominant feature of the lower sound. There are many interesting places to visit in the area around Mount Rainier National Park. The steam-powered ***Mount Rainier Scenic Railroad*** excursion train takes riders on a slow jaunt between Elbe and Mineral, at the mountain's base. On this one-and-a-half-hour round-trip, you'll pass through thick evergreen forests, cross the bubbling Nisqually River, and enjoy spectacular views of the sleeping volcano's summit. Passengers can either sit in an open carriage or, if the weather is cool, relax in a closed, heated car.

Trains leave at 11:00 A.M, 1:15 P.M., and 3:30 P.M. weekends from Memorial Day through the end of September and daily from June 15 through Labor Day. For further information call (360) 569–2351 or (888) 783–2611, or check www.mrst.com. You can also visit the ***Northwest Railway Museum*** (425–888–3030; www.trainmuseum.org), located northeast of Seattle in Snoqualmie.

Back in the Elbe railroad yard, you'll find the two classic dining cars of the ***Mount Rainier Dining Company*** permanently parked on the tracks—a 1922 Southern Pacific and a 1910 Great Northern, offering you a unique railroad dining car experience. There is also a lounge named the Side Track Room located

Mount Rainier Scenic Railroad

PUGET SOUND'S TOP HITS

**American Museum of Radio
and Electricity**
Bellingham

Anacortes Mural Project
Anacortes

Java & Clay Coffeehouse
Gig Harbor

Bair Restaurant
Steilacoom

Bloedel Reserve Gardens
Bainbridge Island

Center for Wooden Boats
Seattle

Hovander Homestead Park
Ferndale

Island County Historical Museum
Coupeville

The Johnson Farm
Anderson Island

La Conner Quilt Museum
La Conner

Lynden Pioneer Museum
Lynden

**Mason County Historical
Society Museum**
Shelton

Meerkerk Rhododendron Gardens
Whidbey Island

Mount Rainier Scenic Railroad
Elbe

Museum of Glass
Tacoma

Pioneer Farm Museum
Eatonville

Point Roberts

**Port Townsend Marine
Science Center**
Port Townsend

Rothschild House
Port Townsend

San Juan Islands

Sidney Art Gallery
Port Orchard

Suquamish Museum
Suquamish

Wolf Haven Wildlife Sanctuary
Tenino

in a late 1930s Chicago, Burlington, and Quincy coach. The dining cars are open Wednesday through Sunday for breakfast, lunch, and dinner. Call (360) 569–2500 or (888) 773–4637 for reservations.

Six miles farther east on Highway 706 is Ashford, a small community of artists, outdoor enthusiasts, and old-timers who appreciate living at the entrance to Mount Rainier National Park. On your way from Elbe to Ashford, however, look for the outdoor sculpture park on the right-hand side of Highway 706. Travelers are welcome to pull into the parking area and enjoy walking among enormous and imaginative metal sculptures, such as elk, deer, and a larger-than-life bicycle. The **Mountain Meadows Inn** (28912 Highway 706 East; 360–569–2788; www.mt-rainier.net) is a friendly and comfortable bed-and-breakfast. Located in a house built in 1910, it was the home of the superintendent of National Mill, once the biggest lumber mill west of the Mississippi River. Guests wake to a hearty, gourmet country breakfast of, perhaps, smoked king salmon and herbed cream cheese omelets. Wildlife is often visible from the generous front porch or as you stroll on trails through the forest.

Another favorite lodging and eatery in these parts is **Alexander's Old Country Inn & Restaurant** (37515 State Route 706 East; 800–654–7615 or 360–569–2300; www.alexanderscountryinn.com), just 3 miles east of Ashford. Luminaries such as Theodore Roosevelt and William Howard Taft have bunked down at this twelve-room homestead, the oldest historic structure in the area. Alexander's Restaurant is touted as one of the best in these parts. The pan-fried trout comes from its own glacier-fed pond, and the baked salmon and beef tenderloin in a green pepper and mango chutney are highly recommended as well. Diners also enjoy freshly baked breads and desserts.

In Ashford, just a few miles from the Nisqually entrance to Mount Rainier National Park, pause to visit **Ashford Creek Pottery** at 30516 Highway 706 (360–569–1000). The charming studio offers functional stoneware enlivened with irises and also displays pottery by local artists.

Before heading up to the mountain, you could also consider being pampered at **Wellspring Spa and Log Cabins** (54922 Kernahan Road; 360–569–2514). Licensed massage therapist Sunny Thompson has created a mountain paradise of saunas, waterfalls, hot tubs, comfortable rooms, and cozy log cabins (and even a treehouse nest). The outdoor hot tubs overlook landscaped gardens with terraced waterfalls and cooing doves. The wood-heat saunas or professional massage can do wonders to revitalize even the weariest traveler.

Jasmer's Guest House (30005 State Route 706 East; 360–569–2682; www.jasmers.com) offers cozy cabins along Big Creek. Other accommodations close to Ashford include **Nisqually Lodge** (360–569–8804) for comfy lodge-style rooms and **Mounthaven Resort** (360–569–2594 or 800–456–9380; www.mounthaven.com) for cabins and RV spaces. On the far north side of Mount Rainier, **Alta Crystal Resort** (68317 State Route 410 East in Greenwater; 800–277–6475) offers cabins and chalets near Crystal Mountain Ski Area and also near hiking and mountain biking trails through an old-growth forest within the Mount Baker–Snoqualmie National Forest.

Mount Rainier National Park celebrated its centennial anniversary in 1999; its capstone, Mount Rainier, rises to a whopping elevation of 14,411 feet. This mountain is not one to take lightly. It commands respect; it makes its own weather. Because it is also an active volcano covered with ice and snow (like Mount St. Helens), geological and weather-related changes can happen here almost without warning. But during summer months, from late June to early September, you can enjoy two scenic drives that lead safely to panoramic locations on the mountain. The first, *Paradise,* is accessed from the Ashford area; the second, *Sunrise,* is accessed from the east side near the Chinook Pass highway. Sunrise is the more arduous and winding drive, but the rewards are many, including wonderful wildflower meadows with environmentally sensitive paths and trails among the native flora. Both Paradise and Sunrise are above 5,000 feet in elevation, so travelers should take warm sweaters and jackets on this trek. There are six developed campgrounds in Mount Rainier National Park; check the Web sites www.nps.gov/mora/ and www.mount.rainier.national -park.com for helpful information about camping, hiking, horse camping, and backpacking in the park. Additional information can be obtained from park headquarters in Ashford (360–569–2211). During winter avid cross-country skiers can contact the *Mount Tahoma Trails Association* about skiing hut-to-hut on some 100 miles of logging road trails; call (360) 569–2451, Mount Tahoma Ski Trail office, for a recorded message and current information.

Good places to grab a bite to eat include *Rainier Overland Restaurant and Lodge,* open summers in Ashford (360–569–0851); *National Park Inn Restaurant* in nearby Longmire (360–569–2275); and *Scaleburgers* at 54109 Mountain Highway in Elbe (360–569–2247). Located in a weigh-station building renovated ca. 1939, Scaleburgers has been serving juicy hamburgers since 1987.

In the lowlands near Eatonville, you can enter a time warp at the *Pioneer Farm Museum* (7716 Ohop Valley Road; 360–832–6300; www.pioneerfarm museum.org). One-and-a-half-hour tours are run from 11:15 A.M. to 4:00 P.M. daily in summer and on weekends during spring and fall. The museum gift shop, housed in an 1888 trading post cabin, brims with old-fashioned treats.

North of Eatonville off Highway 161 is *Northwest Trek* (11610 Trek Drive East; 360–832–6117; www.nwtrek.org), an unusual park where you can see a wide variety of wildlife living in a woodland setting. Sandhill cranes, now an endangered species, and caribou roam free amid moose, bison, and bighorn sheep, while the elusive cougar, lynx, and bobcat prowl in Cat Country. You may catch sight of playful raccoons, river otters, or beavers as you explore the park's nature trails adorned with ferns, native berries, and trees. The park opens at 9:30 A.M. daily from March through October, with tram tours every hour beginning at 10:00 A.M.

The city of *Olympia* is the state capital and the home of Miller beer (orginally the Olympia Brewery). Many visitors simply tour only the capitol building, then move on, but there are many lesser-known sights worth experiencing. Start with a sidewalk tour of downtown as described in *Olympia's Historic Downtown: A Walking Tour,* which highlights outstanding historic buildings, homes, and parks. This brochure is available from the Olympia Thurston County Visitor Information Center at 1600 East Fourth Avenue (360–357–3362; www.olympiachamber.com).

Families with young children will want to stop at Olympia's **Hands-on Children's Museum** (106 Eleventh Street; 360–956–0818). This creative place offers a diverse collection of interactive exhibits for kids ten years old and younger. Call ahead for the current hours. You can also plan to visit the **Washington State Capitol Museum** in the historic Lord Mansion at 211 West Twenty-first Street (360–753–2580; www.wshs.org). The museum offers a look at South Puget Sound's early pioneer and Indian history in interpretive exhibits on two floors of the mansion.

After your visit to the museums, stop downtown and grab a bite to eat at the **Urban Onion** (116 Legion Way SE; 360–943–9242), which reportedly has the best kids' menu in town. If you're there for breakfast, don't pass up the famous U.O. Smoothie, a concoction of orange juice, bananas, and

thevenerable capitol

Olympia's opulent Legislative House, completed in 1927, was one of the last domed capitols built in the United States. Forty-two steps lead to the entrance, symbolizing the fact that Washington was the forty-second state to join the Union. The granite for the steps and foundation was quarried in the town of Index, and the sandstone of its face is also from the Cascade foothills. The dome weighs thirty million pounds and sits 287 feet above the ground. A Visitor Information Center at Fourteenth and Capitol Way offers more information about the Capitol grounds; call (360) 586–3460.

yogurt, or the veggie stir-fry served over hash browns. Lunch and dinner entrees range from traditional burgers to vegetarian burritos.

Stroll along the **Percival Landing** boardwalk on Olympia's waterfront to see the arrival and departure of boats and ships and occasionally view the playful antics of a seal. The boardwalk begins on Fourth Avenue behind Bayview Market. A three-story tower at the landing's north end offers great views of the port, the city, and, on a clear day, the Olympic Mountains. You'll find several places to eat, including the **Olympia Farmers' Market,** located at the north end of Capitol Way, where you can enjoy just-harvested produce, fresh seafood, and locally cooked specialty foods. The spacious, covered market is open from 10:00 A.M. to 3:00 P.M. weekends in April, Thursday through Sunday from May through September, and Friday through Sunday in October.

FAVORITE ATTRACTIONS

American Camp and British Camp
San Juan Island

Ebey's Landing National Historical Reserve
Whidbey Island

Fort Worden
Port Townsend
(360) 385–4730

Mount Rainier National Park
Ashford
(360) 569–2211

Museum of Glass
Tacoma
(866) 468–7386

Peace Arch Park & Gardens
Washington–British Columbia border,
Blaine

Skagit Valley Tulip Festival
Mount Vernon
(360) 428–5959

To absorb the atmosphere of Olympia's past, enjoy a meal at the historic *Spar Cafe, Bar and Tobacco Merchant* (114 East Fourth Avenue; 360–357–6444). The Spar retains many details from its early days; chairs have a clip on the back to hold the patron's hat, sports scores are announced on a chalkboard, and the walls are decorated with old logging photos.

You can enjoy a number of other eateries and coffee shops in the Olympia area, including *Tugboat Annie's Restaurant* located at 2100 West Bay Drive (360–943–1850); *Budd Bay Cafe* at 525 Columbia Street NW (360–357–6963); *Oyster House, Inc.* at 320 Fourth Avenue West (360–753–7000); the drive-through *Capitol Parks Espresso* at 3302 Capitol Boulevard (360–280–3184); *Cafe Vita* at 124 Fourth Avenue East (360–754–8187); and *Wagner's European Bakery & Cafe* at 1013 Capitol Way (360–357–7268).

For fine lodgings near the downtown area, call the innkeepers at *Swantown Inn Bed & Breakfast,* a ca. 1893 Queen Anne/Eastlake Victorian mansion located at 1431 Eleventh Avenue SE (360) 753–9123, www.swantowninn.com. A sumptuous gourmet breakfast is served in the grand dining room, or you can have a continental repast delivered to your door.

From the *Puget View Guesthouse* (7924 Sixty-first Avenue NE; 360–413–9474), located a few miles northeast of Olympia on Puget Sound, guests enjoy wide water views of Nisqually Beach, Anderson Island, and Longbranch Peninsula. They can also walk the nearby beaches and trails of *Tolmie State Park* and watch for marine wildlife. The Nisqually River, which flows from glaciers on Mount Rainier, empties into Puget Sound at the nearby *Nisqually National Wildlife Refuge.* Visitors can enjoy walking on 7 miles of public trails, including the 1-mile Twin Barn Loop to the Education Center (open weekdays from 10:00 A.M. to 2:00 P.M.). For more information contact the refuge office at 100 Brown Farm Road NE, Lacey (360–753–9467) from 7:30 A.M. to 4:00 P.M. weekdays.

More splendid nature trails are found a few miles south of Olympia at *Mima Mounds Natural Area Preserve,* an unanswered "whodunit" carved into the landscape. There is an interpretive center built into one of these 6-foot-high geological wonders. You'll find an observation deck, a barrier-free interpretive path, and hiking trails among the riot of colorful wildflowers and native grasses that bloom in the spring. For a scenic route to the preserve, take Mud Bay Highway west from Olympia and turn south just past the Evergreen Parkway onto picturesque Delphi Valley Road. In about 5 miles veer right on Waddell Creek Road and follow signs south through the Capital Forest. After about 2 miles you'll see the turnoff to Mima Mounds on your right.

A few miles east of Mima Mounds is the *Wolf Haven Wildlife Sanctuary* at 3111 Offut Lake Road, Tenino (360–264–4695; www.wolfhaven.org), open from 10:00 A.M. to 5:00 P.M. daily, May through September, and until 4:00 P.M. Wednesday through Sunday, October through April. Wolf Haven is a privately owned refuge for abandoned wolves and other feral animals that can't be returned to the wild. For a small fee you can take a tour. Volunteers describe wolf biology and lore as well as the personalities of individual wolves living at

Resident Wolves of Wolf Haven

Folks can "adopt" a resident Wolf Haven wolf either singly, as pairs, or as packs. This is a personal way to connect with and make a difference in the lives of these extraordinary animals, which are no longer able to live in the wild. Lone wolves are paired whenever possible for companionship. See www.wolfhaven.org for current information or call (360) 264–4695.

Selected list of resident wolves:

Pairs

Onyx and Tahoma
Solo and Denali
Marius and Morning Star
California Girls: Grey and Brita

Packs

California Boys: Stormy, Cherokee, and Sequoia

Idaho Pack: Kooskia, Siri, Mahina, Miwok, and Zuni

Lone wolves

Ramses
Moose

the sanctuary. You can experience a campfire sing fest and howl-in on Friday and Saturday nights in summer (except in cases of heavy rain) from 7:00 to 10:00 P.M.

Nearby, visit *Lattin's Country Cider Mill & Farm* at 9402 Rich Road (360–491–7328) and purchase freshly made cider, homemade pies, jams, and syrups as well as fresh seasonal fruits and vegetables. Stop by before 10:00 A.M. on weekends to sample homemade doughnuts. If you would like to stay overnight in the Tenino area, call *Blueberry Hill Farm Guest House Bed & Breakfast,* 12125 Blueberry Hill Lane; (360) 458–4726; www.blueberryhillfarm guesthouse.com. The innkeeper makes Grandma's Gourmet Berry Jam and also serves guests delicious farm-style breakfasts (at a nominal charge per person). Travelers in RVs can check with *Offut Lake Resort,* also near Tenino (360–264–2438; www.offutlakeresort.com), for scenic RV sites close to the lake as well as fishing, boating, and canoeing.

South of Wolf Haven on Highway 99 is the town of *Tenino,* a friendly community famous around the turn of the twentieth century for its sandstone quarries. The scenic *Tenino City Park* was built around one of the retired quarries. Water cascades down moss- and vine-covered sandstone walls into a pond, now used each summer as the community's public swimming pool (open from 12:30 to 6:30 P.M., Tuesday through Sunday, from mid-June through August).

Tenino was a railroad town named, some say, after the Number 10-9-0 engine that pulled local trains. The town is on the main north–south line, and all Olympia rail traffic used to change trains here. The *Tenino Depot Museum* (360–264–4321), adjacent to the city park, is one of many local sandstone buildings. Museum exhibits illustrate techniques used in the old quarries to trans-

TOP ANNUAL EVENTS IN THE PUGET SOUND REGION

Bumbershoot
Seattle, Labor Day weekend
(877) 885–9452

Mystery Weekend
Langley, mid-February
(360) 221–5676

Oysterfest & Seafood Festival
Shelton, early October
(800) 576–2021

Scottish Highland Games
Hovander Park, Ferndale, early June
(360) 384–3444

Skagit Valley Tulip Festival
Mount Vernon, all of April
(360) 428–5959

form raw stone into everything from bricks to flower pots, as well as railroad lore and local history. The museum is open Thursday through Sunday, from noon to 4:00 P.M., mid-March to mid-October.

For outstanding dining call *Alice's Restaurant* (19248 Johnson Creek Road SE; 360–264–2887; www.alicesdinners.com). To get there, go south from Tenino on Highway 507, turn left at 184th Avenue (which becomes Skookumchuck Road), and in about 5 miles turn left onto Johnson Creek Road. The menu at Alice's highlights country game—including braised rabbit, catfish, roast pheasant, and venison—in addition to more conventional fare. While waiting to be seated, you can stroll around the trim gardens, complete with gazebo and ponds.

Steilacoom, just northeast of Olympia via Interstate 5, is a small town perched on a bluff overlooking the southernmost part of Puget Sound and nearby Anderson Island. Established in 1854 by Maine sea captain Lafayette Balch, Steilacoom was the first incorporated town in the Washington Territories, and during the late nineteenth century, it was an important seaport, county seat, and commercial center. Stroll through the downtown National Historic District, with more than thirty buildings on the historic register.

The *Bair Restaurant,* located at 1617 Lafayette Street (253–588–9668; www.thebairrestaurant.com), offers great breakfasts, delicious lunches, and Northwest-style gourmet dinners. The former hardware store and pharmacy, built in 1895 by W. L. Bair, was a popular gathering spot for those early commuters who caught the Tacoma trolley that stopped across the street. The store's lights would dim just before the trolley arrived, giving patrons a few minutes' warning to pay their bills. The restaurant is open daily, but call for seasonal hours.

The indigenous people of south Puget Sound, the Coastal Salish, had a main village where the town of Steilacoom is now situated. You can learn more by visiting the *Steilacoom Tribal Cultural Center,* in a lovely old church in downtown Steilacoom (1515 Lafayette Street; 253–584–6308). The center is open daily except Monday from 10:00 A.M. to 4:00 P.M. The gift shop sells Indian crafts and artwork.

Steilacoom's history is rich with stories of fast ships, quick business deals, and slow trains. To learn more about the town, visit the *Steilacoom Historical Museum,* in the basement of the Town Hall at 112 Main Street (253) 584–4133. The museum, open from 1:00 to 4:00 P.M., Tuesday through Sunday, offers a glimpse of the town's 140-year history, including displays of a turn-of-the-twentieth-century kitchen, a blacksmith's shop, and a barber shop.

To visit another historic site that takes visitors back to the days of early American settlement and of the British Hudson's Bay Company, find *Fort Steilacoom Museum* on the grounds of Western State Hospital, 9601 Steilacoom

Boulevard (253–756–3928). Of the original twenty-six wood-frame structures, four have survived over the years and now form the museum complex. Quarters 1 is furnished for a married officer and his family; Quarters 2 was home to fort commander Silas Casey and his family from 1858 to 1861; Quarters 3 is furnished as bachelor officers lived; and Quarters 4, once the chapel and chaplain's quarters, is now the fort's interpretive center. Call ahead for current hours.

Then, for a comfortable overnight stay in this tiny historic village, call the friendly innkeepers at *Above the Sound Bed & Breakfast,* located at 806 Birch Street (253–589–1441). Two cozy guest rooms and a spacious common room with fireplace offer a warm welcome to travelers. Breakfast is served in the pleasant sunroom on the main level with commanding views of the water and ferry landing.

From Steilacoom you can take a twenty-minute ferry ride across the waters of Puget Sound to Anderson Island. The island is only 4 miles from end to end, but there are plenty of little nooks to explore. At the center of the island you'll find the *Johnson Farm,* which was operated by the Johnson family from 1912 to 1975 and is now maintained by the Anderson Island Historical Society to display the labors and comforts of traditional rural life. A community garden on the property brims with homegrown vegetables and fruit in summer and fall. Tools and artifacts are on display, including the wheelhouse of the ferry **Tahoma,** which plied the Anderson Island route for decades. The farm is always open, and tours of the farmhouse are available on summer weekends. Browse in the cozy gift shop nestled in one of the farm's renovated chicken coops.

Anderson Marine Park, on the island's southwest shore, is a delightful and secluded place to explore. The park offers a nature trail through the woods and down to Carlson's Cove. Well-marked signs point out the diverse plant life and bird activity in the evergreen forest. Along the way you'll walk on short stretches of the trail marked "skid road," "corduroy," and "puncheon." These terms, which describe the shape of the logs under your feet in the muddier parts of the walk, demonstrate historic road surfacing techniques to show how logging roads were once built. The last stretch includes a steep descent down to a small dock floating in the secluded cove rich with intertidal life. Beware of the poison oak beyond the marked path along the shore, and be sure to wear good walking shoes.

Ken and Annie Burg offer families the fun and comfort of their large log home, *Inn at Burg's Landing Bed & Breakfast* (8808 Villa Beach Road; 253–884–9185), located near the Anderson Island ferry dock. From the inn's large decks, you can watch the boat traffic passing on the waters of Puget

Sound, with a backdrop of Mount Rainier and the Cascades on blue-sky days. The inn's private beach is ideal for strolling and seashell collecting. Ken Burg, who grew up on Anderson Island and attended its one-room school, can tell stories of island life "back in the good old days." Annie guarantees that no guest goes hungry for breakfast.

Inner Sound

Historically the home of the Puyallup and Nisqually Indian tribes, the Tacoma area did not see white settlers arrive until 1833, when the British Hudson's Bay Company established a fur-trading post, Fort Nisqually. In the early 1850s the first permanent settlers, mainly lumbermen, arrived. These workers built sawmills along the Commencement Bay waterfront, which soon bustled with cargo ships and workers of many nationalities, including American, English, Scottish, Irish, Hawaiian, Native American, and Chinese. Back then the old Whiskey Row area sported saloons, brothels, and gambling houses. By the early 1870s the fledgling town successfully courted the Northern Pacific Railroad to designate Tacoma its western terminus. The railroad was completed in 1883, thus linking Tacoma to the rest of the country, and the city's population soared from some 5,000 in 1884 to 50,000 by 1892.

And what about today? A twenty-first-century renaissance is under way in Tacoma, the welcome mat is out, and travelers will find many new shops, cafes, restaurants, and hotels downtown and in several historic neighborhoods. A new museum district is in the making along the Thea Foss Waterway, where visitors can find one of its stunning centerpieces, the newly opened **Museum of Glass** at 1801 East Dock Street (866–468–7386 or 253–284–4750; www.museum ofglass.com). Its impressive tilted 90-foot-tall cone wrapped in shimmering stainless steel offers a reminder of the sawmill wood burners of the mid-1800s and symbolizes the city's transformation from an industrial to a cultural enclave. Reflecting pools, walkways, and outdoor spaces invite visitors to linger along the waterway. Indoors you can see glassblowing demonstrations in the Hot Shop Amphitheater and enjoy rotating exhibits in the gallery spaces, as well as browse in the museum store, which overlooks the waterway. For good eats with views of the waterway, try the **Blue Olive Cafe,** located nearby at 715 Dock Street (253–383–7275).

The **Washington State History Museum** at 1911 Pacific Avenue (888–238–4373; www.wshs.org), is connected to the Museum of Glass by the spectacular Chihuly Bridge of Glass, a 500-foot pedestrian walkway over Interstate 705 that showcases the work of renowned glass artist and Tacoma native Dale

Chihuly. Next door is historic Union Station, also displaying Chihuly glass in its rotunda. The **Tacoma Art Museum** (253–272–4258; www.tacomaartmuseum .org) has moved to its splendid new home at 1701 Pacific Avenue. Other nearby museums include the **Working Waterfront Museum** at 705 Dock Street (253–272–2750; www.wwfrontmuseum.org); **Karpeles Manuscript Library Museum** at 407 South G Street (253–383–2575); and the **African American Museum** at 925 C Court (253–274–1278). You can also explore downtown Tacoma's historic **Broadway Theater District** and, adjacent to it, Antiques Row on Broadway between Seventh and Ninth Streets. In this area you'll see two restored ca. 1918 theaters and a contemporary theater, along with several architectural treasures such as the 1886 Old City Hall clock tower and the 1888 Northern Pacific Railroad headquarters.

From here head north to the Stadium District, named for the imposing 1906 chateaulike fortress that began as an elegant hotel but now houses Stadium High School. Continue to Old Town to see the **Job Carr Cabin Museum** at 2305 North Thirtieth Street (253–627–5405), a replica of the 1864 home of Tacoma's first mayor, public notary, and postmaster. Next you can visit the **Proctor Historic District,** with its intriguing shops, cafes, and restaurants. At the far northern tip of the city, **Point Defiance Park** at 5400 North Pearl Street offers a zoo, an aquarium, and colorful perennial gardens, along with **Camp 6 Logging Exhibit & Museum** (253–752–0047) and **Fort Nisqually Living History Museum** (253–591–5339; www.fortnisqually.org). You can also find a flock of antiques shops along North Pearl Street, including **Ruston Galleries & Vintage Clothing** (253–759–2624), **Claudia Smith Antiques & Collectibles** (253–759–6052), and **Now & Then Shop & Art Deco** (253–759–7206).

For exceptional eating and libation in the Tacoma area, there are several options: **Antique Sandwich Company** at 5102 Pearl Street (253–752–4069) serves good specialty sandwiches and is a popular hangout; and **Spar Tavern** at 2121 North Thirtieth Street (253–627–8215) offers tasty pub fare and local microbrews and ales. **The Swiss,** a blues pub and coffeehouse offering polka breakfasts with live accordion music, is located near Union Station at 1904 Jefferson Avenue (253–572–2821). **From the Bayou Restaurant,** located at 506A Garfield Street (253–539–4269) east of I–5 in east Tacoma and open for lunch and dinner, offers Cajun cuisine such as crab-stuffed halibut with Cajun roux. Nearby at 516 Garfield Street, **Marzano's** (253–537–4191) offers tasty Italian fare.

Pearl Street ends to the north at Point Defiance, where a ferry leaves every hour until late evening for **Vashon Island,** one of the largest of Puget Sound's islands. When you ferry over to visit this relaxing island, stop at the **Blue Heron Art Center** (19704 Vashon Highway; 206–463–5131; www.vashonallied arts.com) to get a feel for their thriving arts community and its myriad events.

Vintage Automobiles Galore

The city of Tacoma will soon add another museum near the Thea Foss Waterway to its already-stellar lineup. The *LeMay Museum* (www.lemaymuseum.org) will showcase the vintage automobile collection of longtime Tacoma resident Harold LeMay. Tours of the collection are possible Tuesday through Saturday 10:00 A.M. to 5:00 P.M. and can be arranged by calling the museum office (253–779–8490).

Next, call the **Brian Brenno Blown Glass Studio & Gallery** (17630 Vashon Highway; 206–463–4525) to ask when their artists are blowing glass. Among the creations at the gallery you'll see life-size glass hats in fabulous colors. If you're ready for a snack, pop into **Homegrown Restaurant & Deli** (17614 Vashon Highway; 206–463–6302). Then don't miss visiting **The Country Store and Gardens** (20211 Vashon Highway; 888–245–6136; www .tcsag .com) to enjoy the Ceiling Museum of antique kitchen implements and kitchenware as well as all kinds of natural foods, preserves, and garden goodies. Head down to **Point Robinson** at the southeast tip of the island, called Maury Island, to see the working lighthouse there. Call the president of the Keepers of Point Robinson (206–463–6672) well ahead if you'd like to arrange a tour.

Linger overnight on Vashon Island by arranging for cozy rooms at the **Betty MacDonald Farm Bed & Breakfast** (206–567–4227; www.bettymacdonald farm.com). For additional lodging information browse the Visitor Information Center site, www.vashonchamber.com.

Gig Harbor is a delightful fishing village nestled in a protected bay on the northwest side of the Tacoma Narrows. The harbor is crowded with both pleasure and fishing boats. Harborview Drive, which hugs the shore, is lined with shops, sidewalk cafes, and galleries, making it a great place to stroll.

Gig Harbor's **Rent-A-Boat and Charters** (8829 North Harborview Drive; 253–858–7341) offers several fun ways to explore Puget Sound, from pedal boats and seagoing kayaks to large sailboats and powerboats. The operation is open daily (weather permitting) in spring and summer from 9:00 A.M. to 7:00 P.M. and by reservation in winter. Galleries featuring local artisans are scattered throughout town. The **Ebb Tide Co-operative Gallery** (3106 North Harborview Drive; 253–851–5293), open daily from 10:00 A.M. until 5:00 P.M., displays colorful woven clothing, jewelry, watercolors, wood carvings, and pottery. You'll find great gifts also at the **Beach Basket** (253–858–3008), **Seasons on the Bay** (253–858–8892), and **Strictly Scandinavian** (253–851–5959)—all located in the heart of Gig Harbor. For a good selection of regional wines as well as gifts, stop by *The Keeping Room* at 7811 Pioneer Way (253–858–9170). The owners host a fun party each year, and the guests who attend dressed and looking most like the legendary Marilyn Monroe win a special bottle of Marilyn Merlot wine. It's great fun. Call for current dates.

Estates, Mansions, Villas, and Castles

A number of Pacific Northwest timber, ship, and industrial barons of the late 1800s and early 1900s exhibited a tendency to the immense, ornate, and showy when it came to building their houses. Many of these palatial homes eventually fell into disrepair; some were razed, but a number of these fine structures have recently been renovated. Here are six among the top-drawer variety, five of them open as bed-and-breakfast inns and one as a splendid estate garden, also open to the public. Each offers a fascinating history.

Branch Colonial House Bed & Breakfast Inn
6,000 square feet
Ca. 1904 home restored by
Robin Soto Korobkin
2420 North Twenty-first Street
Tacoma
(253) 752–3563 or (877) 752–3565
www.colonialhousebnb.com

Chinaberry Hill Victorian Inn
6,000 square feet
Ca. 1889 home restored by
Cecil and Yarrow Wayman
302 Tacoma Avenue
North Tacoma
(253) 272–1282
www.chinaberryhill.com

Ca. 1907 Lakewold Gardens Estate
Ten-acre estate gardens developed in 1938 by owners Corydon and Eulalie Wagner. Gardens and Georgian-style manor house now conserved by Friends of Lakewold; splendid gardens and gift shop open to the public.
12317 Gravelly Lake Drive SW
Tacoma
(253) 584–3360 or (888) 858–4106
www.lakewold.org

DeVoe Mansion Bed & Breakfast Inn
6,000 square feet
Ca. 1911 home restored by
Dave and Cheryl Teifke
208 East 133rd Street
Tacoma
(253) 539–3991 or (888) 539–3991
www.devoemansion.com

Thornewood Castle Inn Bed & Breakfast
27,000 square feet
Ca. 1911, renovation ongoing by
Wayne and Deanna Robinson
8601 North Thorne Lane SW
Lakewood
(253) 584–4393
www.thornewoodcastle.com

Villa Bed & Breakfast
10,000 square feet
Ca. 1925 home
705 North Fifth Street
Tacoma
(253) 572–1157 or (888) 572–1157
www.villabb.com

OTHER FRIENDLY B&Bs, TACOMA–GIG HARBOR–VASHON ISLAND AREA

Aloha Beachside Bed & Breakfast
8318 Highway 302
Gig Harbor
(888) 256–4222
www.alohabeachsidebb.com

Bear's Lair Bed & Breakfast
13706 Ninety-second Avenue NW
Gig Harbor
(877) 855–9768
www.bearslairbb.com

**The Betty MacDonald Farm
Bed & Breakfast**
12000 Ninety-ninth Avenue SW
Vashon Island
(206) 567–4227 or (888) 328–6753
www.bettymacdonaldfarm.com

The Fountains Bed & Breakfast
926 120th Street NW
Gig Harbor
(253) 851–6262
www.fountainsbb.com

Green Cape Cod Bed & Breakfast
(ca. 1929)
2711 North Warner Street
Tacoma
(253) 752–1977
www.greencapecod.com

Waterfront Inn Bed & Breakfast
9017 North Harborview Drive
Gig Harbor
(253) 857–0770
www.waterfront-inn.com

For comfortable lodgings, most of them with views of Henderson Bay, Carr Inlet, or Colvos Passage, check with the friendly volunteers at the Gig Harbor Visitor Information Center, 3125 Judson Street (888–843–9444; www.gigharbor guide.com).

Recommended eating spots in the Gig Harbor area include **Narrows Landing Restaurant,** at the Tacoma Narrows Airport, 1208 Twenty-sixth Avenue NW (253–853–4114); **Anthony's Homeport Restaurant** at 8827 North Harborview Drive (253–853–6353); **Tides Tavern** at 2925 Harborview Drive (253–858–3982); and **Java & Clay Coffeehouse** at 3210 Harborview Drive (253–851–3277). For those interested in live local theater, check out the local plays and outdoor summer musicals offered by **Encore! Theatre Company** (253–858–2282) and **Paradise Cabaret Theatre** (253–851–7529).

From Gig Harbor you can backtrack a few miles to Tacoma via the Tacoma Narrows Bridge and rejoin I–5 heading north to the Seattle environs. **Seattle's International District,** south of downtown, includes a large and well-established Asian community. Visitors enjoy touring the many small shops and sampling the excellent food. **Uwajimaya,** at 519 Sixth Avenue South, is a unique department store where you'll find an amazing assortment of Asian foods, artwork, furniture, books, and household goods. To learn about Seattle's Chinese community, contact **Chinatown Discovery Tours** (425–885–3085), which offers both day and night guided tours of the Chinese/Asian Museum, specialty shops, and the district's best restaurants. ***Bill Spiedel's Underground Tour*** (206–682–4646) takes an intriguing look at subterranean passages, about three blocks in all, that were the original streets and storefronts of Seattle's mid-1800s downtown. The Underground Cafe features buffalo burgers, ribs, salads, snacks, and espresso drinks. *Note:* Wear sturdy shoes; the terrain is dimly lit and uneven, and you'll negotiate several flights of stairs on the two-hour tour.

At the south end of Lake Union, the ***Center for Wooden Boats*** (1010 Valley Street; 206–382–2628; www.cwb.org) has a fleet of classic wooden boats, which are available for rent by the hour or the day. You can explore waterway attractions and join the colorful flotilla of small boats on the lake. The center also sponsors workshops where enthusiasts share ancient skills and historical knowledge, from boatbuilding and knot work to traditional music and lore of the seven seas. The center's pavilion is an ideal place to enjoy a picnic and view lakeside activities.

Also located along the shores of Lake Union, northwest of the Center for Wooden Boats, is the free-spirited ***Fremont Neighborhood.*** On Fremont Avenue you'll discover a number of funky, bohemian, and fun gift shops, boutiques, cafes, and coffeehouses.

For bedding down in the Seattle area, try ***Chambered Nautilus Bed & Breakfast Inn,*** a Georgian colonial inn located in the University District at 5005 Twenty-second Avenue NE (206–522–2536; www.chamberednautilus .com); ***Mildred's Bed & Breakfast,*** in the Capitol Hill area at 1202 Fifteenth Avenue East (206–325–6072); or the homey but elegant ***Salisbury House Bed & Breakfast,*** also in the Capitol Hill area at 750 Sixteenth Avenue East, Seattle (206–328–8682; www.salisburyhouse.com).

The ***University of Washington*** (UW) and its environs offer numerous day and evening activities. Explore paths and nature areas on the campus and wander among colorful perennials in the ***Medicinal Herb Garden*** (take the Fifteenth Street and Fortieth Avenue entry gate into the campus near Meany Hall, then bear right onto Stevens Way to the garden). Spend hours walking pathways and waterside boardwalks at the renowned ***Washington Arboretum,*** visit several fine museums on campus, and attend performances at the university's several concert halls. Sporting events range from crewing races on nearby Lake Washington to Husky football and basketball games. The UW Visitor Information Center (206–543–9198) can provide maps and current information about cultural and sporting events. Nearby University Village Center offers interesting shops, delis, cafes, galleries, bookstores, and an excellent weekend farmers' market.

The Capitol Hill area is also great for walking, with all sorts of parks, shops, cafes, and coffee shops. ***Volunteer Park,*** located nearby and designed by the

For Wine and Microbrew Aficionados

The grand duchess of wineries in the Seattle area is the elegant **Chateau Ste. Michelle,** at 14111 Northeast 145th in Woodinville. Reach them at (425) 415-3300 or www.ste-michelle.com for events and directions. Tall Douglas fir, colorful rhododendrons, and lush beds of annuals and perennials greet visitors entering the chateau gates. There are shady picnic areas, and folks also can browse in the gift shop, attend seasonal events, and take a tour of the wine-making process. Wine and microbrew aficionados can also check out other fine establishments:

Bear Creek Pub and Grill
7950 164th Avenue NE
Redmond
(425) 895-9088

Columbia Winery
14030 Northeast 145th
Woodinville
(800) 488-2347
www.columbiawinery.com

Hedges Cellars
195 Northeast Gilman Boulevard
Issaquah
(800) 859-9463
www.hedgescellars.com

Redhook Ale Brewery
14300 Northeast 145th Street
Woodinville
(425) 483-3232

Rock Bottom Brewery and Restaurant
550 106th Avenue NE
Bellevue
(425) 462-9300
www.rockbottom.com

For additional information check the informative Web site www.eastkingcounty.org.

East Coast Olmstead brothers, offers paths for walking, places to picnic, and a superb orchid collection at the park's handsome glass conservatory. At the western edge of the extensive grounds, you can enjoy marvelous views of the city and Puget Sound and also take in gorgeous sunsets. Also plan an hour or more to enjoy the splendid ***Bellevue Botanical Gardens,*** at 12001 Main Street, Bellevue 98005 (425–452–2750; www.bellevuebotanical.org). Here folks stroll along a lush perennial border garden, a summer dahlia display, a traditional knot garden, a meditative Japanese garden, an alpine rock garden, and a loop trail through the reserve. For other helpful information about the Bellevue-Redmond-Kirkland area, browse the informational Web site www.east kingcounty.org. For a pleasant day trip, head down to the Seattle waterfront and board the ferry for a thirty-minute ride to nearby ***Bainbridge Island.*** Browse the shops and boutiques in ***Winslow,*** the island's main town, and enjoy eats or beverages at one of these friendly spots located in downtown Winslow along Winslow Way: ***Streamliner Diner*** (206–842–8595) near the ferry landing; ***Blackbird Bakery*** (206–780–1322); and ***Winslow Way Cafe*** (206–842–0517).

To stay overnight on the island, check with the friendly folks at **Captain's House Bed & Breakfast** in Winslow (206–842–3557). From Bainbridge Island you can access other Kitsap Peninsula destinations such as Poulsbo, Port Orchard, and Gig Harbor.

The picturesque **Snoqualmie Valley,** about 30 miles east of Seattle, is surrounded by the foothills of the Cascade Mountain range. The Snoqualmie River, flowing down the valley, creates the spectacular 270-foot Snoqualmie Falls. Above the falls is a public overlook and the posh **Salish Lodge & Spa** (6501 Railroad Avenue; 800–826–6124).

The **Snoqualmie Valley Railroad & Northwest Railway Museum,** at 38625 Southeast King Street in downtown Snoqualmie, offers train rides from the restored Victorian train station through scenic evergreen forests, to the nearby community of North Bend and past Snoqualmie Falls. There are runs each weekend from April through October (Sunday only before Memorial Day and after Labor Day). Call (425) 888–3030 for the current schedule and fare information, or go to www.trainmuseum.org and www.snovalley.org.

For toothsome treats after visiting the railway museum, be sure to stop by **Snoqualmie Falls Candy Factory** (8102 Railroad Avenue SE; 425–888–0439) for not only delicious fudge and taffy but also hamburgers, sandwiches, espresso, and a great selection of ice cream. You could also plan a stop at **Gilman Village** in nearby Issaquah to sample chocolate confections at **Boehm's Candies** (255 Northeast Gilman Boulevard; 425–392–6652). Gilman Village offers a gaggle of shops, boutiques, and eateries. For a cozy place to spend the night, call the friendly folks at **The Roaring River Bed & Breakfast,** 46715 Southeast 129th Street, North Bend (425–888–4834 or 877–627–4647; www.theroaring river.com). All four rooms have private entrances, sitting areas, and decks overlooking the bubbling Middle Fork of the Snoqualmie River. For evening dining in the North Bend area, try **Gordy's Steakhouse** at the Cascade Golf Course (425–831–2433) and **Rob-**

bloedelreserve

Brimming with rich scenery and history and just a thirty-minute ferry ride from Seattle, Bainbridge Island is the perfect day-trip destination. It's also the gateway for the get-away-from-it-all activities on the Kitsap and Olympic Peninsulas. One of the most lovely and historic places on the island is the **Bloedel Reserve** (7571 Northeast Dolphin Drive; 206–842–7631). Once a private estate, the 150-acre reserve offers a feast for the senses with its beautifully maintained grounds, including a bird marsh, an English landscape garden, a moss garden, a reflection pool, a Japanese garden, and woodlands. The reserve is open to the public Wednesday through Sunday; reservations are required.

Family Excursions on the Kitsap Peninsula

Anna Smith Children's Park
Creative demonstration garden
7601 Tracyton Boulevard NW
Bremerton
(360) 337–4595

Northwest Electric Boat Rentals
Poulsbo
(360) 265–8300

Point Defiance Zoo & Aquarium
Picnic and play areas, gardens
5400 North Pearl Street
Tacoma
(253) 591–5337
www.pdza.org

More information:

Kitsap County Parks & Recreation
(360) 337–4595
www.kitsapgov.com/parks

Kitsap Peninsula Visitor Information
(360) 297–8200
www.visitkitsap.com

Washington State Ferries
(206) 464–6400
www.wsdot.wa.gov/ferries

ertiello's Italian Cafe in old-town North Bend (425–888–1803), both recommended by the locals.

Near Carnation, 6 miles north of Fall City on Highway 203, *Remlinger Farms* is a diverse 270-acre fruit, vegetable, and berry farm that welcomes families to visit. There's a farm-animal petting zoo for children, picnic tables, a farm-fresh produce store, restaurant, and bakery. Remlinger Farms offers a Ripe 'n Ready Report of in-season produce by calling (425) 451–8740 or browsing the farm's Web site, www.remlingerfarms.com. The farm is located half a mile off Highway 203 on Northeast Thirty-second Street, just south of Carnation.

From Seattle take a ferry to Bremerton, and from here explore the *Kitsap Peninsula* and the western sections of Puget Sound. Kitsap County has 236 miles of shoreline, more than any other county in the state. Most of its towns have splendid water views. When you reach Gorst, a tiny town on the edge of Sinclair Inlet, you'll find an ex-landfill and log dump transformed into the remarkable *Elandan Gardens and Gallery* at 3050 West State Highway 16, Bremerton (360– 373–8260). The garden's extensive bonsai collection and its gallery, which offers elegant antiques and art treasures, are open from 10:00 A.M. to 5:00 P.M. Tuesday through Sunday.

Port Orchard, a few miles east of Gorst on Highway 116, has a hospitable downtown ideal for window shopping. Bay Street, the main commercial street, has old-fashioned sidewalks with a wooden canopy for comfortable strolling, rain or shine. Murals on downtown walls illustrate life during the late nineteenth century, when Port Orchard was a major stop for the mosquito fleet, the small steamboats that were once a common form of transportation on the sound. At the north end of Sidney Avenue, you can catch the modern version of the fleet, which carries pedestrians and bicycles across the bay to Bremerton every half hour. A waterfront observation deck offers views of marine activities in the bay and across the water to Bremerton's naval shipyards.

To get a taste of Port Orchard's early days as well as the richness of local artistic talent, stroll a few blocks south on Sidney Avenue to the **Sidney Art Gallery** at 202 Sidney Avenue (360–876–3693), open Tuesday through Saturday from 11:00 A.M. to 4:00 P.M. and on Sunday from 1:00 to 5:00 P.M. The first floor of this former Masonic Temple, built in 1903, features monthly exhibits highlighting the works of northwestern artists. The second floor houses the **Sidney Museum** (360–876–3693), featuring exhibits of turn-of-the-twentieth-century stores and coastal scenes. Learn more about Port Orchard history at the **Log Cabin Museum,** located just up the hill at 416 Sidney Street.

Bicyclists can enjoy a splendid ride on the **Manchester Bike Route.** This quiet, winding, beachfront road goes 15 miles to Manchester. Along the way you'll find beaches to explore, a restaurant where you can refuel, and a pleasant state park for play. For an all-day adventure, you can bicycle approximately 8 miles farther to the Southworth Ferry Dock and ride a ferry to Vashon Island or to downtown Seattle.

Reflections Bed and Breakfast (3878 Reflection Lane East, Port Orchard; 360–871–5582; www.portorchard.com/reflections), a spacious home filled with New England antiques, offers wide views of Bainbridge Island and Port Orchard Passage from each guest room, the deck, or the hot tub. Guests can choose from the Chesapeake Room, the Sudbury Room, the Fairfax Room, and the honeymoon suite, complete with a private sitting room and deck.

Poulsbo is a friendly community on the shores of Liberty Bay. It was settled in the 1880s by Norwegians, and the Poulsbo business community has revived this heritage to create a Scandinavian-theme town. Scandinavian delights await at every turn in the town's historic district, from potato *lefse* (pancakes) to the painted folk art designs (rosemaling) adorning shutters and doorways. Be sure to visit **Sluy's Poulsbo Bakery** (360–779–2798) on Front Street, Poulsbo's main street and also close to the water and the marina, for delicious Poulsbo bread and Scandinavian pastries galore.

You'll find a number of eateries and coffeehouses in Poulsbo to tempt the palate and quench the thirst with a freshly brewed cup of coffee or a steaming latte, among them **Checkers Espresso and Gallery** at 18881 Front Street, Suite

E (360–697–2559); the funky and fun *Poulsbohemian Coffeehouse* in the Egan Rank Building at 19003 Front Street (360–779–9199; www.silverlink .net/pbch/); *JJ's Fish House* at 1881 Front Street (360–779–6609); and *Sheila's Bay Cafe* at 18776 Front Street NE (360–779–2997).

After browsing in the shops or learning about marine biology, head for *Anderson Parkway,* with its large wooden gazebo (Kvelstad Pavilion), where you can relax and see the marina, the boats, Liberty Bay, and the green hills beyond. A 612-foot boardwalk leads from the Viking statue, along the shore, and up the forest-covered bluff to the serene *Arboretum Conservatory.* As you stroll you may see loons or cormorants dive for fish offshore.

After all this waterside exploration, you may want to take to the waves yourself. The *Olympic Outdoor Center* (18971 Front Street; 360–697–6095), across from Poulsbo's Marina and Waterfront Park, can outfit and prepare you for an adventure on Liberty Bay. The shop rents kayaks and canoes of all sizes for $10 to $20 per hour with instruction. Experienced naturalists are also available for scheduled or self-designed day (or full-moon) trips.

The *Cascade Marine Trail* links more than fifty kayak-accessible sites, from comfy bed-and-breakfasts to campgrounds, throughout Puget Sound. Kayaking visionaries foresee the day when this network of trails and campsites will take paddlers from Olympia north as far as Skagway, Alaska. Trail updates are available at the Olympic Outdoor Center, or you can contact the *Washington Water Trails Association* at 4649 Sunnyside Avenue North, Room 305, Seattle; (206) 545–9161; www.wwta.org.

berries

Western Washington's climate is conducive to growing a wide array of fresh berries, beginning in early summer with strawberries and raspberries and ending in the fall with wild blackberries and huckleberries. You'll find U-pick farms and stands throughout your journeys in the Puget Sound area. Berries are especially abundant in the Pierce, Skagit, Snohomish, Snoqualmie, and Whatcom County areas. When you're at a restaurant and the server says there's fresh berry pie, don't pass it up. You could also try the loganberry, a cross between a blackberry and a raspberry.

To find out more about the early people who first used these waters for food and travel, take a right (south) turn off Highway 305, south of Poulsbo, to the *Suquamish Museum* at 15838 Sandy Hook Road, Suquamish (360–394–8495; www.suquamish.nsn.us/museum). The museum's premier exhibit, *The Eyes of Chief Seattle,* will introduce you to the history and traditional lifestyle of the Suquamish Nation. The museum is open daily from 10:00 A.M. to 5:00 P.M.,

May 1 to September 30; and during the rest of the year on Friday through Sunday 11:00 A.M. to 4:00 P.M.

Just three miles northeast of the museum off Highway 305 is **Old Man House State Park,** where Chief Seattle (who gave his name to the city of Seattle) lived and died. The Old Man House was a huge plank building that once

Live Local Theater in the Puget Sound Region

From producing *Laughter on the Twenty-Third Floor* (Neil Simon) and *Ten Little Indians* (Agatha Christie) to *Crazy for You* (George Gershwin) and *South Pacific* (Rogers & Hammerstein), live local theater groups are alive and well in the greater Puget Sound region. These avid thespians also offer warm welcomes to visitors traveling to their towns and cities. Call for seasonal play dates.

American Cabaret Theatre
Seattle
www.americancabarettheatre.com

Bellingham Theatre Guild
Bellingham
(360) 733–1811
www.bellinghamtheatreguild.com

Driftwood Players
Aberdeen
(360) 538–1213

Everett Community Theater
Everett
(425) 257–6766

Fifth Avenue Musical Theatre Company
Seattle
(206) 292–2787
www.5thavenuetheatre.org

Key City Players
Port Townsend
(360) 385–7396

Paradise Cabaret Dinner Theatre and Summer Theatre
Gig Harbor
(253) 851–7529
www.paradisetheatre.org

The Playhouse Theatre
Bainbridge Island
(206) 842–8578

San Juan Island Community Theatre
Friday Harbor
(360) 378–3211
www.sanjuanarts.org

Seattle Children's Theatre
Seattle
(206) 441–3322
www.sct.org

Snoqualmie Falls Forest Theater
Snoqualmie
(425) 222–7944

Tacoma Little Theatre
Tacoma
(253) 272–2281
www.tacomalittletheatre.com

Whidbey Playhouse
Oak Harbor, Whidbey Island
(360) 679–2237;
www.whidbeyplayhouse.com

stretched along the beach. A display explains how local tribes built and used the gigantic house. The small park is ideal for picnics and quiet reflection alongside Agate Passage.

For a relaxing rural interlude, contact the **Manor Farm Inn** (26069 Big Valley Road NE, Poulsbo; 360–779–4628), a comfortable country-style bed-and-breakfast. The inn offers seven spacious guest rooms. See the rooms and pastoral grounds on the inn's Web site, www.manorfarminn.com. For other comfortable overnight stays in the Poulsbo area, contact **Murphy House Bed & Breakfast** near the bustling waterfront at 425 Northeast Hostmark Street (360–779–1600 or 800–799–1606; www.murphyhousebnb.com) and **Foxbridge Bed & Breakfast,** an elegant Georgian-style manor close to town at 30680 Highway 3 NE (360–598–5599; www.sfox.com/foxbridge).

Shine Road becomes Paradise Bay Road north of Highway 104, which winds through the forests above Hood Canal, offering occasional glimpses of the water along the way. Past Port Ludlow and Oak Bay, you can turn off to Indian Island and Fort Flagler, or you can continue straight toward Port Townsend. The bridge to **Indian Island** offers great views of the narrow strait separating this island from the mainland. The road beyond the bridge follows the southern shore, with several places to pull off and admire the scenery. Turn right at the JEFFERSON COUNTY DAY USE sign and follow the gravel road down to the beach to explore the pebbly tidelands, scattered with driftwood and salt marsh plants. Waterbirds are especially abundant during their fall migration. Just above the shore you'll find the trailhead to the South Indian Island Trail, an ideal hike if you want to explore more of the island's beauty.

The causeway from Indian Island to **Marrowstone Island** crosses lush wetlands and a lagoon between the two islands. Nearby sits the **Ecologic Place Beach Cottages** at 10 Beach Drive, Nordland (360–385–3077; www.beachcottagegetaway.com), a rustic retreat surrounded by tall grass and wild beaches, ideal for wildlife lovers. Eight cedar guest cabins encircling the meadow come with kitchens and windows that offer views of Oak Bay. The caretakers recommend that guests bring boots, warm clothing, blankets, and, if possible, a canoe or kayak. Linens, towels, basic kitchen utensils, and firewood for the woodstoves are provided.

Fort Flagler covers the entire north end of Marrowstone Island with forests, former gun batteries, and rugged coastline. The fort was used off and on for military training until it became a park in 1954. Although the campground is busy during the summer (call 888–226–7688 and see www.parks .wa.gov for information and campsite reservations), the park is big and diverse enough to offer seclusion for those who seek it. Numerous hiking trails go through the forest to cliffs overlooking Admiralty Inlet, where you might spy colorful harlequin ducks feeding offshore or perhaps watch a peregrine falcon soaring overhead. The *Roots of a Forest* interpretive trail, a short distance past the campground entrance, provides an inside look into forest ecology. There's an indoor interpretive display, open weekends from 1:00 to 4:00 P.M., across from the park office and a wild, expansive beach to explore at *Marrowstone Point,* down the road at the northeast corner of the park.

The *Ajax Cafe* in Port Hadlock (271 Water Street; 360–385–3450; www .ajaxcafe.com) is an unexpected delight. With its funky decor the much-loved cafe offers superb dinners, including shark, scallops, salmon, duck, and beef. The public wharves, ships, and boatyards across the street add to the ambience. A sign at the dock tells of the history of this now-quiet oceanside spot as a booming industrial site from 1878 to 1916. The cafe is open daily for dinner from 5:00 to 9:00 P.M. and for lunch Friday to Sunday from 11:30 A.M. to 3:30 P.M.

In *Port Townsend* there's plenty of northwest history to discover and also a plethora of arts events, open houses, and festivals. Contact the Port Townsend Visitor Center at 2437 East Sims Way (360–385–2722; www.enjoypt.com) for seasonal information. Residents enjoy meeting one another and visitors for coffee and delicious sweets at *Tyler Street Coffee House* (215 Tyler Street; 360–379–4185) or for a fresh, healthful breakfast at the *Salal Cafe* (634 Water Street). Both establishments open onto *Franklin Court,* a courtyard with flowers, wooden walkways, and fruit trees. On the bluff above the downtown area, *Sweet Laurette & Cyndee's Café & Patisserie* at 1029 Lawrence Street (360–385–4886) offers French-inspired goodies such as tarts, galettes, truffles, cheesecake, and lunch indoors and alfresco.

Because Port Townsend's scenic location has spawned a lively community of artists, visitors find many fine galleries located downtown in the waterfront area as well as uptown, on the bluff overlooking Puget Sound. Try *Ancestral Spirits Gallery* at 701 Water Street (360–385–0078) for Inuit and Native American art and *Northwinds Gallery,* located near the visitor center at 2409 Jefferson Street (360–379–1086).

The *Jefferson County Historical Museum* is located at 540 Water Street (360–385–1003; www.jchsmuseum.org) in the ca. 1891 city hall building. The four-story brick structure houses exhibits that describe the area's nautical, native, and Victorian history. The museum is open Monday through Saturday from 11:00 A.M. to 4:00 P.M. and Sunday from 1:00 to 4:00 P.M. Admission is by donation.

Be sure to explore the historic neighborhoods on the hill above downtown Port Townsend. Just follow the stairs up Taylor Street or take either Quincy or Monroe Street up the hill to see the many Victorian homes that once housed the cultural and financial elite of territorial Washington. Stop to see the Old Bell

Tower on Tyler Street on the bluff, which once summoned the volunteer fire department. At the corner of Jefferson and Taylor Streets, you'll find the ca. 1868 **Rothschild House,** which has been preserved as it was a century ago, when it was home to the Rothschild family. You can tour the house from 11:00 A.M. to 4:00 P.M. daily during spring and summer to see the large kitchen, the formal dining room and parlor, and bedrooms filled with the family's original furniture and clothing. Be sure to stroll through the rose garden with its fragrant, many-petaled varieties, some dating to the early 1800s. Call the visitor information center (360–385–2722) for the current dates of Port Townsend's favorite annual events, including the **Annual Victorian Festival** in mid-March, the **Secret Garden Tour** in late June, the **Historic Homes Tour** in mid-September, and the **Cabin Fever Quilt Show** in early September.

If you can't spend a night at the opulent **Ann Starrett Mansion Victorian Bed and Breakfast Inn** (744 Clay Street; 360–385–3205; www.starrettmansion .com), you may call to see if tours are currently scheduled. It is a splendid example of Victorian architecture, complete with an octagonal tower, a sweeping circular staircase, and formal sitting rooms. Ask about the comfortable carriage house guest rooms on the garden level.

Within walking distance, on Jackson Street, find lovely **Chetzemoka Park** and its rose gardens, including a splendid rose arbor walkway, large swings, and views of Admiralty Inlet and the Cascade Mountains to the east. Picnics are a favorite pastime here. Other comfortable places to stay overnight in Port Townsend include **James House Bed & Breakfast,** a home built by a prominent businessman ca. 1889 and now renovated, located on the bluff at 1238 Washington Street (360–385–1238; www.jameshouse.com), and **Ravenscroft Inn Bed & Breakfast,** also located on the bluff, at 533 Quincy Street, and overlooking Puget Sound (360–385–2784; www.ravenscroftinn.com). From the bluff you can walk down a series of concrete stairs to the downtown wsaterfront area and its eclectic assortment of shops, galleries, boutiques, and eateries.

Consider the **Fountain Cafe** at 920 Washington Street (360–385–1364) for seafood and pasta specialties; **Fins Restaurant** at 1019 Water Street (360–379–3474) for superb seafood; **Nifty Fifties** at 817 Water Street (360–385–1931) for juicy hamburgers and old-fashioned sundaes, shakes, malts, and sodas; and **Elevated Ice Cream & Candy Shop,** 627 Water Street (360–385–1156), to enjoy homemade ice cream, Italian ices, espresso, and pastries and to see local art on display.

While you are in Port Townsend, be sure to inquire about events at **Fort Worden State Park** (360–344–4400). Like Fort Flagler to the east, Fort Worden was once part of the fortifications that protected Puget Sound from sea invasion. Located just 2 miles north of downtown, the fort is the site of **Port**

The Nautical Life: Wooden Boats, Tall Ships, Schooners, Wooden Boatbuilding, and Wooden Boat Festivals

Center for Wooden Boats
Located on Lake Union, offering exhibits, programs, and classic wooden boats to rent for informal paddling excursions on the lake
1010 Valley Street
Seattle
(206) 382–2628
www.cwb.org

Northwest Maritime Education Alliance
Offers collaborative programs: lecture series, summer workshops, restoration projects, and historic vessel tours
www.nwmaritime.org

The Northwest School of Wooden Boatbuilding
Offers classes and workshops
251 Otto Street
Port Townsend
(360) 385–4948
www.nwboatschool.org

Sound Experience
Offers environmental sailing programs in the waters of Puget Sound aboard the historic schooner *Adventuress*
2310 Washington Street
Port Townsend
(360) 379–0438
www.soundexp.org

The tall ship *Lady Washington*
Scheduled ports of call along the West Coast on the ship's Web site
www.ladywashington.org

Wooden Boat Festival
Held the first weekend of September in Port Townsend; includes the Symposium on Wooden Boatbuilding
www.woodenboat.org

The Wooden Boat Foundation
A center for maritime education located in the Cupola House at Point Hudson
380 Jefferson Street
Port Townsend
(360) 385–3628
www.woodenboat.org

Townsend Marine Science Center (360–385–5582) and of Centrum Foundation (360–385–3102; www.centrum.org). Events offered by Centrum include writing, music, and dance conferences, which usually offer activities open to the public. There is also a rhododendron garden, an artillery museum, nature walks, and a public beach to explore. You can stay in the old barracks or in comfortable officers' quarters, in the youth hostel, or at the campground. For information about vacation housing or camping at Fort Worden State Park, call (360) 385–4730.

Whidbey Island, the largest of the Puget Sound islands, has been popu-lated for 10,000 years by Native peoples and was one of the first areas on the sound to be settled by Europeans. Its extensive coastline, lush forests, and loca-tion midway between the snowcapped Olympic and Cascade mountain ranges create outstanding views everywhere you look. Whidbey Island has long been a favorite retreat for city dwellers, offering visitors plenty to do and see. Small working farms, artist studios, and innovative home businesses are scattered among meadows, shoreline, and evergreen forests. There are several historic communities and small-scale resorts. Whidbey Island is accessible from both the Seattle and Port Townsend areas by short ferry rides and also from the north across the Deception Pass bridge. To get to Whidbey Island from the Seattle area, take exit 189 (Mukilteo Ferry) from I–5 and follow signs through Mukilteo to the ferry terminal. Join the lineup in the right-hand lane. Ferries leave about every half hour and take twenty minutes to reach the island. If you need more infor-mation, call Washington State Ferries at (360) 464–6400 or the statewide toll-free number at (800) 843–3779.

Highway 525, which becomes Highway 20 north of Keystone, runs down the center of the island, carry-ing most through-traffic. You can also take the meandering local roads that follow the shoreline for better views and less traffic.

Langley, on Saratoga Passage, is a favorite island community to visit. To get there, turn right on Lan-gley Road off Highway 525 and fol-low signs into town.

whidbeyisland trivia

Living on an island is somewhat different from living on the mainland. For example, when the locals leave the island they often say, "We're going shopping over in America."

Note from the islanders: Do not under any circumstances try to cut your automobile into the ferry line—you will incur the wrath of not only the islanders but also everyone else in line.

Washington State Ferries
(360) 464–6400
www.wsdot.wa.gov/ferries

On the way, stop to visit *Whidbey Island Vineyard and Winery* (5237 South Langley Road; 360–221–2040; www.whidbeyislandwinery.com), where you can taste samples of its rhubarb, pinot noir, and siegerrebe varieties, as well as others. The tasting room is closed on Tuesday during July and August.

Langley has many antiques and art galleries, and you might want to sam-ple one of them, the *Gaskill/Olson Gallery* at 302 First Street (360–221–2978; www.gaskillolson.com). Although a busy tourist town during summer week-ends, Langley is always pleasant, with plenty of spots to sit and view the nautical scenery on Saratoga Passage. On First Street you can join the bronze statue of a sea-gazing boy leaning over the railing above Saratoga Passage, with his dog lying at his side. From here a wooden staircase leads down to the beach, where you can stroll along a grassy walkway or descend farther to the pebbly shore, below a bulkhead sculpted with images of salmon and whales.

You'll find cafes, restaurants, espresso bars, and bistros to suit every taste on First and Second Streets. Try *Mike's Place* at 219 First Street (360–221–6575) and *Cafe Langley* at 113 First Street (360–221–3090). *The Braeburn Restaurant,* at 197 Second Street (360–221–3211), is one of the locals' favorite breakfast hangouts. Also on Second Street is *Useless Bay Coffee Company,* which you can pop into for coffee and espresso.

For fine dining locals suggest *Fish Bowl* at 317 Second Street (360–221–6511). For more casual fare try *Edge Cliff Restaurant,* 510 Cascade Avenue (360–221–8899).

For a spin on live theater, plan to attend the *Langley Mystery Weekend* sponsored by the Chamber of Commerce (360–221–6765; www.whidbey.com/langley/lc/mystery) and held during the last full weekend of February. Mystery buffs meet over coffee in local cafes and coffee shops to pore over clues in order to nab the character that did the nefarious deed. Previous mysteries, all locally written, have included *A Taste for Murder, Much Ado about Kitties or the Cat's Revenge,* and *A Murder of Crows.* It's great fun, with locals dressed in vintage garb and helping with the special effects. You can also arrange for tickets to attend plays and musicals by the *Island Theatre Players* at Whidbey Island Center for the Arts, at 565 Camano Avenue in Langley (360–221–8268; www.whidbey.net/wica). Recent offerings included the backstage farce *Moon over Buffalo* and the musical thriller *Little Shop of Horrors.*

To stay overnight in the Langley area, call the innkeepers at *Country Cottage of Langley Bed & Breakfast,* located at 215 Sixth Street (360–221–8709; www.acountrycottage.com) and one of the first vintage homes to be remodeled for bed-and-breakfast travelers. Innkeepers Jerry and Joanne Lechner offer fine hospitality at *Eagles Nest Inn Bed & Breakfast,* a contemporary octagonal-shaped home situated with a fine view of Saratoga Passage at 4680 Saratoga Road (360–221–5331; www.eaglesnestinn.com). You can also find amenable lodgings in and close to Langley at the *Cat and the Fiddle Bed & Breakfast,* 430 Fourth Street (360–221–5460) and at *Inglewood Haven,* 5010 Inglewood Drive (360–221–8641; www.inglewoodhaven.com).

The rhododendron, Washington's state flower, is especially prolific on Whidbey Island. If these pique your interest, you'll want to visit *Meerkerk Rhododendron Gardens* at 3531 South Meerkerk Lane, Greenbank (360–678–1912; www.meerkerkgardens.org). The rhododendron blooms are usually at their peak the last two weeks of April and the beginning of May, but the gardens are lovely at any time. Featuring more than 800 mature rhododendron and companion plants, the forested landscape includes ponds, forest, and waterside nature trails. To get there, turn east off Highway 525 on Resort Road, 1½ miles south of Greenbank, or follow the scenic Honeymoon Bay Road for 5 miles north from Freeland along Holmes Harbor.

You could check to see if the charming log cottages are available at *Guest House Log Cottages* (24371 State Route 525, Greenbank; 360–678–3115; www.guesthouselogcottages.com). If these cottages are not available, you could try *Farmhouse Bed & Breakfast,* 2740 East Sunshine Lane in Clinton (360–321–6288; www.farmhousebb.com). Or call innkeeper Peggy Moore to ask about the romantic *Seacliff Cottage,* 727 Windmill Drive in Freeland (360–331–1566; www.cliffhouse.net/cottage/).

Hillsides covered with vines at the historic *Whidbey's Greenbank Berry Farm & Winery* (360–678–7700; www.greenbankfarm.com) are a pleasant setting for a picnic, and visitors are welcome to tour the farm, where loganberries (a raspberry/blackberry cross) are distilled into a popular liqueur, Whidbey's Loganberry Liqueur. The gift shop sells snacks for your picnic basket in addition to a selection of Washington State wines. The farm, on Wonn Road off Highway 525, a quarter mile north of Greenbank, is open daily from 10:00 A.M. to 4:30 P.M.

For tasty takeout entrees, try the deli at *Coupe's Greenbank Store* (360–678–4326) located at the corner of Wonn Road and Highway 525.

Historic *Coupeville* is located several miles to the north, about midway up the island on scenic *Penn Cove.* Saratoga Passage lies to the east, and Admiralty Inlet lies to the west. Look for a gaggle of mussel rafts floating out on Penn Cove where the famous Penn Cove mussels are grown and harvested. The annual *Penn Cove Mussel Festival,* with much eating of local seafood and deliciously prepared mussels, takes place the first weekend in March.

To learn about Coupeville's Native American, pioneer, and maritime history and to pick up a walking tour guide, visit the *Island County Historical Museum,* at 902 Northwest Alexander Street (360–678–3310) at the end of Front Street by the wharf. The museum is open Tuesday through Sunday from 11:00 A.M. to 5:00 P.M.

After browsing the museum go across the street to the wharf, which overlooks Penn Cove and the mussel-growing rafts. Poke around the *Gallery at the Wharf* and also the *Harbor Store Cafe* (360–678–6905) for breakfast or lunch fare. Walk along Front Street and up Main Street to see more historic buildings, then stop at *Miriam's Espresso* on Main Street (360–678–5600), if you're ready for steaming lattes or cups of Tully's freshly brewed coffee. Or detour into **Mariti Chocolate Company,** 12 Northwest Front Street (360–678–5811), for locally made fudge and chocolates. If you are in the area on Saturday, take in the **Coupeville Farmers' Market** (from April through October; 360–678–5434) on the corner of Main and Eighth Streets to mingle with friendly locals and load up on fresh berries, flowers, and vegetables. For fabulous freshly baked cinnamon rolls, soups, and salads, stop at **Knead & Feed Restaurant** on Front and Main Streets (360–678–5431), a former storehouse and laundry built in 1871 and nestled one level down the bluff facing Penn Cove under the Tartan and Tweed Store. Its original post-and-beam structure adds to the ambience of this pleasant waterside spot. Local folks swear by the steamed mussels and garlic bread at **Toby's Tavern** on Front Street (360–678–4222).

To stay overnight in the Coupeville area, contact **Anchorage Inn Bed & Breakfast,** 807 North Main Street (360–678–5581 or 877–230–1313; www .anchorage-inn.com), where children over ten are welcome; the **Compass Rose Bed and Breakfast,** 508 South Main Street (360–678–5318; www.compass rosebandb.com); and **Garden Isle Guest Cottages,** 207 Northwest Coveland Street (360–678–5641; www.gardenislecottages.com), near the downtown area. For evening dining in Coupeville, check out local restaurants that do great things with mussels, seafood, and steaks, including **The Oystercatcher** (360–678–0683) and **Christopher's** (360–678–5480). Another pleasant dining and lodging alternative is the ca. 1907 **Captain Whidbey Inn** (2072 West Whidbey Island Inn Road; 360–678–4097; www.captainwhidbeyinn.com) situated on the west shore of Penn Cove. The lodge, built of madrona logs, has comfortable rooms, a cozy beachstone fireplace, and a restaurant. Cabins and cottages are also available.

You'll find the impressive **Admiralty Head Lighthouse** interpretive center located near the Keystone ferry landing at **Fort Casey State Park;** call the staff at (360) 678–4519 for seasonal tours. The park is open year-round for camping on a first-come, first-served arrangement. There are old forts to explore, long stretches of undeveloped public beaches to walk, and major tracts of protected forest and farmland to see in the area, which includes **Ebey's Landing National Historical Reserve.**

Before continuing north to scenic Deception Pass at Whidbey Island's north end, an awesome sight in practically any kind of weather, you can find pleasant eateries in the community of **Oak Harbor.** Or replenish your cooler, put together an impromptu picnic, and continue north to **Deception Pass State Park.** Pull into any large grocery outlet for supplies, or stop at **Pot Belly Deli** (32070 Highway 20; 360–675–5204) for gargantuan sandwiches, or **Seabolt's Smokehouse** (31640 Highway 20; 360–675–6485) for fresh seafood deli fare. You could also pick up espressos and goodies at **Daily Grind** (1351 Southwest Barlow Street; 360–675–2767) and at **Dairy Valley Old Fashioned Ice Cream Parlor** (296 Northeast Kettle Street; 360–675–5300). Look for the large Dutch windmill and try **Auld Holland Motor Inn** (800–228–0148) on Highway 20 for a comfortable overnight stay in Oak Harbor. **Zorba's** (360–279–8322) at 841 Southeast Pioneer Way offers pleasant dining with Italian and Greek fare. If you're in the area on the weekend,

check with **Whidbey Playhouse** (360–679–2237; www.whidbeyplayhouse .com) to see what the local thespians are offering in the way of drama, comedy, musical, or children's theater productions.

One of the best ways to see Deception Pass is from the water. **Mosquito Fleet Enterprise** (800–325–6722; www.clippervacations.com) offers scenic day cruises and daylong whale-watching excursions from Everett up Saratoga Passage through the steep canyon walls of Deception Pass and on through the San Juan Islands. The boat carries 150 passengers and offers snacks to purchase from an onboard galley; you can also bring your own snacks in nonglass containers. Also bring your cameras and binoculars.

Northern Sound

Just across the Deception Pass bridge from Whidbey Island, travelers reach Fidalgo Island. For a bird's-eye view of this island, turn west from Highway 20 just south of Pass Lake and follow Rosario Road as it forks right, away from Burrows Bay. At the Lake Erie Grocery take an acute left onto Heart Lake Road, then turn right to enter **Mount Erie Park**. The steep road (not recommended for trailers or RVs) has several trails and observation points along the way, and the wide-angle views of northern Puget Sound and its islands from the 1,300-foot summit is spectacular. Continue right on Heart Lake Road to reach the town of Anacortes, the main gateway to the San Juan Islands. But before you head for the large ferry terminal, take time to explore this eclectic community. Anacortes also makes a great base camp where you can leave your bags and car to board the ferry for a day trip to Friday Harbor on San Juan Island.

During your walking tour, you'll meander past the **Burlington Northern Railway Station** at Seventh Street and R Avenue. The revitalized station

Anacortes Mural Project

Anacortes resident Bill Mitchell initiated the idea for the life-size cutouts and life-size townsfolk figures that appear all over town. His goal is to create murals that represent one hundred years of the community's history. Enjoy more than one hundred, with a map and numbered list from the Anacortes Visitors Information Center at 819 Commercial Avenue (360–293–3832; www.anacortes.org). Here are some favorites:

Alfred Jorgeson
the barn door halibut, 1946

Ann Bessner and Guemes Island girls
in a North Beach canoe, 1934

Bill Mitchell
self-portrait with 1954 Autoette electric cart and wheelchair

Cecil Weyrich
Black Ball Line & Washington State ferries, 1928 to 1972

Dancing flapper
by John Held Jr., 1920s cartoonist

Dennis Mapes
birthday jeep and American flag, July 4, 1944

Edna Whitney
tandem bicycle and friends, ca. 1910

First train in town
1890

Hubert Crosby
Empire Theater assistant manager, 1925 to 1928

Ken Moore
Anacortes Seahawks basketball player, 1960

1947 Harley Davidson
two-sided

Rainier Bar bartender
with two puppies, ca. 1908

Robert Sund
Ish River poet, musician, and Bohemian, 1993

Skagit Saloon window
1891

Toulouse-Lautrec poster lady
Paris, France, 1895

Wild Bill Bessner
his Indian motorcycle, 1920

houses an arts center, the ***Depot Gallery*** (360–293–3663), open from mid-May to mid-October Tuesday through Friday and Sunday from 1:00 to 4:00 P.M. and on Saturday from 10:00 A.M. to 4:00 P.M.

Located nearby and a local favorite, ***Gere-a-Deli*** (502 Commercial Avenue; 360–293–7383) offers tasty clam chowder, salads, and sandwiches from 8:00 A.M. to 5:00 P.M. Monday through Saturday. ***Calico Cupboard Cafe and Bakery*** at 901 Commercial Avenue (360–293–7315) offers tasty luncheon fare, and ***Anacortes Chocolate Factory & Cafe*** at 2302 Commercial Avenue (360–293–8042) is well known for its sinful chocolates, scones, and espresso, as well as salads, sandwiches, and homemade soups. ***Penguin Coffee,*** 2119 Commericial Street (360–588–8321), is a good spot for fresh-brewed coffee and espresso. ***Randy's Pier 61*** at 209 T Avenue (360–293–5108) offers waterfront dining with great views of Guemes Channel; it's open daily for lunch and dinner and Sunday for brunch. ***Rock Fish Grill & Anacortes Brewery*** at 320 Commercial Avenue (360–588–1720) is a local favorite for microbrews and ales, seafood, and pizza done in a wood-fired oven.

One of the best-kept secrets in Anacortes is ***SeaBear Specialty Seafoods*** (605 Thirtieth Street; 360–293–4661). Here you'll discover alderwood-smoked salmon, soups, chowders, and barbecued salmon. The warehouse store is in an industrial complex just east of Commerical Avenue and off Thirtieth at T Street.

You'll find the older neighborhoods just west of Commercial Avenue on Sixth through Twelfth Streets. ***Causland World War I Memorial Park,*** on Eighth Street between M and N Avenues, is a pleasant green hideaway surrounded by mosaic walls made of white quartz and red argillite swirling in brown and gray sandstone. Across the street you can review the history of Fidalgo Island at the ***Anacortes History Museum*** (1305 Eighth Street), once the town's Carnegie Library. For a pleasant overnight stay, you could call the hospitable innkeepers at ***Nantucket Inn Bed & Breakfast,*** close to downtown at 3402 Commercial Avenue (360–299–2011; www.whidbey.com/nantucket); at ***Autumn Leaves Bed & Breakfast,*** 2301 Twenty-first Street (866–293–4929); at ***Heron House Guest House,*** 11110 Marine Drive (360–293–4477); and at ***Ship Harbor Motor Inn,*** 5316 Ferry Terminal Road (800–852–8568). For splendid evening dining try ***Charlie's Restaurant*** (360–293–7377), also near the ferry landing, and ***Flounder Bay Café*** at 2201 Skyline Way (360–293–3681). You could also check with the local players at ACT, ***Anacortes Community Theater*** (360–293–4373), to see what's on the current playbill.

For a pleasant drive or bicycle ride, take Twelfth Avenue westward past the ferry exit. Follow Sunset Avenue onto Loop Road around ***Washington Park,*** where you'll find access to several public beaches. At Fidalgo Head stop at the viewpoint on a high promontory overlooking Burrows Island and Bay. When you can tear yourself away from the great views, circle back to Sunset Drive. Before departing Anacortes consider it somewhat mandatory to visit the splendid San Juan Islands (www.wsdot.wa.gov/ferries).

All four islands with regular ferry service—Lopez, Shaw, Orcas, and San Juan—offer plenty to explore. Lopez and Shaw Islands are the most off the beaten path. Shaw, the smallest San Juan island accessible by public ferry, offers a pleasant step back in time. Franciscan Sisters used to run the ferry dock and the adjacent ***Shaw General Store*** (360–468–2288). This is the only place on Shaw to buy provisions, so stock up here for a picnic. The charming old store, now run by a local family, also offers coffee, espresso, and ice cream. Old baskets, fruit boxes, and nautical paraphernalia decorate the walls.

The *Shaw Island Public Library,* in the center of the island on Blind Bay Road, is a sunny little building, open from 2:00 to 4:00 P.M. Tuesday and Saturday and from 10:00 A.M. to noon on Thursday. Inside, the smell of cedar fills the air as you sit back in a cozy spot with a good book and a view of the surrounding forest. The children's corner is full of old favorites and new storybooks arranged around a colorful rug peppered with pillows and child-size chairs. Opposite the library you can see the old red schoolhouse, more than one hundred years old. A new school was built in the 1980s for the island's small number of elementary-age students.

Head south along Hoffman Cove Road, then left on Squaw Bay Road past secluded Squaw Bay. Past the bay is the turnoff to *South Beach County Park,* with several campsites overlooking the bay. The small beach provides a quiet picnic spot with ample supplies of driftwood logs for rustic benches in the sand. From here follow Squaw Bay Road through a scenic valley back to Blind Bay and the ferry dock.

Lopez Island is larger and more developed than Shaw but still offers many opportunities for quiet and seclusion. Located 4 miles from the ferry landing, Lopez village, with a museum, a store, and several restaurants, is the island's commercial center. The *Lopez Historical Museum* (360–468–2049), full of island history and lore, is worth a stop. The museum is open from May through September Friday to Sunday, noon to 4:00 P.M. For good eateries in Lopez village, try *Love Dog Cafe* (360–468–2150), *Holly B's Bakery* (360–468–2133), *Isabel's Espresso* (360–468–4114), and *Lopez Old Fashioned Soda Fountain* (360–468–4511) located in the pharmacy. *Bay Cafe* at 9 Old Post Road (360–468–3700) is an island favorite for fine dining and offers breakfast on weekends. At scenic Fisherman Bay try *The Galley* (360–468–2713) for the best water views along with tasty fish-and-chips, juicy hamburgers, and good Mexican dishes.

For a comfortable overnight stay in Lopez village, call the friendly folks at *Edenwild Inn Bed & Breakfast* (800–606–0662; www.edenwildinn.com), who offer eight guest rooms, cozy fireplaces, and delicious country breakfasts. At *MacKaye Harbor Inn Bed & Breakfast* (ca. 1904), 949 MacKaye Harbor Road (360–468–2253 or 888–314–6140; www.mackayeharborinn.com), travelers find five guest rooms, bountiful breakfasts, and great water views along with kayak rentals and the use of the inn's mountain bikes during their stay. Or if you're tucked into the woods, you might welcome eagles and ravens for neighbors, along with two pleasant resident cats, at *Ravens Rook Guest Cabin,* located off Shark Reef Road (360–468–2838 or 877–321–2493; www

.rockisland.com/~ravensrook/) and done in rustic Northwest post-and-beam style. From here a short walk through adjacent Shark Reef Sanctuary takes you to the rocky beach, which offers large tidal pools filled with intriguing sea creatures.

Public beaches on Lopez Island include the west side of Fisherman Bay off Bay Shore Road, **Shark Reef Park** (good tide pools here but rocky) at the end of Shark Reef Road on the island's southwest tip, and **Agate Beach** off MacKaye Harbor Road at the island's south end. **Spencer Spit State Park and Campground** (360–468–2251; www.parks.wa.gov) on the island's east shore is a scenic spot with hiking trails and nearby rocky beach areas to beachcomb. **Odlin County Park** (360–378–1842) is closer to the water and offers camping and RV spaces (no hookups) about 4 miles from Lopez village.

The next ferry stop in this watery region of some 175 islands is Orcas Island. By now any stressed city dwellers are beginning to relax into island time. The salt water and crisp breezes open to wider and wider vistas of small islands covered with tall, red-barked madrone, low-lying manzanita, and weathered rocks covered with myriad algae in soft hues of cream, yellow, and green. The wide, green and white ferry lumbers to the dock at Orcas Island, bumping against tall wooden pilings and lurching to a stop. Crew members attach the huge lines and ready the debarkation process. Those departing onto Orcas are in their vehicles and ready to motor carefully from their section of the ferry's lower and midlevels.

You can easily spend two or three days on Orcas exploring its nooks and crannies. Drive over to **Moran State Park and Campground** (360–376–2326; www.parks.wa.gov), hike its many trails, and then drive up to nearby **Mount Constitution.** One of the grandest views of the islands is from atop the tower here, especially fine at sunset. Poke into the small communities of Deer Harbor, Eastsound, Westsound, Olga, and Doe Bay. Have a picnic by the water. Visit art galleries and artists' studios.

Hopefully, you have called well in advance to make overnight reservations at one of the welcoming bed-and-breakfast inns on Orcas Island. Not far from the ferry landing, **Turtleback Farm Inn** (Crow Valley Road; 360–376–4914; www.turtlebackinn.com) offers guests pastoral views and excellent cuisine along with resident sheep, chickens, and geese. At **Kingfish Inn Bed & Breakfast** and **West Sound Cafe** (360–376–4440; www.kingfishinn.com), located 3 miles from the ferry landing, at the intersection of Deer Harbor and Crow Valley Roads, Lori and Mike Breslauer offer four light and airy guest rooms with water views on the second floor of a historic building they restored in 1997. Your night's stay includes the option of a breakfast basket delivered to your room or, better yet, tasty morning fare served in the couple's pleasant cafe

Orca Whales 101

It's no wonder that *Free Willy* was filmed in the San Juans, as three pods of orca whales make their home in these waters. You can whale-watch by sea, by land, and by air in the San Juans, and you might see one without even trying. Here are some facts you can use to embellish your own whale tales:

Males average 29 feet in length; females average 24 feet. Females outnumber males four to one and can live to age eighty. The average male lives to about thirty.

Males weigh up to 16,000 pounds, females up to 12,000 pounds.

Whales give birth to one calf at two- to six-year intervals.

Typical whale diet is fish, squid, sea lions, seals, and other whales. Orcas eat from 100 to 300 pounds of food a day.

The whales "talk" to each other with a dialect unique to each pod.

Orcas navigate the waters at about 2 to 6 mph.

(open 9:00 A.M. to 3:00 P.M.) on the first floor, along with great views of the small marina, the water, and islands beyond. For those who like getting farther away from it all, contact the innkeepers at **Otters Pond Bed & Breakfast,** located beyond Eastsound and near Moran State Park (360–376–8844; www.otterspond.com).

If you're interested in private cottages available by the day or week on Orcas Island, call **Buckhorn Farm Bungalow** at 17 Jensen Road (360–376–2298; www.buckhornfarm.com). The bungalow is close to the beach, sleeps four, and comes with a woodstove, cozy sitting areas, and a cheerful kitchen. At the **Old Trout Bed & Breakfast** at 4272 Orcas Road (360–376–7474; www.oldtroutinn.com), ask about the **Water's Edge Cottage,** where a couple can snuggle up with a view of the pond.

For great coffee and dining in and near Eastsound, the largest community on Orcas, try **Teezer's Coffee Shop** at the corner of North Beach and A Streets (360–376–2913), **Bilbo's Festivo** (360–376–4728) for regional Mexican, and **Christina's** (360–376–4904) for Northwest seafood. For morning, midday, or takeout, locals suggest **Rose's Bread & Specialties** (360–376–5805). Enjoy a scenic drive past Rosario Resort and beyond Moran State Park and Campground to try **Cafe Olga at Artworks** (360–376–5098) for an international flair, or **Olga's Cafe** nearby (360–376–5862) for tasty regional fare (plus food to go for your picnic basket) and great views from its deck overlooking the bay. For a comfortable overnight stay right in the village of Eastsound, contact the friendly inkeepers at **Kangaroo House Bed & Breakfast** (360–376–2175 or 888–371–2175; www.kangaroohouse.com).

Getting off the island takes a bit of planning. Double-check the ferry departure you want and plan to arrive at the ferry landing a couple of hours early, particularly during the busy summer season. Vehicles line up in a first-come, first-served arrangement. From Orcas you can either ferry back to Anacortes, on the mainland, or continue on to San Juan Island and, even farther, on to Vancouver Island, British Columbia (U.S. and Canadian Customs personnel meet the ferries at the Sidney, B.C., ferry terminal). Check the current ferry schedule for the international sailings (206–464–6400; www.wsdot.wa.gov/ferries).

Bustling Friday Harbor is the largest town on **San Juan Island,** which is the largest of the inhabited islands in the San Juans. Folks find a busy marina, the ferry landing, and a plethora of shops and eateries. From mornings to midday try **San Juan Coffee Roasting Co.** at the Cannery Landing (360– 378–4443) and **Garden Path Cafe** on Second Street (360–378–6255). For casual and fine dining in Friday Harbor, check with **The Place Bar & Grill** on Spring Street next to the ferry landing (360–378–8707), **Haley's Bait Shop & Grill** on Spring Street near the local movie theater (360–378–4434), **Vinny's Italian** on West Street (360–378–1934), and **Friday Harbor House** on West Street overlooking the harbor and marina (360–378–8455). For fine dining away from town, try the much-loved **Duck Soup Inn** on Roche Harbor Road (360–378–4878) and, at **Roche Harbor Resort** at the northwest tip of the island, **Madrona Grill** or **McMillan's Dining Room** (360–378–5757).

thepigwar

In 1859 on San Juan Island, a long-standing border dispute between British and American residents nearly resulted in an all-out war. The catalyst and only casualty, however, was an Englishman's pig. An American shot the pig when he found the errant animal rummaging in his potato patch. The resulting "Pig War" lasted until 1872, when the island's ownership was awarded to the United States.

Today you can visit American Camp at the south end of the island, where the American troops were stationed, and British Camp, on Garrison Bay at the north end, where the Royal Marines of Britain were posted. Both offer interpretive displays, hiking trails, and scenic beaches.

Nearby, **Lime Kiln Cafe** (360–378–6809) is a good spot for breakfast or lunch. *Note:* Some island eateries close during the winter months and reopen around Memorial Day weekend.

For bedding down on lively San Juan Island, call well ahead for information and reservations. On the water at the marina, you can arrange accommodations on **Wharfside Bed & Breakfast,** which is aboard the *Slow Season*

(360–378–5661; www.slowseason.com). There are two cozy staterooms aboard the 60-foot ketch-rigged sailboat. You tend to get seasick sleeping aboard? Well, not to worry; for other spots on dry land in Friday Harbor, check with the Schutte family at **Panacea Bed & Breakfast,** 595 Park Street (360–378–3757; www.panacea-inn.com) or with **Harrison House Suites** at 235 C Street (360–378–3587; www.harrisonhousesuites.com). Outside of Friday Harbor try **Highland Inn Bed & Breakfast** near Lime Kiln Whale Watch Park (360–378–9450; www.highlandinn.com); **Oak Ridge Bed & Breakfast** at 141 Glen Oak Lane (360–378–6184; www.oak-ridge.net) on the way out to Cattle Point;

and **Lakedale Resort Log Cabins,** 4313 Roche Harbor Road (360–378–2350; www.lakedale.com). You can also find scenic camping and RV sites on the island by checking with the visitor information center in Friday Harbor (360–378–5240; www.sanjuanisland.org) and with www.guidetosanjuans.com. For those who like the hinterlands, call the friendly innkeepers at **Olympic Lights Bed & Breakfast,** located several miles from Friday Harbor (360–378–3186). The renovated 1895 farmhouse sits in a wide meadow near the bluff that overlooks the Strait of Juan de Fuca. From here you can walk to the site of **American Camp** and enjoy scenic walks at 4th of July Beach. Check out **British Camp** and its historic displays about the infamous Pig War. Don't miss a visit to the **Whale Museum** in Friday Harbor at 62 First Street (360–378–4710; www.whalemuseum.com). *Note:* The public is encouraged to report any signs of stranded marine mammals by calling the Whale Museum.

nativeamerican terms

The ferries that sail from Anacortes to Shaw, Lopez, Orcas, and San Juan Islands have Native American names. The most well-known and best-loved island ferries:

Elwha, meaning "elk"

Illahee, meaning "land, place, or location"

Kaleetan, meaning "arrow"

Washington State Ferry information
(360) 464–6400
www.wsdot.wa.gov/ferries

After returning to the Anacortes ferry terminal from the San Juan Islands, you can head east for a few miles to the communities of La Conner and Mount Vernon. During April some 1,100 acres are carpeted with blooming tulips and daffodils, which thrive in the rich loamy soil of the Lower Skagit Valley. On clear days views of snowcapped Mount Baker in the distance frame the colorful scene. Tulips and bulbs are sold at roadside stands, and you can tour some of the fields. Check (360) 428–5959 and www.tulipfestival.org for information on the annual Skagit Valley Tulip Festival in April. *Note:* Visit midweek to avoid busy weekends, when the narrow farm roads are often clogged with traffic.

The **White Swan Guest House** (1388 Moore Road; 360–445–6805; www .thewhiteswan.com) provides accommodations on pastoral Fir Island, just a few miles from La Conner. The restored 1890s Victorian farmhouse offers colorful perennial gardens and the charming Garden Cottage, ideal for families with children or for a romantic retreat.

Then follow Chillberg Road west to **La Conner,** which sits on the bank of the Swinomish Channel. The scenic waterway carries a parade of small boats between Padilla Bay to the north and Skagit Bay to the south. Once a quiet village serving local farmers and fishermen, La Conner is now a popular tourist destination, with restaurants, antiques shops, and boutiques clustered along First Street. Be sure to stop and visit the **Skagit County Historical Museum** at 501 Fourth Street (360–466–3365), which includes exhibits on the area's history, industries, and fashions. The museum is open from 1:00 to 5:00 P.M. Wednesday through Sunday and charges a small admission fee. Also, don't miss visiting the **La Conner Quilt Museum** located in the ca. 1891 Gaches Mansion at 703 South Second Street (360–466–4288; www.laconnerquilts.com). The museum houses a wonderful collection of quilts from the Northwest and also offers ongoing exhibits of quilts and fiber art throughout the year. Afterward,

---

Blueberry-Lemon Muffins

These Blueberry-Lemon Muffins are from the White Swan Guest House (360–445–6805) near La Conner and Mount Vernon:

Dry ingredients	Wet ingredients
2 cups flour	1 egg, beaten
½ cup sugar	1 8-oz. container fat-free lemon yogurt
1 teaspoon baking soda	2 tablespoons milk
2 teaspoons baking powder	½ cup vegetable oil
1 teaspoon salt	
1 cup fresh or frozen blueberries	

Preheat oven to 400 degrees. Fold wet ingredients into flour mixture until just mixed and lumpy. Spoon into lined muffin cups in muffin pan. Sprinkle sugar on top. Bake for 18 to 20 minutes until golden brown on top. "These muffins are a favorite of guests," says innkeeper Peter Goldfarb, "just next to my chocolate chip cookies!"

you can pause for a bite to eat at **Calico Cupboard Cafe & Bakery** (720 South First Street; 360–466–4451), at **La Conner Brewing Company** (117 South First Street; 360–466–1415), and **Whiskers Waterfront Cafe** (128 South First Street; 360–466–1008).

Head north from La Conner on Whitney–La Conner Road and cross Highway 20 onto Bayview Edison Road, which offers views of the islands and marine wildlife of **Padilla Bay.** If you have time, walk or bicycle along the 2¼-mile Padilla Bay Shore Trail. You'll pass Bay View State Park, Padilla Bay National Estuarine Research Reserve, and **Breazeale–Padilla Bay Interpretive Center,** located at 1043 Bay View–Edison Road (360–428–1558). In addition to fish tanks and displays of local birds and mammals, the kids can enjoy environmental games and hands-on activities. Because of its fertile waters, Padilla Bay is a major stop for migrating birds. Breazeale is open year-round from 10:00 A.M. to 5:00 P.M. Wednesday through Sunday.

amoveablewinter feast

During February on the tidal flats and fields of Fir Island, visitors can marvel at some 30,000 Arctic snow geese, 1,500 trumpeter swans, and hundreds of tundra swans in addition to more than twenty species of ducks that pause to munch and rest while winging it along the Pacific Flyway. For maps and directions to best viewing spots, contact

La Conner Visitor Information Center
413 Morris Street
(360) 466–4778 or (888) 642–9284
www.laconnerchamber.com.

Small, comfortable inns entice travelers to pause in the Skagit Valley area, and among them are the romantic **Skagit Bay Hideaway Bed & Breakfast** at 17430 Goldenview Avenue, La Conner (360–466–2262; www .skagitbay.com); family-friendly **Arts Place Guesthouse** at 511 Talbot Street, La Conner (360–466–3033); **Benson Farmstead Bed & Breakfast** at 10113 Avon–Allen Road, Bow (360–757–0578 or 800–441–9814; www.bbhost.com/ bensonbnb); and **Alice Bay Bed & Breakfast** for intimate waterside views at 11794 Scott Road on Samish Island, Bow (360–766–6396 or 800–652–0223; www.alicebay.com).

Chuckanut Drive (Highway 11) is one of those scenic drives that everyone should experience. Continuing north from Padilla and Samish Bays for about 20 miles, you will discover that the winding road skirts high bluffs, offers distant glimpses of the San Juan Islands, and brings you into the Bellingham environs. Bellingham Bay, Fairhaven Park and Rose Gardens, and Fairhaven Historic District come into view soon after you pass Larrabee State Park. Many of Bellingham's old commercial and residential buildings have been renovated to their nineteenth-century grandeur, especially in the **Fairhaven Historic Dis-**

trict and downtown **Bellingham.** To reach Fairhaven from I–5 take exit 250 and follow Highway 11 west to Twelfth Street. From Old Fairhaven Parkway you can access and stroll along the Interurban Trail; its route follows a section of the 1920s electric trolley line. You can also take a passenger water shuttle express (360–734–8180; www.islandcommuter.com), near Marine Park, for a day trip over to bustling Friday Harbor on San Juan Island. Or, just west of downtown follow signs to the **Lummi Island** ferry landing, take the eight-minute ferry ride, and enjoy a leisurely drive on this scenic little island. While exploring the eclectic Fairhaven District near Bellingham's waterfront, pause at **Colophon Cafe,** 1208 Eleventh Street (360–647–0092), with its funky cow memorabilia and bovine decor; at **Skylark's Cafe,** 1308-B Eleventh Street (360–715–3010) for courtyard dining; or at **Mannino's** (360–715–3010) for tasty Italian dishes. On Wednesday afternoons browse **Fairhaven Farmers' Market** at Eleventh and Mill Streets for fresh seafood, veggies, fruits, baked goodies, and crafts. Visit splendid **Sehome Hill Arboretum,** also located nearby at Western Washington University, and plan to take in a university **Summer Stock Theater** production (360–650–3876; www.wwu.edu/depts/theatre).

The **Whatcom Museum of History and Art** (360–676–6981), in the Old City Hall at Prospect Street, is a good place to pick up a walking map of downtown Bellingham and the Fairhaven Historic District. The museum is open noon to 5:00 P.M. Tuesday through Sunday, and admission is free. **Allied Arts of Whatcom County** operates a bright, friendly gallery at 1418 Cornwall Street. Be sure to take in the **Art Walk** offered on the first Friday of every month. Also check out the **American Museum of Radio and Electricity** located at 1312 Bay Street (360–738–3886; www.antique-radio.org). From 11:00 A.M. to 5:00 P.M. Wednesday through Saturday, history buffs can browse the museum's collection of more than 1,000 radios and broadcasting memorabilia dating from the

Historic Fairhaven's Dirty Dan Harris

He sported the customary beard, mustache, and longish hair worn in the 1880s. It's said that he was a sailor, trader, and rumrunner. He wore a shabby frock coat over a red undershirt. A dusty black plug hat was jammed on his head. On his feet he wore a pair of dirty boots. He didn't bother to lace them. He also didn't bathe very often. But the man, Dirty Dan, or Daniel Harris, in 1883 filed the original plan to create the community of Fairhaven. Dirty Dan is memorialized at 1211 Eleventh Street at Dirty Dan Harris' Steakhouse (360–676–1011). The place opens daily at 5:00 P.M. and offers slow-cooked prime rib, seafood, steaks, fine wines, and spirits. Wear clean shoes and call for reservations.

early 1940s. The museum also houses an FM station that broadcasts locally radio shows from the World War II era. For dining in the Bellingham area, innkeepers and locals suggest finding pasta, seafood, and great desserts at *Pastazza* (2945 Newmarket Street; 360–714–1168; www.pastazza.com); fresh southwestern fare at *Pepper Sisters* (1055 North State Street; 360–671–3414); and delicious Asian and Northwest cuisine at *Pacific Cafe* (100 North Commercial Street; 360–647–0800). *Chocolate Necessities,* located just off Meridian Street and Horton Road (360–676–0589 or 800–804–0589), offers fine chocolates and decadent chocolate truffles. You'd like a great view while dining? Head to *Harborside Bistro* at 1 Bellwether Way (360–392–3200) in the Bellwether Hotel. At *Schnauzer Crossing Bed & Breakfast* (4421 Lakeway Drive; 360–733–0055 or 800–562–2808; www.schnauzecrossing.com) longtime innkeepers Donna and Vermont McAllister offer one guest room, one large suite, and a cottage—two of the rooms are wheelchair-accessible. Guests also enjoy saying hello to the three resident standard schnauzers, Marika, Klipsun, and Ellie.

A beautiful and peaceful attraction worth a visit is *Big Rock Garden City Park* (360–676–6985), located just outside the Bellingham area at 2900 Sylvan Street. This large Japanese garden features northwestern and Oriental garden

Lummi Island

Lummi Island, near Bellingham and a six-minute ferry ride from Gooseberry Point across Hale Passage, is one of the smaller San Juan isles. It's about 9 miles long and 2 miles wide, but it offers a few surprises. For one, during the month of August, you can watch the ancient fishing technique of reef-netting from boats at Legoe Bay on the west side of the island. Riley Starks and Judy Olsen, owners of **Nettles Organic Farm** and of **Willows Bed & Breakfast and Tap Root Cafe** (360–758–2620; www .willows-inn.com), employ workers who reef-net for wild salmon that later appear in gourmet entrees at the inn's cafe Thursday through Sunday. Call for lunch or dinner reservations and for cozy rooms. At **West Shore Farm Bed & Breakfast** (360–758–2600), Carl and Polly Hanson offer comfortable rooms in their octagonal home overlooking Rosario Strait. For a special treat, guests can also ask Carl to play his Scottish bagpipes. You can also call Sandy and Howard McCandles at scenic **Cottage by the Sea Bed & Breakfast** (360–758–7144). Near the ferry landing **Beach Store Cafe** (360–758–2233) offers hamburgers and casual fare, and **Islander General Store** (360–758–2190) carries beverages and grocery supplies. On Memorial Day or Labor Day weekend, attend the annual artist tours to see splendid watercolors, oils, sculpture, jewelry, glass, pottery, and fiber arts for sale at artists' studios around the island.

art. Grab a seat on the deck or patio, relax, and enjoy the lush surroundings. It's open from March through November.

The small community of **Ferndale** is a great place to explore both history and nature. Two blocks south of Main Street on First Avenue, you'll find **Historic Pioneer Park** (360–384–0792), home to the largest collection of nineteenth-century log structures in the state. You and the kids can tour these sturdy buildings, hewn from giant cedars, from noon to 5:00 P.M., May 1 through September 30.

Housed in the restored turn-of-the-twentieth-century Nielsen Farmhouse, the **Tennant Lake Natural History Interpretive Center** (360–384–3064; www.co.whatcom.wa.us/parks/tennantlake) provides information about the wetland environment surrounding Tennant Lake. Next to the ca. 1906 farmhouse and its beds brimming with summer perennials, stroll the paths of the Fragrance Garden. Touch and smell the leaves of curry, gingermint, chamomile, lavender, sage, and woolly thyme. The garden is wheelchair accessible, and braille signs are posted on the inside of the handrails. Then follow the path out past the viewing tower and toward the lake. Walk along the half-mile system of boardwalks to see a wide variety of wetlands vegetation along with raptors and waterfowl, including large flocks of trumpeter swans in winter. To get to the nature center, follow the signs from downtown Ferndale.

Find another historic destination by following the marked ½-mile road from Tennant Lake to **Hovander Homestead Park** (5299 Nielsen Road; 360–384–3444). The restored family farmhouse was built in 1896 by Hakan Hovander, a Swedish architect who helped rebuild Chicago after the Great Fire of 1871. Volunteers in period-style clothing will show you through the elegant rooms from noon to 4:30 P.M. on Saturday and Sunday in May and Thursday through Sunday from June through Labor Day. There are farm animals on the grounds in summer and antique farm equipment at the big red barn, as well as a demonstration garden. On the park's 200 acres you'll find hayfields, orchards, walking trails, river views, playground equipment, and picnic tables. You can also experience traditional Scottish fun when the park hosts the **Bellingham Highland Games** in June.

You could now detour from I–5 and head east into the Cascade Mountain foothills on Highway 542 and follow the road for glorious views of 10,778-foot **Mount Baker.** At Glacier, near milepost 38, stop at the USDA Forest Service/National Park Service Visitor Center (360–499–2714 or 360–856–5700) for current information on scenic hiking trails and campgrounds in the North Cascades. From here it's an easy summer drive up to the Shuksan Picnic Area, Heather Meadows, and on to **Artist Point Viewpoint** at road's end, 58 miles from Bellingham, at a brisk elevation of 5,140 feet. The nearby **Mount Baker**

Ski Area is open during the winter; call (360) 671–0211 for ski reports.

You'd rather retreat from these imposing mountain vistas to sea level, you say? If so, just beat a path to *Birch Bay* just northwest of Ferndale (exit 270 from I–5) and close to the U.S.–Canadian border. Plan your visit for Thursday through Monday between mid-June and Labor Day so that you can stop at *The C Shop* (4825 Alderson Road and Birch Bay Drive; 360–371–2070), a combina-

Quick Guide to Victoria and Vancouver, British Columbia

Victoria, located at the tip of Vancouver Island, and the city of Vancouver, situated on the mainland and not far from the U.S.–Canadian border, are destinations worth exploring if your travel arrangements include this part of Puget Sound just over the border of Washington State. Both cities offer splendid public gardens, wide water vistas, awesome scenic drives, great coffeehouses and eateries, and comfortable overnight lodging options. You can travel to Victoria by passenger ferry from Seattle; by passenger and vehicle ferries from Port Angeles, at the tip of the Olympic Peninsula; by vehicle ferries from Anacortes, in northern Puget Sound; and by ferry from Tsawwassen, located just a few miles across the Canadian border from Blaine. Check these helpful resources to implement your planning:

Victoria Clipper
(from Seattle)
(206) 448–5000
from outside Seattle call (800) 888–2535
www.clippervacations.com

Victoria Express
(from Port Angeles)
(800) 633–1589
www.victoriaexpress.com
www.bcferries.com

Distance and driving time from Seattle to Vancouver, B.C., via border crossing at Blaine: 117 miles/3 hours

Vancouver highlights
Downtown, Yaletown, Gastown, Chinatown, Queen Elizabeth Gardens, Granville Island on False Creek, English Bay, Burrard Inlet, Stanley Park, Sooke, and Lions Gate Bridge to North Shore, Grouse Mountain, Whistler Ski Area
(604) 683–2000
www.tourismvancouver.com

Victoria and Vancouver Island highlights
Inner Harbour, Empress Hotel, British Parliament Buildings, Royal Provincial Museum, Butchart Gardens, Sidney/Swartz Bay and up-island to Nanaimo, Tofino, Campbell River, and Port Hardy
(250) 953–2033
www.tourismvictoria.com

Tourism British Columbia
(800) 435–5622
www.HelloBC.com

tion bakery, candy shop, and hometown cafe. After munching sticky buns, cinnamon rolls, pizza (available after 5:00 P.M.), and handmade chocolates, take a brisk walk along the beach at **Birch Bay State Park and Campground** (360–371–2800; www.parks.wa.gov). Here you'll see seabirds and shorebirds, beachcombers, and wonderful water views of Birch Bay, Georgia Strait, and the San Juan Islands; go to www.birchbay.net for current tide tables, annual events, and other helpful information about this welcoming seaside community. You can also pause for good eats and wide-angle water views of Birch Bay at **Shores Restaurant** (360–371–3464). For overnight stays inquire with **Driftwood Inn Motel** on Birch Bay Drive (360–371–2620) and with **B&D Cottages** (360–371–2084).

Lynden, a friendly community with a proud Dutch heritage, is located in the fertile Nooksack Valley farmlands east of Birch Bay. Stroll down Front Street, bedecked with flowers and quaint Dutch decor, and stop in for fresh pastries at **Lynden Dutch Bakery** (360–354–3911) or authentic European cuisine at **Dutch Mothers Restaurant** (360–354–2174).

At **Lynden Pioneer Museum,** 217 Front Street (360–354–3675), you can stroll through a re-created turn-of-the-twentieth-century main street, with stores, a cafe, doctor and dentist offices, a school, a church, and a train station. Then take a look at the collection of early automobilies, more than forty restored horse buggies and wagons, and antique farm machinery. In midsummer you'll see the steam tractors and threshing machines getting fired up at the Puget Sound Antique Tractor and Machinery Association's Threshing Bee.

Plan one more adventure, this time to visit **Point Roberts** by heading north via I–5 to Blaine, **Peace Arch State Park,** and the U.S.–Canadian Customs for entering British Columbia.

A tiny peninsula situated just below the 49th parallel, south of British Columbia, Point Roberts became U.S. territory in the late 1840s. Finding Point Roberts is easy. First proceed through Canadian Customs at the U.S.–Canadian border at Blaine, some 20 miles north of Bellingham. While the driver waits in the customs line, members of your party can walk alongside and through the gorgeous gardens of Peace Arch Park. Continue north into British Columbia and follow the signs to Tsawwassen, about 23 miles. Here follow signs to Point Roberts and proceed through a small U.S. Customs station to reenter the United States and this small resort community, population about 860. *Note:* Heightened security will cause longer lines at the U.S.–Canadian border at Blaine. Carry a current voter registration card or passport; your driver's license alone is not enough proof of citizenship but can be used for a photo ID. For pets you will need proof of up-to-date rabies vaccination.

For a spectacular water view, stop at **Lighthouse Marine Park** (811 Marine Drive, 360–945–4911) at the peninsula's southwest corner. The windswept park has camping and picnic sites adjacent to the beach. A 30-foot wooden tower above the boardwalk offers great views of Georgia Strait and the Canadian Gulf Islands.

At **Point Roberts Marina** (360–945–2255), at the south end of Tyee Drive, you can inspect a flotilla of sailboats and motor craft, then stop for a snack at the **Dockside Cafe** (360–945–1206). A fine place to have dinner while still taking in the splendid views is **South Beach House** (360–945–0717) east of the marina at 725 South Beach Road. They serve Wednesday through Sunday from 5:30 P.M.

Call ahead to arrange a room at **Maple Meadows Bed and Breakfast,** located at 101 Goodman Road, Point Roberts (360–945–5536; www.travel-wise .com/maple/index.html). Innkeepers Terrie and Keith LaPorte welcome visitors to their comfortable ca. 1910 Victorian farmhouse near Boundary Bay. "Just forty minutes north of us is Vancouver, British Columbia," says Terrie. Large old-fashioned maples shade the grounds and lawn areas. Folks can also arrange to stay in the Old Pumphouse, a secluded and romantic getaway separate from the main house.

Places to Stay on Puget Sound

ANACORTES

Fidalgo Bay Resort RV Park
1107 Fidalgo Bay Road
(360) 293–5353
(800) 727–5478

Ship Harbor Motor Inn
5316 Ferry Terminal Road
(800) 852–8568

ANDERSON ISLAND

Above the Sound Bed & Breakfast
806 Birch Street
Steilacoom
(253) 589–1441

Inn at Burg's Landing Bed and Breakfast
8808 Villa Beach Road
(253) 884–9185

ASHFORD

Mountain Meadows Inn
28912 State Route 706 East
(360) 569–2788

Nisqually Lodge
Highway 706
(860) 569–8804

BELLINGHAM

Days Inn
215 Samish Way
(360) 734–8830

Schnauzer Crossing Bed & Breakfast
4421 Lakeway Drive
(360) 733–0055

BIRCH BAY

Birch Bay Beachside RV Park
7630 Birch Bay Drive
(800) 596–9586

Driftwood Inn Motel
Birch Bay Drive
(360) 371–2620

GIG HARBOR

Best Western Wesley Inn
6575 Kimball Drive
(253) 858–9690

Fountains Bed & Breakfast
926 120th Street NW
(253) 851–6262

Gig Harbor RV Resort
9515 Burnham Drive
(800) 626–8311

LA CONNER/MOUNT VERNON/BOW

**Benson Farmstead
Bed & Breakfast**
10113 Avon-Allen Road
Bow
(360) 757–0578

Katy's Inn
503 South Third Street
La Conner
(866) 528–9746

**The White Swan
Guest House**
1388 Moore Road
Mount Vernon
(360) 445–6805

LOPEZ ISLAND

Raven's Rook Cabin
58 Wildrose Lane
(360) 468–2838

LUMMI ISLAND

**West Shore Farm
Bed & Breakfast**
2781 West Shore Drive
(360) 758–2600

ORCAS ISLAND

Bay Side Cottages
65 Willis Lane
Olga
(360) 376–4330

Buckhorn Farm Bungalow
17 Jensen Road
Eastsound
(360) 376–2298

Cayou Cove Cottages
Deer Harbor
(360) 376–3199

**Turtleback Farm Inn
Bed & Breakfast**
Crow Valley Road
(800) 376–4914

POINT ROBERTS

**Maple Meadows
Bed & Breakfast**
101 Goodman Road
(360) 945–5536

PORT ORCHARD

**Reflections Bed
and Breakfast**
3878 Reflection Lane East
(360) 871–5582

PORT TOWNSEND

**Ravenscroft Bed
& Breakfast**
533 Quincy Street
(360) 385–2784

POULSBO

Foxbridge Bed & Breakfast
30680 Highway 3 NE
(360) 598–5599

SAN JUAN ISLAND

Harrison House Suites
235 C Street
Friday Harbor
(360) 378–3587

**Lakedale Resort
Log Cabins**
4313 Roche Harbor Road
Friday Harbor
(360) 378–2350

Tucker House Cottages
206 B Street
Friday Harbor
(360) 378–2783

HELPFUL WEB SITES IN THE PUGET SOUND REGION

Bellingham & Whatcom County
www.whatcom.kulshan.com

Ferry Information
www.wsdot.wa.gov/ferries

Kitsap Peninsula
www.visitkitsap.com

Mount Rainier National Park
www.mount.rainier.national-park.com

Port Townsend Area
www.enjoypt.com

San Juan Islands
www.guidetosanjuans.com
www.emilysguides.com

Seattle and Tacoma Area
www.seeseattle.org

Washington State Parks
www.parks.wa.gov

Whidbey Island
www.whidbey.net/islandco

TACOMA

Chinaberry Hill
Bed & Breakfast
302 Tacoma Avenue North
(253) 272–1282

DeVoe Mansion
Bed & Breakfast
208 East 133rd Street
(253) 539–3991

VASHON ISLAND

Betty MacDonald Farm
Bed & Breakfast
12000 Ninety-ninth
Avenue SW
(206) 567–4227

WHIDBEY ISLAND

Anchorage Inn
Bed & Breakfast
807 North Main Street
Coupeville
(360) 678–5581

Auld Holland Motor Inn
33575 Highway 20
Oak Harbor
(800) 228–0148

Guest House Log Cottages
24371 State Route 525
Greenbank
(360) 678–3115

Inglewood Haven
Bed & Breakfast
5010 Inglewood Drive
Langley
(360) 221–8641

Places to Eat on Puget Sound

ANACORTES

Anacortes Chocolate
Factory & Cafe
2302 Commercial Street
(360) 293–8042

Gere-a-Deli
502 Commercial Avenue
(360) 293–7383

Penguin Coffee House
2119 Commercial Street
(360) 588–8321

BAINBRIDGE ISLAND

Blackbird Bakery
210 Winslow Way East
(206) 780–1322

Pegasus Coffee
House & Gallery
131 Parfitt Way
(206) 842–6725

BELLEVUE/REDMOND

Rock Bottom Brewery &
Restaurant
550 106th Avenue NE
Bellevue
(425) 462–9300

Bear Creek Pub
7950 164th Avenue NE
Redmond
(425) 895–9088

BELLINGHAM

Colophon Cafe & Deli
1208 Eleventh Street
(360) 647–0092

Harborside Bistro at
Bellwether Hotel
1 Bellwether Way
(360) 392–3200

Skylark's Fairhaven Cafe
1308-B Eleventh Street
(360) 715–3642

BIRCH BAY

The C Shop Bakery & Cafe
4825 Alderson Road
(360) 371–2070

SELECTED VISITOR INFORMATION CENTERS

Anacortes Visitor Information Center
819 Commercial Street
(360) 293–3832

Gig Harbor Visitor Information Center
3125 Judson Street
(888) 843–9444

Langley Visitor Information Center
Whidbey Island
(360) 221–5676

San Juan Islands Visitor Information
(888) 468–3701

Oak Harbor Visitor Information Center
Whidbey Island
(360) 675–3535

ALSO WORTH SEEING

Microsoft Visitor Center
Redmond
(425) 703–6214
www.microsoft.com

Pacific Rim Bonsai Collection
Weyerhaeuser Campus
Federal Way
(253) 924–5206

Shores Restaurant
Birch Bay Drive
(360) 371–3464

GIG HARBOR

Java & Clay Cafe
3210 Harborview Drive
(253) 851–3277

Tides Tavern
2925 Harborview Drive
(253) 858–3982

ISSAQUAH

**Boehm's Candies at
Gilman Village**
255 Northeast Gilman
Boulevard
(425) 392–6652

LA CONNER

**La Conner Brewing
Company**
117 South First Street
(360) 466–1415

LOPEZ ISLAND

The Galley Cafe
Fisherman Bay
(360) 468–2713

Holly B's Bakery
Lopez Village Plaza
(360) 468–2133

LYNDEN

Lynden Dutch Bakery
421 Front Street
(360) 354–3911

OLYMPIA

Budd Bay Cafe
525 Columbia Street NW
(360) 357–6963

Tugboat Annie's
2100 West Bay Drive, #3
(360) 943–1850

ORCAS ISLAND

Bilbo's Festivo
Eastsound
(360) 376–4728

Olga's Waterfront Cafe
Olga 98279
(360) 376–5862

Teezer's Coffee Shop
North Beach and A Streets
(360) 376–2913

POINT ROBERTS

The Breakers Bar & Grill
531 Marine Drive
(360) 945–2300

PORT HADLOCK

Ajax Cafe
271 Water Street
(360) 385–3450

PORT TOWNSEND

**Elevated Ice Cream &
Candy Shop**
627 Water Street
(360) 385–1156

Manresa Castle
Edwardian Lounge
651 Cleveland Street
(800) 732–1281

Nifty Fifties Cafe
817 Water Street
(360) 385–1931

POULSBO

JJ's Fish House
1881 Front Street
(360) 779–6609

Shelia's Bay Cafe
18779 Front Street
(360) 779–2997

SAN JUAN ISLAND

Garden Path Cafe
Second Street
Friday Harbor
(360) 378–6255

Haley's Bait Shop & Grill
Spring Street
Friday Harbor
(360) 378–4434

**San Juan Coffee
Roasting Co.**
Cannery Landing
Friday Harbor
(360) 378–4443

SEATTLE

Pike Place Public Market
Pike Street to Virginia Street
(206) 682–7453

SNOQUALMIE

Snoqualmie Falls Candy Factory & Cafe
8102 Railroad Avenue SE
(425) 888–0439

STEILACOOM

The Bair Restaurant
1617 Lafayette Street
(253) 588–9668

TACOMA

Engine House #9 Powerhouse
611 North Pine Street
(253) 272–3435

Over the Moon Cafe
709 Opera Alley Court C
(253) 284–3722

VASHON ISLAND

Sound Food Café & Bakery
20312 Vashon Highway SW
(206) 463–0888

WHIDBEY ISLAND

Deception Cafe & Grill
5596 Highway 20, north
of Deception Pass bridge
(360) 293–9250

Knead & Feed Cafe
Front Street
Coupeville
(360) 678–5431

Pot Belly Deli
3207 Highway 20
Oak Harbor
(360) 675–5204

North Cascades and North Central Washington

The forces of nature raised huge chunks of granite thousands of feet into the air to form the far north section of the Cascade mountain range. We're talking *big* mountains that reach some 8,000 and more feet into the sky as well as craggy snow-covered peaks that fill the horizon from left to right, that cause tingles up the spine, and that also awaken a bit of fear and wonder in the heart and soul.

Abundant water, rich volcanic soil, and hot summers make the Okanogan, Chelan, and Wenatchee river valleys on the east side of the Cascades ideal for fruit growing. Depending on the season, you'll find juicy cherries, apples, pears and peaches, as well as field-ripened vegetables.

Farther east, the landscape mellows into dry, tan hills covered either with sagebrush and bitterbrush or pine and mazanita. You can explore back roads, ghost towns, and a scattering of small lakeside fishing resorts. Okanogan and North Cascades National Forests offer thousands of miles of trails, making it easy to hike, cross-country ski, trail ride, or mountain bike your way off the beaten path.

CANADA
UNITED STATES

Mount Baker,
10,775 feet
+

N O R T H C A S C A D E S

Baker
Lake

Newhalem

Winthrop

Okanogan R.

97

Tonasket

20

O K A N O G A N
VALLEY

20

20

Twisp

Stehekin

Glacier Peak
10,541 feet
+

153

Okanogan

97

155

Columbia R.

Lake
Chelan

C A S C A D E   R A N G E

MOUNTAIN PASSES,
VALLEYS
AND
CANYONS

17

174

97A

Chelan

17

2

Leavenworth

202

97

2

18

90

169

W E N A T C H E E   M O U N T A I N S

517

Wenatchee

28

410

N

0   35 mi
0   35 km

Ellensburg

90

82

North Cascades

The North Cascades are high, craggy mountains, covered with green forests and cut by dozens of rivers, waterfalls, and lakes. If you're approaching from the west, you'll see lush forests of western red cedar, Douglas fir, and western hemlock along with those towering summits often clothed in snow until July.

At the timberline between 4,500 and 5,500 feet elevation, alpine meadows carpeted with brightly colored wildflowers and rugged outcroppings sprout stands of mountain hemlock and alpine fir. Crossing over the passes to the eastern side of the Cascades, you'll see how the wrung-out clouds leave the hills and canyons to drought-tolerant species of lodgepole, western white pine, and ponderosa pine.

Highway 20, Washington's only paved road across this northern wilderness, was completed in 1972. The highway closes with the first heavy snowfall, usually around Thanksgiving. It normally opens again for the fishing

NORTH CENTRAL WASHINGTON'S TOP HITS

Baker Lake
Concrete

Bonaparte Lake Resort
Tonasket

Cascadian Farm Organic Market
Wauconda

Chimposiums
Ellensburg

Ginkgo Petrified Forest State Park
Vantage

Historic Molson School
Molson

Iron Horse Inn and Cabooses
South Cle Elum

John Wayne Pioneer Trail
Ellensburg

Lake Chelan and Stehekin
Chelan

Leavenworth Outdoor Summer Theater
Leavenworth

Lower Yakima River Canyon
Yakima

Ohme Gardens and Rocky Reach Dam Gardens
Wenatchee

Osprey River Adventures
Methow River and Skagit River

Ross Lake Floating Cabins
Highway 20, Newhalem

Run of the River Bed and Breakfast
Leavenworth

Skagit River Bald Eagle Natural Area
Rockport

Wren's Nest Bed and Breakfast
Ellensburg

FAVORITE ATTRACTIONS

Iron Horse Trail State Park and John Wayne Pioneer Trail System
Cle Elum

Lake Chelan

Lower Yakima River Canyon

Methow Valley, Highway 20

North Cascades National Park

Ohme Alpine Gardens
Wenatchee

season in April. For current highway conditions check www.wsdot.wa.gov or call the Washington State Department of Transportation at (800) 695–7623. Late spring or early fall are the best times to view displays of colorful spring flowers or gorgeous autumn leaves. The USDA Forest Service and the *North Cascades National Park* office complex at 810 State Route 20 in Sedro-Woolley (360–856–5700) are good places to stop for information as you approach from the west. The office is open Saturday through Thursday from 8:00 A.M. to 4:30 P.M. from Memorial Day weekend through mid-October and Monday through Friday (same hours) during the rest of the year.

The *North Cascades Institute,* also in the same office complex, offers yearly seminars that delve into the natural, cultural, and aesthetic diversity of the North Cascades, its wilderness areas, and the Skagit Valley. The institute is taught by enthusiastic experts and offers classes and field experiences. You and the kids can learn about butterflies, wildflowers, Native carving, naturalist journals, wilderness poetry, photography, alpine ecology, and more. For the current program guide, contact North Cascades Institute, 810 State Route 20, Sedro-Woolley 98284-9394; (360–856–5700; www.ncascades.org).

Many visitors to north-central Washington enjoy river-rafting adventures. More than a dozen rivers from Rockport to Wenatchee are popular for rafting, ranging from a relaxing Class I to suicidal Class VI rapids. Several professional rafting companies supply the equipment, information, and confidence beginners need to tackle a river. Most guided rafting trips concentrate on Class III and IV rivers—that is, rivers that have enough riffles, rapids, and white water to guarantee a great adventure. Some easy float trips are scheduled to observe eagles and osprey. For current information about trips on the Skagit River and Methow River, contact Dave Ward at *Osprey River Adventures* (800–997–4116; www.ospreyriveradventures.com) and the North Cascades National Park office complex in Sedro-Woolley (360–856–5700).

Traveling east on Highway 20 from Sedro-Woolley, you'll follow the winding Skagit River, a designated National Wild and Scenic River, colored blue-green with glacial meltwaters. Take the turnoff north on Baker Lake Road if you wish to visit **Baker Lake,** a lovely mountain reservoir with campsites, trails, and lake access. You'll enjoy spectacular views of Mount Baker, due north, known to the local Nooksack Tribe as Koma Kulshan, "the steep white mountain." **Shadow of the Sentinels,** on your right just past the Koma Kulshan Guard Station at Baker Lake's south end, is a pleasant half-mile, wheelchair-accessible trail and interpretive hike through old-growth forest. For information about forest and lakeside campgrounds in the North Cascades, contact the Cascades National Park Visitor Information Center on Highway 20 just west of Newhalem (206–386–4495; www.nps.gov/noca). Inquire about water sources, because in some instances campers need to pack in freshwater.

Located about 23 miles east of Interstate 5, the town of **Concrete** is worth a stop before you continue traveling east on Highway 20. The Superior Portland Cement plant here was once the largest in the state, producing nearly half the cement used to build the Grand Coulee Dam and supplying plenty more for construction of the local dams on Diablo and Ross Lakes. The plant closed in 1968, and Concrete now serves as a jumping-off point for recreation in the Skagit Valley and North Cascades. The 1916 concrete bridge that spans the Baker River at the town's east end is listed in the National Register of Historic Places. Today, a jaunt across the bridge leads to East Shannon Road and an overlook to Baker Dam. **Shannon Lake,** the reservoir behind the dam, is the site of the largest nesting osprey colony in the state.

There are a couple of places to bed down in the Concrete–Birdsview area, making this a good jumping-off spot for exploring the scenic North Cascades Highway and mountainous regions to the east. At **Ovenell's Heritage Inn Bed & Breakfast and Log Cabins,** located at 46276 Concrete Sauk Valley Road (360–853–8494; www.ovenells-inn.com), travelers are greeted by a noisy but cheerful welcoming committee—a gaggle of ducks, geese, and farm animals, including several resident dogs and cats, four ponies, two quarter horses, and about 180 head of cattle. There are four comfortable guest rooms in the main house and several new log cabins to choose from. The best view is from the morning deck; this is especially fine on sunny mornings when breakfast can be served outdoors. At **Cascade Mountain Inn Bed & Breakfast** (40418 Pioneer Lane; 360–826–4333; www.cascade-mtn-inn.com), the environment is a bit more quiet although just as inviting. The innkeepers enjoy sharing their corner of the North Cascades with travelers. Guests find five comfortable rooms on the second floor of the large home, each with country-style decor and views of Sauk Mountain, South Twin Mountain, or of nearby pastures and meadows.

Birding on the North Cascades Loop

From eagles, great blue herons, and common loons to western tanagers, golden-crowned kinglets, and Steller's jays, birding is big in the North Cascades. Check these resources, make sure you don't forget the binoculars and long-range camera lenses, wear sturdy shoes and protective clothing, pack a picnic and freshwater, use state maps to plan your treks, and hit the road to spy more than 200 bird species.

Tennant Lake Wildlife Area is near Ferndale, northwest of Bellingham. Use the 1-mile-long elevated boardwalk Loop Trail around lush wetlands and a marshy lake. There is an observation tower, as well as a fragrance garden, perennial beds, and an interpretive center.

Bayview State Park (www.parks.wa.gov), part of 10,000-acre Padilla Bay National Estuarine Reserve near Mount Vernon, offers gravel beaches, salt marsh, mud flats, and offshore beds of eelgrass. For best bird viewing and to avoid crowds, visit in late summer and early fall.

Larrabee State Park (www.parks.wa.gov; www.bellingham.org), north of Mount Vernon via scenic Chuckanut Drive, offers 2,683 acres of mountain lookouts, lakes, conifers, saltwater coves, and rocky tidepools. Try the 8 miles of trails that start at the day-use area.

Rockport State Park, near Rockport, has 465 acres with 5 miles of trails through old-growth conifers. Spring visits are best.

Pearrygin Lake State Park (www.parks.wa.gov), north of Winthrop, is a 580-acre park with a large lake; bird viewing is best along its east side. Try spring and summer mornings.

Chelan Riverwalk Park, in the city of Chelan (www.lakechelan.com), is a municipal park located where the Chelan River flows out of Lake Chelan. Try the 1-mile walking loop in spring and summer.

Waterfront Park in Leavenworth (www.leavenworth.org) is the location for the planned Leavenworth Audubon Center. Mornings are best along the river path, two island trails, and bridge.

Resources: Get a copy of the *Great Washington State Birding Trail map,* which details these and some sixty other sites for hiking and viewing bird species on the North Cascades Loop. Check www.wa.audubon.org; www.wos.org; www.birdweb.org; and Washington Department of Fish and Wildlife in Mount Vernon (360–445–4441).

For good eats along Highway 20 in the Concrete area, try the **Cajun Bar & Grill** (360–853–8518) at the corner of Main and Baker Streets for tasty Cajun-style favorites; **Annie's Pizza Station** (360–853–7227) for good pizza and other Italian fare; and, a bit farther east, **Perks** (360–853–9006) for espresso drinks and sandwiches.

You'll see snowcapped peaks as you continue east on Highway 20. For spectacular views, **Sauk Springs Trail,** just north of the highway at **Rockport State Park,** provides an easy hike on a barrier-free path. Five miles of trails surround the park's old-growth Douglas fir trees, which are more than 300 years old.

The **Bald Eagle Interpretive Center** (open weekends from mid-December to mid-February) is located in Rockport, 1 block south of Highway 20 on Alfred Street in the Rockport Fire Hall (360–853–7009). Contact the center in January for information about the early February Upper Skagit Bald Eagle Festival (www.skagiteagle.org). Guided float trips on the Skagit River (Osprey River Adventures; 800–997–4116) allow folks to see the eagles during this yearly event. This is home to one of the largest wintering bald eagle populations in the continental United States. Some 350 or so eagles are counted here annually, with January and February being the best times to see the majestic birds in the Skagit River area.

About 3 miles east on Highway 20, just past the town of Rockport, is the **Skagit River Bald Eagle Natural Area** with its viewpoints and interpretive signs overlooking the river. Designated sites such as this are the best places to watch eagles without disturbing them. The great birds flock here in autumn from as far away as Alaska to feast on chum salmon that are exhausted and dying after navigating many miles upstream from the Pacific Ocean.

At milepost 101 you'll find the **Cascadian Farm Organic Market** (55749 Highway 20, Rockport; 360–853–8173), a roadside stand that sells the Cascade Farm company's outstanding organically grown products. Cascadian Farm's organic foods are shipped all over the country. At this busy little stand, you can taste delicious berry shortcakes, low-sodium pickles and sauerkraut, fresh salads, sweet corn, all-fruit sorbets, and espresso. There are shaded picnic tables and self-guided tours of the experimental gardens. The market is open May through mid-September from 10:00 A.M. to about 6:00 P.M. weekdays and to 9:00 P.M. on weekends.

Skagit River Resort & Clark's Eatery, at 58468 Clark Cabin Road near Rockport (360–873–2250), offers pleasant overnight accommodations—cabins, bed-and-breakfast guest rooms, a number of RV sites, tent sites, and laundry facilities. The owners seem to love rabbits; there are some 175 of the furry critters living in the woods and on the grounds of the resort. In the small cafe find such tasty fare as pumpkin pancakes, homemade apple syrup, and homemade soups.

Near the confluence of the Skagit and Cascade Rivers, the town of Marblemount has been the last-chance stop for food, fuel, and news for travelers heading into the high wilderness ever since miners trekked through these rugged mountains in the 1880s. **Buffalo Run Restaurant,** open for breakfast, lunch, and dinner at 60084 Highway 20 (360–873–2461), features buffalo steaks and burgers as well as venison and elk. Or for a more traditional menu, stop at "family and fisherman friendly" ***Marblemount Diner*** (360–873–4503) at the east end of Marblemount.

Are you ready for a hardy and strenuous hike to reach awesome and panoramic vistas in the North Cascades? If you don't mind steep trails of 3 to 5 miles in length that end in superb views of alpine lakes, craggy mountains, and long-range vistas that on clear days can stretch as far as Puget Sound and Mount Rainier to the south, then contact the USDA Forest Service Marblemount Ranger Station and ***Marblemount Wilderness Information Center*** (360–873–4500) for maps, helpful advice, information, and backcountry permits for the Pasayten Wilderness and for North Cascades National Park. Also ask about hiking trails to high vistas from nearby Cascade Pass trailhead and Thornton Lakes trailhead. *Note:* Do not attempt backcountry hikes without being completely prepared with adequate maps, clothing, sturdy hiking shoes, food, water, and shelter. Also see "Ten Essentials for Backcountry Hikers" on page 95.

The Skagit River Valley widens at milepost 120, ***Newhalem,*** a company town just off Highway 20. Stop at the historic ***Skagit General Store*** (206–386–4489), ca. 1922, to gather picnic goodies and try samples of delicious flavors of Skagit fudge made on the premises, such as chocolate walnut, chocolate orange swirl, chewy praline, and coconut chocolate. Then find a shady picnic spot near Old Number Six, a restored Baldwin locomotive engine that ran between Newhalem and Rockport before the highway was built. Pop into the Skagit Visitor Center (206–233–2709; www.skagittours.com) to inquire about scenic boat trips on Diablo Lake aboard the *Alice Ross III.* On the two-and-one-half-hour tour, you'll see Ross Dam, Diablo Dam, craggy mountain peaks, North Cascades wildlife, and learn the history of the Skagit hydroelectric project including the old Incline Railway, which took project workers 560 feet up and back down Sourdough Mountain in the early 1920s. The boat tours are offered on weekends in June and September and on Thursday through Monday during July and August. *Note:* Highway 20 closes from Ross Dam east over 5,477-foot Washington Pass and down to Mazama with the first winter snows in late October or November and opens again, usually, by mid-April.

Just past Skagit General Store, cross the Skagit River on a small suspension bridge and walk the ***Trail of Cedars,*** a 1-mile self-guided and wheelchair-accessible nature trail that loops through old-growth forest. Cross the river on another pedestrian suspension bridge next to the gorge powerhouse and continue a short distance on a woodland trail with benches and native plantings for close-up views of ***Ladder Creek Falls.*** The frothy water plunges about 75 feet through a narrow chasm of basalt.

If you'd like to check your e-mail while in the remote North Cascades area, pop into the **J.D. Ross Library** in Newhalem, open Tuesday and Wednesday from 4:00 to 6:30 P.M. and log onto the Internet. The open-grate bridge at the **Gorge Creek Scenic Lookout,** between mileposts 123 and 124 on Highway 20, provides breathtaking views of the 242-foot gorge below. The big parking lot makes this spot easily accessible to highway travelers.

To get farther from the crowds and thoroughly enjoy yourself in the process, stay at the floating **Ross Lake Resort.** To reach the resort you must either hike on a 2-mile mountain trail from Highway 20 or enjoy a three-part journey that begins with a boat ride from the Ross Lake Resort parking lot, on Diablo Lake, at 8:30 A.M. or 3:00 P.M. Piles of food (visitors must bring their own since there is no store or restaurant at the resort), ice chests, baggage, and people all jumble together in the Seattle City Light boat, *The Cascadian,* as it chugs past rocky islands and into a narrow passageway between steep canyon walls up to Ross Dam. Then, with gear and everyone safely loaded onto open trucks, it's a short but bumpy ride up switchbacks through the forest to Ross Lake. Speedboats from the resort ferry guests across the lake to the cluster of twelve comfortable wood cabins floating on huge cedar logs off the northwestern shore. *Note:* There are nominal fees per person for the journey to the floating resort.

The cabins, built in the 1930s for logging crews, have been modernized with kitchens, plumbing, and electricity. Hardy hikers can arrange water-taxi service to trailheads for backcountry adventures. The resort is open from mid-June through the end of October and gets especially busy when fishing season starts in early July. *Note:* Pets are not allowed, and boat rental is required for cabins on weekends; rental options include 14-foot boats with outboard

Ross Lake Resort

motors, 17-foot aluminum canoes, 17-foot single kayaks, 20-foot double kayaks, and fishing rods and reels for rainbow trout. Instruction is provided for all equipment. Check their Web site, www.rosslakeresort.com, for photos of the cabins and other helpful information. For reservations contact the staff at Ross Lake Resort at (206) 386–4437.

Back on Highway 20 heading east, you can stop for sweeping views of Diablo Lake and the hanging glaciers of Colonial and Pyramid peaks beyond from the overlook at milepost 131.8. A few miles farther, the *Happy Creek Forest Walk,* south of the highway, provides a barrier-free boardwalk a third of a mile long past huge fallen and standing old-growth trees. Interpretive signs tell the forest's story amid the sounds of the bubbling creek. Ross Lake stretches before you from the *Ross Lake Overlook,* north of the highway. A few miles farther east, at the *East Bank trailhead,* a quarter-mile hike will take you to Ruby Creek, an important spawning area for native trout (no fishing allowed). After 3 miles on the trail, you reach the shore of Ross Lake, and in 28 miles hardy backpackers can reach the Canadian border. *Canyon Creek trailhead,* where Highway 20 veers southeast, marks the beginning of a short walk over a bridge to a turn-of-the-twentieth-century mining site. About 2 miles up the trail, you'll see Rowley's Chasm, a 200-foot cleft in the rocky hillside.

The roadside scenery gets even more spectacular as you approach the high mountain passes. Creeks cascade down avalanche chutes—steep alpine meadows are dotted with purple fireweed and red Indian paintbrush in the summer. There are several places to pull off the road to ogle at the awesome mountain views, such as the *Whistler Basin Overlook* at milepost 160, the barrier-free *Rainy Lake Trail,* or the point at which the 2,600-mile *Pacific Crest National Scenic Trail* from Mexico to Canada crosses the highway at 4,855-foot-high Rainy Pass. Cast your gaze on 7,720-foot Liberty Bell Mountain, a jagged-edged precipice that looms above *Washington Pass Overlook* (milepost 162.2), a spot with wide-angle views perched 700 feet above the highway. The wheelchair-accessible loop path to the overlook offers close-up views of alpine plants and geology, from spiral-grained trees to smooth, glacier-carved stones. At an elevation of 5,477 feet above sea level, Washington Pass is the North Cascades Highway's uppermost point. From here the highway winds down a steep U-shaped valley into the drier terrain below Liberty Bell.

A semiarid landscape is dominated by tall cinnamon-barked ponderosa pine on the Cascade Mountains' eastern slopes as you descend into the *Methow Valley.* There are pleasant, streamside campgrounds along the way at *Klipchuck* and *Early Winters.* Near Newhalem, a National Park Service Visitor Center and Ranger Station (206–386–4495) is open daily, June 19 through Labor Day, from 10:00 A.M. to 4:00 P.M. It provides helpful maps and campground information for the North Cascades. Some 45 miles farther east, the tiny village of *Mazama* is located a quarter mile north of the highway at the upper end of the scenic Methow Valley. At first glance, Mazama's country store, gas station, and post office appear to be all that is left of this once-booming mining town. Look just beyond the village center to discover *Mazama Country Inn* (509–996–2681; www.mazamacountryinn.com), an all-season retreat nestled in the forest between mountains. Located at the edge of the *Pasayten Wilderness,* the inn's eighteen-room wood lodge and comfortable cabins open onto miles of hiking and mountain-bike trails. In the winter, you can cross-country ski out your door on the second-largest groomed trail system in the United States. The inn's restaurant is open to travelers as well as overnight guests. In Mazama other eateries include the *Freestone Inn Dining Room* (31 Early Winters Drive; 509–996–3906) for Northwest gourmet specialties and *Mazama Country Store* (509–996–2855), which offers homemade soups and baked goods along with deli sandwiches, pizza, and information about seasonal recreation in the area. During the winter when Highway 20 is closed, Mazama is accessible only from Highways 97 and 153 from Wenatchee to the southeast.

There's lots to do in this area during all four seasons. *Rendezvous Outfitters* (www.methow.com/huts) offers backcountry hut-to-hut ski touring on

Ten Essentials for Backcountry Hikers

1. Flashlight, spare batteries
2. Map of your hiking area
3. Compass and GPS (global positioning system) device
4. Extra food, water
5. Extra clothing
6. Sunglasses and sunscreen
7. First aid supplies, medications
8. Pocketknife
9. Matches in waterproof container
10. Fire starter

Avid Pacific Northwest Orienteering groups offer outdoor workshops in how to find your way in all types of terrain and weather. Locate regional orienteering activities at www.pnwo.org. Ask about the essentials for hikers when you call or visit regional USDA Forest Service ranger stations on your travels. The Mount Baker–Snoqualmie National Forest headquarters in Sedro-Woolley (360–856–5700; www.fs.fed.us/r6/mbs) provides helpful maps, information, and advice for camping and hiking in the North Cascades.

the **Methow Valley Winter Trail System** in the Okanogan National Forest for a combination of daytime adventure and overnight comfort. If scenic horse-back-riding adventures are your style, consider a summer or fall wilderness pack trip or cowboy wagon dinner ride with **Early Winters Outfitting & Saddle Co.,** located nearby. Contact Aaron Lee or Judy Burkhart in Mazama (800–737–8750; www.earlywintersoutfitting.com). Scenic horseback rides are also available for guests staying at the **Freestone Inn at Wilson Ranch,** 31 Early Winters Drive near Mazama (800–639–3809; www.freestoneinn.com) and at **Sun Mountain Lodge** about 10 miles south of Winthrop (800–572–0493; www.sunmountainlodge.com).

Hikers and mountain bikers can obtain current information for all types of trails from the Methow Valley Visitor Information Center and USDA Forest Service Ranger District (509–996–4000) and from **Methow Valley Sports Trails Association** (509–996–3287; www.mvsta.com).

Even if you're not camping, the **Methow River KOA Campground** (509–996–2258) is worth a detour from Highway 20 about a mile east of Winthrop for a look at its display of license plates from around the world, all collected by local resident Mike Meyers.

Highway 20 traffic slows as it winds through the small town of **Winthrop,** an early 1900s trading post now spruced up with a touristy western theme. The **Schafer Museum,** in a historic log home on the hill 1 block above town, is worth a visit to glimpse some of the town's early history. The museum is open from 10:00 A.M. to 5:00 P.M. daily from Memorial Day to Labor Day. Also, stop and say hello to Carol and D.J. Stull at **Winthrop Blacksmith Shop** at 236 Riverside Avenue (509–996–2703). You can often see D.J. working at his small gas-fired forge, and you can also browse their gallery of hand-forged gifts and home accessories.

Good eateries along Winthrop's main street, Riverside Avenue (Highway 20), include **Rocking Horse Bakery & Coffee** (509–996–4241) for awesome baked goods and java; **Boulder Creek Deli** (509–996–3990) for great specialty sandwiches; **Grubstake & Co.** for gourmet pizza (509–996–2375); **Sheri's Sweet Shoppe** (509–996–3834) for freshly made fudge, chocolates, cinnamon rolls, and handmade ice cream; **Winthrop Brewing Company** (509–996–3183) for fine handcrafted ales and tasty pub fare; and **Heenan's Burnt Finger Bar-B-Q & Steakhouse** (509–996–8221) for Texas-style ribs, chili, and steaks along with news of the Methow River. For a gourmet feast at a crisp altitude of 2,850 feet with a great view of the Methow Valley, 1,000 feet below, try the elegant dining room at **Sun Mountain Lodge** (509–996–2211), some 10 miles from town via Twin Lakes and Patterson Lake Roads.

Comfortable places to bed down in the scenic Winthrop area include the inviting, family-oriented *WolfRidge Resort* (509–996–2828; www.wolfridge resort.com), the casually elegant *Chewuch Inn Bed & Breakfast* (509–996–3107 or 800–747–3107; www.chewuchinn.com), and *River Run Inn & Cabins* (800–757–2709; www.riverruninn.net), located close to the Methow River.

Those who hanker to learn the art of catch-and-release flyfishing can find an able teacher near Winthrop. On a private pond at *Fly Rod Ranch,* at 494 Rendezvous Road (509–996–2784; www.flyrodranch.com), Ben Dennis teaches folks the art of fly casting. If golf's your passion call the Court family at *Bear Creek Golf Course* (509–996–2284) to set up a tee time. About 3 miles out on Eastside County Road from Winthrop, the scenic and somewhat hilly course offers nonstop views of Mount Gardner and Studhorse Mountain as well as the distant Sawtooth Range and Pasayten Wilderness. On your round of golf, you'll likely hear birds twittering along Bear Creek or spy evidence of local wildlife such as deer, moose, bears, and coyotes.

The Eastside Winthrop–Twisp Road is a pleasant, less-traveled route to the small community of Twisp. On the way, about 5 miles east of Winthrop, you can explore the world of firefighting at the *North Cascades Smokejumpers Base* operated by the U.S. Forest Service. Contact the base (509–997–2031) Monday through Friday, 7:45 A.M. to 4:30 P.M., for tour information. The USDA Forest Service Methow Valley Ranger Station (509–996–4003, www.fs.fed.us/r6/oka) offers maps and information for backcountry hikes in the region.

In the small community of *Twisp,* pause for espresso drinks and superb pastries at *Cinnamon Twisp Bakery,* at 116 Glover Street (509–997–5030), and for waist-bulging entrees at *BJ's Branding Iron Restaurant & Saloon,* 123 Glover Street (504–997–3576). For an overnight stay here in the scenic Twisp Valley, call *Methow Valley Inn Bed & Breakfast,* 234 Second Avenue (509–997–2253; www.methowvalleyinn.com), and *White Tail Crossing Bed & Breakfast,* 147 Twisp–Winthrop Eastside Road (509–997–9422; www.white tailcrossingbb.com). You could also ask about what's currently playing onstage by the professional summer stock players at *Merc Playhouse,* in the historic Twisp Mercantile building at 101 Glover Street (509–997–2306, www.merc playhouse.com).

A couple miles past Twisp, the highway forks. Highway 20 continues east to Okanogan. Highway 153 proceeds southeast along the Methow River as it winds and bubbles over its pebbly bed to Pateros. On this route you'll pass the pleasant community of Methow, then plunge into orchard country as the river gorge deepens before its confluence with the Columbia River.

Okanogan Valley

The Okanogan Valley stretches from the British Columbia border at Oroville south to the Columbia River. Much of the land along the river is planted with fruit orchards. The area above the river valley is drier, covered with rolling grass and sagebrush meadows dotted with occasional stands of ponderosa pine, glacially deposited boulders, and pristine lakes. *Okanogan* is the Kalispel Tribe's word for "rendezvous," or "gathering place."

Highway 20 merges with U.S. Highway 97 in the city of **Okanogan.** You can visit the **Okanogan County Historical Museum,** located in Legion Park on Second Avenue, open daily from 11:00 A.M. to 5:00 P.M. Fine displays cover local geography and history of Indian and pioneer life. Outside, poke into the Okanogan Visitor Information Center (509–422–9882) and inspect a collection of log buildings, including a settlers' cabin, a blacksmith's shop, and a saloon.

If time allows linger in Okanogan so you can visit **Granny Mae's Gift Emporium & Coffee Bar** at 111 Second Avenue South and also **The Rusty Shovel** at 123 Second Avenue South (509–422–0558), where the owners offer all kinds of western-style gifts and rustic handmade treasures for homes and gardens. For tasty eats, especially if you like lots of sports action and activity, try **Okanogan Old Mill & Irish Pub,** 96 Pine Street (509–422–2282), fashioned from Okanogan's old flour mill building. You could also check out the 1940s-style **On the Avenue Restaurant & Ice Cream Parlour,** 134 Second Avenue South (509–422–2278), open Wednesday to Sunday.

The **Breadline Cafe** (509–826–5836), a few miles north at 102 South Ash Street in **Omak,** offers a soda fountain, espresso drinks, a bakery, and a deli. Also in Omak, stop by **Novel Delights Inc.** at 19 North Main Street (509–826–1113) for tasty espressos, bagels and cream cheese, or delicious cookies home-made by the owner. You can also browse the large selection of used books that are arranged by categories such as gardening, travel, and mystery. **Magoo's Restaurant** at 24 North Main Street (509–826–2325) is a good choice for breakfast and lunch. Locals suggest **Rancho Chico's** at 22 North Main Street (509–826–4757) for an excellent Mexican feast.

Heading north again on US 97, stop at the small town of **Riverside** on any day except Saturday. Pull up and park at **Historic Detro's Western Store,** hunkered down on Main Street (509–826–2200), but remember that it's open every day but Saturday. You'll see hats, boots, jeans, shirts, belts, jewelry, and all sorts of western wear for cowboys, cowgirls, and kids too. You can inspect all kinds of tack supplies like ropes, bridles, bits, and saddles. You might even meet a real cowboy or cowgirl. For good eats try the neighboring **Riverside Bar & Grill.**

Conconully Jail, Sam's Story

Although it was built for impenetrability, the Conconully jail became the butt of many a local joke for the frequent prisoner escapes it endured between 1891 and 1915. Perhaps the most amusing is the story of Sam Albright, who found out that two of his friends were guests of the hoosegow and went with another man to pay them a visit. Finding the jailer absent, he and his partner unlatched the window and climbed through. The four friends proceeded to engage in a lively poker game, after which Sam and his friend left candy and books for the inmates, then exited back through the window, latching it behind them.

For a pleasant overnight campout, head north and west of Omak a few miles to **Shady Pines Resort Cabins and RV Park,** located at 125 West Fort Salmon Creek Road (800–552–2287) on the shores of 350-acre Conconully Reservoir. Steve and Dena Byl and their son Jake offer small cabins that sleep four and a log cabin duplex that sleeps six, all shaded from summer's heat by tall pines. All cabins come with full kitchens, queen-size beds, and cozy sitting areas. Beach-front RV sites offer full hookups, and a few tent sites are also available. You can bring your own motorboat, or you can rent rowboats to fish for rainbow trout or go for a relaxing paddle around the scenic lake. Inquire about fishing regulations.

There's tasty regional food in **Conconully.** Try **Tamarack Historic Saloon** at 316 North Main Street (509–846–8137) for good hamburgers, ales, and pub grub; **Lucky D's Restaurant** at 215 North Main Street (509–826–2573) for hearty breakfasts and lunches; and **Sit'N Bull's** at 308 North Main Street (509–826–2947) for steaks and hamburgers.

East of Tonasket about 23 miles on Highway 20, the tiny community of **Wauconda** offers a great introduction to the open beauty of the Okanogan high desert. You'll pass a scattered collection of homes, old homestead cabins, and barns set on the 3,000-foot-high desert plateau. The **Wauconda Store and Cafe** (509–486–4010), a one-stop store/cafe/post office, is worth a stop. The wood-paneled cafe, decorated with local art and historical photos, offers great views of the rolling valley and high desert tree species including western larch, ponderosa pine, lodgepole pine, Engelmann spruce, and aspen.

Bonaparte Lake Resort, located near Tonasket at 695 Bonaparte Lake Road (509–486–2828), has cabins (with kitchens), camping, gas, and a lodge with a small store and cafe famous for its great hamburgers. To get there, turn north about 3 miles west of Wauconda off Highway 20 onto a 6-mile country road that winds along Bonaparte Creek through meadows and forests. The Okanogan National Forest also has several campgrounds in the area. **Lost Lake**

Campground, about 8 miles beyond the resort, offers several fine hiking trails, including the easy Big Tree Trail, where you can see 600-year-old western larches, and the Strawberry Mountain Trail, offering panoramic views from hillsides covered with wild strawberries. For maps and current information, contact the Tonasket Ranger Station at 1 West Winesap; (509) 486–2186; www.fs .fed.us/r6/oka.

Located about 20 miles east and north of Oroville, Molson's two historical museums are worth seeing. The *Molson School Museum,* open daily from 10:00 A.M. to 5:00 P.M. Memorial Day weekend through Labor Day, offers three floors of well-organized displays highlighting local history. After browsing through the classrooms and library upstairs, the vintage clothing and furniture on the main floor, or the huge tool collection downstairs, you can enjoy homemade treats and lemonade provided by museum volunteers in a breezy main-floor classroom. The *Old Molson Outdoor Museum* (509–485–3292; leave a message), open during daylight hours for self-guided tours from April through December, exudes an Old West feeling with its nineteenth-century cabins, shingle mill, mining and farm tools, and storefronts. Both museums are free, but donations are requested. *Sidley Lake* and *Molson Lake,* just north of town, are popular with travelers who like to fish. Bird-watchers also delight in the array of waterfowl, from blue-billed ruddy ducks to long-necked canvasbacks, feeding amid reeds and islands in the tiny lakes. From Molson retrace your route back to *Oroville* and US 97.

Oro, Spanish for "gold," bespeaks this town's early history as a miner's mecca. Oroville's original Great Northern Depot has been restored as a museum and community hall on the corner of Twelfth and Ironwood Streets. The *Oroville Old Depot Museum* (509–476–2303 or 509–476–2739), open Thursday from 1:00 to 4:00 P.M. and Saturday from 10:00 A.M. to 4:00 P.M., pro-

Old Molson Outdoor Museum

TOP FIVE ANNUAL EVENTS IN NORTH CENTRAL WASHINGTON

Skagit Eagle Festival
Rockport, early February

Spirit of the West Cowboy Gathering
Ellensburg, mid-February

Leavenworth Spring Bird Fest
early May

'49er Days
Winthrop, May

Ellensburg Rodeo
Ellensburg, late August–early September

vides insight into the town's history as a railroad, mining, and agricultural center buffeted by changing times.

For good eats in Oroville try *Fat Boy's Diner* at 1518 Main Street (509–476–4100) for hamburgers, malts, and shakes amid a nostalgic 1950s decor; *Espressions Espresso* at 817 Apple Way (509–476–2970) for light sandwiches, baked goods, and soft ice cream; *Home Town Pizza* at 1315 Main Street (509–476–2410) for made-from-scratch pizza, Italian pastas, and gourmet desserts to die for. At nearby *Osoyoos State Park,* stop at the McDaniel's open-air stand for their twelve varieties of fabulous homemade breads and soups along with German hot dogs. Eat at picnic tables with outstanding views of Osoyoos Lake, then enjoy the 3-mile *River Park Walkabout* loop trail that takes in more great views of the lake and the mouth of the Okanogan River.

Continue southwest to *Loomis,* traversing dry hillsides above the green Sinlahekin Valley. Loomis is another quiet village that boomed during the gold rush of the 1890s and busted soon after. You'd never know from the orchards, old houses, and 1-block main street that this was once the largest city in the county. South from Loomis you can take a primitive but scenic road through the *Sinlahekin Valley and Wildlife Area* back to Conconully. *Note:* Before heading into the hinterlands by car, get a full tank of gasoline; check the water and oil; and always pack water, beverages, and healthful snacks.

East from Loomis on the Loomis–Oroville Road is narrow Spectacle Lake, rimmed with cattails, dry hills, and remnants of an old wooden irrigation flume. There are several rustic resorts along this roadside lake, but the best one is hidden away to the north on secluded Wannacut Lake. Watch for the sign past Spectacle Lake for *Sun Cove Resort and Guest Ranch,* located at 93 East Wannacut Lane (509–476–2223). You can also get there directly from Oroville on a 10-mile, partially gravel road by following signs on Twelfth Avenue west of the Oroville Depot Museum. The log cabins and larger cottages are comfortable and offer splendid lake views. Besides excellent fishing opportunities, including plenty of rainbow and Lahonton cutthroat trout, there are wooded grounds that provide plenty of fun activities for both children and adults, including hiking trails, a swimming pool, a playground, and sports equipment. The Bear's Den (the resort office and meeting area) offers snacks, groceries, and reading and laundry facilities. The resort is open from April through November.

If you don't take the turnoff to Sun Cove, you can continue straight on the Loomis–Oroville Road past Whitestone Lake and merge right onto the Tonasket–Oroville Westside Road. This less-traveled route traverses the hills west of the Okanogan River, parallel to US 97. During summer, keep an eye out for fresh-fruit stands along the way to refill your picnic hamper with locally grown apples, pears, peaches, cherries, and apricots. You can cross the river to US 97 at *Tonasket*, but before heading south toward Lake Chelan, pause for refreshments at *All Perked Up Espresso* on Main Street (509–486–8325) or at *Shannon's Ice Cream Parlor & Cafe* at 626 South Whitcomb Avenue (509–486–2259). You'll find delicious ice cream in many flavors plus tasty sandwiches, soups, salads, and desserts in this welcoming oasis. An option for hearty meals is *Whistler's Family Restaurant* (509–486–2568) at 616 South Whitcomb Avenue, and also *Tonasket Saloon & Tovie Cafe* (509–486–2459).

If you are in the area during the winter ski season, the Tonasket Ranger District at 1 West Winesap (509–486–2186; www.fs.fed.us/r6/oka) can provide information about the *Sitzmark Ski Area*, the Highland Cross Country Snow Park, and nearby snowmobile trails.

Mountain Passes, Valleys, and Canyons

You don't mind being surrounded on three sides by rugged, 8,000-foot-high mountain peaks, dense alpine forests, and miles of hiking trails? You don't mind a four-hour boat ride to the end of a 55-mile-long lake that reaches deep into the *Lake Chelan Recreation Area* and the *Sawtooth Wilderness*? You love the allure of winter moonlight snowshoe treks? And you like the idea of staying overnight in rustic tent-cabins or cozy lodge rooms without TVs, telephones, daily newspapers, or Internet access? If so, this qualifies you for an extraordinary outdoor adventure to *Stehekin* and the scenic Stehekin Valley, one of the most isolated outposts in the central Washington Cascades. The good news is that Stehekin also offers a small restaurant (in the lodge), a bakery, mountain-bike rentals, and shuttle van rides up-valley to trailheads—but that's about it. We're talking small here; we're talking low key and down-home friendly. This is way too much wilderness or too much lakeside scenery, you

Skiing Washington

Individual Web sites offer specific information about downhill runs; the extent of cross-country trail systems; snowboarding areas; snowshoeing; day lodge amenities; directions, weather, snow conditions, Sno-Park fees; and overnight accommodations in the area.

49 Degrees North Ski Area
Located 42 miles north of Spokane
via US 395
(509) 935–6649
www.ski49n.com

Hurricane Ridge
Located 18 miles south of Port Angeles
in Olympic National Park
(360) 417–4555
www.hurricaneridge.net

Loup Loup Ski Area
Located between Okanogan and Twisp off
Highway 20
(509) 826–2720
www.skitheloup.com

Methow Valley Winter Trail System
Located north of Wenatchee and near
Mazama, Winthrop, and Twisp via
Highways 97, 153, and 20
(509) 996–3287
www.mvsta.com and
www.methow.com/huts

Mission Ridge
Located 12 miles from Wenatchee
(509) 663–6543
www.missionridge.com

Mount Baker
Located 56 miles east of Bellingham
via Highway 542
(360) 734–6771
www.mtbakerskiarea.com

Mount Spokane Ski & Snowboard Park
Located 23 miles north of Spokane
(509) 238–2220
www.mtspokane.com

Sitzmark Ski Area
Located 17 miles northeast of Tonasket
off US 97
(509) 485–3323
www.skiresortsguide.com/stats.cfm/
wa09.htm

Snoqualmie Pass Summit
Located 45 miles east of Seattle via
Interstate 90
(425) 434–7669
www.summit-at-snoqualmie.com

Stevens Pass
Located between Seattle and
Leavenworth via Highway 2
(206) 812–4510
www.stevenspass.com

White Pass
Located 90 miles southeast of Olympia
and near Mount Rainier National Park via
Interstate 5 and Highway 12
(509) 672–3100
www.skiwhitepass.com

Further information
www.skiwashington.com
October through March

say? Not to worry; you can go back to Chelan for your overnight stay, as long as you remember to catch the boat for the return trip.

Two passenger ferries sail daily between the town of Chelan and the village of Stehekin. The *Lady of the Lake* takes four hours to travel each way. The *Lady Express* does the same trip in a little over two hours. If time allows take the slower trip, which provides more time to enjoy the fine views. During the trip, Forest Service rangers offer presentations on local natural history and the mountain wilderness environment. For schedules, contact Lake Chelan Boat Company, (509–682–4584; www.ladyofthelake.com). Chelan Airways (509–682–5065) offers floatplane trips from Chelan to Stehekin.

If you're interested in camping and hiking in the Stehekin Valley area, first call the National Park Service/USDA Forest Service Visitor Information Center in Stehekin (360–856–5700, extension 340, then extension 14)—this is a satellite telephone, so callers will need to be patient; online information is available at www.nps.gov/noca. Park rangers can help with trail maps, weather conditions, campgrounds and camping sites, other lodging in Stehekin, equipment lists, guide services, and permits for backcountry excursions. The center is open daily from 8:00 A.M. to 4:30 P.M. from mid-May through mid-October. There is also a National Park Service and Lake Chelan Recreation Area information center in Chelan, at 428 West Woodin Avenue (509–682–2549). *Note:* Do

Recreation and Picnicking in the Lake Chelan Area

Chelan Falls Park
Picnic area, swimming beach, boat ramp, and docks about 5 miles north of Chelan

Chelan Riverwalk Park
Scenic 1-mile shoreline trail along the Chelan River near downtown

Lake Chelan Mural Walk
Over a dozen murals in and around the downtown area, each containing an apple in some form. Pick up a mural map from the visitor information center.
(509) 682–3503; www.lakechelan.com

Old Mill Park
Picnic sites, boat launch, short-term moorage, and marine wastewater station located in the Manson area about 10 miles up the north lakeshore

Willow Point
Scenic and quiet lakeside spot near Manson

not hike into wilderness areas without being fully equipped and fully informed about the areas you plan to explore. See "Ten Essentials for Backcountry Hikers" on page 95.

For a gentler outdoor adventure, try the **Stehekin Valley Ranch** (509–682–4677; www.courtneycountry.com), open from mid-June to the last week of September. At the ranch 9 miles up-valley from the boat landing, the Courtney family offers rustic one-room tent-cabins—a few of them come with electricity and baths. In the open-air dining lodge, guests hunker down at huge log slab tables to enjoy steaming cups of coffee and hearty meals cooked by ranch staff. There are no water views here, but you can arrange for scenic horseback rides and rafting trips.

Folks can also contact **North Cascades Stehekin Lodge** (509–682–4494; www.stehekin.com) to bed down near the boat landing in Stehekin. The lodge offers a restaurant and a small convenience store. **Silver Bay Inn,** located at 10 Silver Bay Road (509–687–3142; www.silverbayinn.com), offers cozy and self-contained accommodations in the Lake Cabin (sleeps four), the Bay Cabin (sleeps six), the River View Room (sleeps two), and the Lakeview House (comes with two bedrooms, two baths, and a full kitchen). The property offers panoramic views of Lake Chelan and those 8,000-foot-high steep mountains.

Bring sturdy walking shoes and bottles of water so you can enjoy the easy 3½-mile hike up-valley from Stehekin to view **Rainbow Falls.** Just a short walk from the main road brings you to a good viewpoint to see some 312 feet of cascading water. For a taste of history, explore the old one-room Stehekin School, down the road from the falls, then walk a short distance to the Buckner orchard and their early 1900s homestead. On your return walk, stop at the **Stehekin Bakery** for delicious, fresh-baked treats (open May 15 through October 15). If you can hold off munching everything, carry your snack the 2 miles back to Stehekin and enjoy your pastries with grand views of the lake at one of the picnic tables on the large deck near the boat landing.

applesapples apples

Nearly 10,000 acres of the Chelan Valley are devoted to growing apples, with smaller crops of other luscious fruit such as cherries, pears, apricots, and peaches. Apple varieties that folks love to munch include

Red Delicious

Golden Delicious

Granny Smith

Gala

Fuji

Jonagold (available September through March)

Braeburn (available October through July)

Look for fruit stands throughout the valley on your travels.

The Columbia River is tamed in the center of the state by the Rocky Reach, Rock Island, Wanapum, and Priest Rapids dams, which create long, narrow reservoirs, generate electricity, and provide irrigation for the Wenatchee Valley region. Like the Okanogan Valley to the north, nearly all available plots of land along the east side of the Columbia River and several smaller valleys to the west toward Cashmere are planted in orchards, making this one of the nation's prime sources of apples, pears, peaches, and apricots. Boating, swimming, fishing, and bicycling are popular during the long, sunny summers; skiing and snowshoeing are popular in winter.

The town of *Chelan,* set on the southeast shore of 55-mile-long Lake Chelan, is a popular tourist destination. The downtown area is a pleasant place for strolling, shopping, and leisurely eating. *Chelan Riverwalk Park* offers a shoreline walking trail and a pavilion where outdoor concerts are scheduled during the summer. Among the many good eateries in the area, try the historic *Campbell House* in downtown Chelan (104 West Woodin Avenue; 509–682–2561), with a full-service dining room on the main floor. But the best place to eat is in the pub on the second floor, which offers outdoor seating on its veranda along with superb views of the lake. For a casual family-style eatery, stop at *Apple Cup Cafe* at 804 East Woodin Avenue (509–682–2933), which serves breakfast all day; for good takeout pizza try *Local Myth Pizza* at 122 South Emerson (509–682–2914); and for giant cinnamon rolls, bagel sandwiches, salads, and specialty espressos, find *Latte Da Coffee Stop Cafe* at 303 East Wapato Avenue (509–682–4196).

In the *Manson* area on the north lakeshore a few miles from Chelan, sample Mexican specialties at *El Vaquero Restaurant* at 75 Wapato Way (509–687–3179). For Italian pastas, garden salads, freshly baked subs, and burgers, head out to *Uncle Tim's Pizzeria & Pasta House/Sports Bar* at 76 West Wapato Way, also in Manson (509–687–3035). If you have a deli picnic planned, follow the signs to scenic *Willow Point Park* near Manson. While the city parks can get lively and noisy with kids and families, this small shoreside park offers a quiet alternative and great views of the lake. If you're in the area on a Monday between late June and the end of September, you could drive about 4 miles from Manson to *Banjo Creek Farms* (509–687–0708; www.banjocreek farms.com) for the weekly farmers' market from 9:30 A.M. to 12:30 P.M. Here you find local fresh vegetables and fruits, cut flowers, and homemade cinnamon rolls, pies, and breads—along with homemade jams and jellies, quilts, and crafts. For a pleasant round of golf, call for tee times at the scenic *Lake Chelan Municipal Golf Course* (800–246–5361; www.lakechelangolf.com).

If you head east on U.S. Highway 2 from the Columbia River, about 25 miles south of Chelan, you'll climb about 6 miles above the river to the town of *Waterville.* The ***Douglas County Historical Museum*** on US 2 on the west side of town has interesting displays, including an extensive rock collection. In front of the museum, you can see a large metal bucket that was once part of an overhead conveyor system that in the early 1900s carried wheat 2,400 feet down to the river, where it was loaded onto grain barges. Waterville is a pleasant community with many old houses and a fine county courthouse. Directly across from the museum at 102 East Park, the ca. 1903 ***Waterville Historic Hotel*** (888–509–8180; www.watervillehotel.com) is in the process of being restored by owner Dave Lundgren. One large suite and ten comfortable rooms (some with private baths and claw-footed tubs) are now open for travelers. You'll see some of the original oak and leather Mission-style furnishings on the main floor in the cozy lobby and tearoom area, where a light continental breakfast is served to guests. Ask Dave about the Nifty Vaudeville Theater in town, which occasionally screens old movies. It's a short downhill drive from here to return to Wenatchee, Leavenworth, and Chelan.

Heading south on U.S. Highway 97A from the Chelan area and away from the dense forests of the North Cascades, the Columbia River is on your left as you drive toward **Wenatchee.** Tan-colored hills looming on your right (west) are now clothed in sagebrush, bitterbrush, and aromatic juniper. But across the river

trivia

At 2,640 feet, Waterville boasts the distinction of being the town with the highest altitude in the state.

to the east, you see compact orchards that are lush and green from irrigation. Detour at ***Rocky Reach Dam*** (509–663–7522; www.chelanpud.org) and enjoy a rest stop and perhaps an impromptu picnic amid a splendid perennial garden, hanging baskets of summer flowers, and a children's playground. With camera in hand, climb the steps to the top of the children's slide and snap a picture of the large floral U.S. flag, Old Glory Garden, planted in red, white, and blue annuals in the lawn. More than 5,000 annuals bloom on Petunia Island surrounding the fish ladders.

Just prior to reaching Wenatchee, look for the sign to ***Ohme Gardens*** and detour to 3327 Ohme Road (509–662–5785; www.ohmegardens.com) to visit this lush and cool alpine wonderland. Beginning in 1929 Herman and Ruth Ohme developed the family gardens on their barren hilltop 600 feet above the Columbia River. Ten years later, friends and community members urged the Ohmes to allow public visits to their splendid garden. Travelers still flock to this nine-acre alpine garden atop the bluff that allows wide views of the Columbia River, Cascade Mountains, and Wenatchee Valley. Irregular stepping stones and narrow flagstone pathways meander up and down and around shaded fern-lined pools, next to large ponds, and around immense boulders. You'll see many varieties of sedum along with creeping thyme, creeping phlox, alyssum, and dianthus. Tall western red cedar, mountain hemlock, grand fir, Douglas fir, and alpine fir grow around the garden's perimeter. The garden is open from April 15 to October 15, 9:00 A.M. to 6:00 P.M. There's a nominal admission fee. *Note:* The upper garden is handicapped accessible. Wear sturdy walking shoes here.

For other things to see and do in the area, stop by the Wenatchee Valley Visitor Information Center at 25 North Wenatchee Avenue; (800) 572–7753. Browse the Web sites www.wenatcheevalley.org and www.appleblossom.com for additional information. A pleasant overnight option is *Apple Country Bed & Breakfast,* located at 524 Okanogan Avenue; (509) 664–0400; www.applecountryinn .com. Innkeepers Jerry and Sandi Anderson welcome guests to their ca. 1920 Craftsman-style home with its deep and inviting porch. Guest rooms in the main house are named for the apples that grow in the valley—Gala, Fuji, Red Delicious, and Golden Delicious. A separate carriage house offers a cozy and private haven.

About 4 miles from downtown and toward Mission Ridge Ski Area is the *Rimrock Inn Bed & Breakfast,* at 1354 Pitcher Canyon Road, where Dave and Mary Cook welcome guests to their three spacious guest rooms (509–664–5113 or 888–664–5113; www.rimrockinn.com).

For good eats in the Wenatchee area, try *Jeepers It's Bagels* at 619 South Mission Street (509–663–4594) in the Victorian Village; the *Cellar Cafe* in a vintage house at 249 North Mission Street (509-662–1722); *Lemolo Cafe & Deli,* 114 North Wenatchee Avenue (509–664–6576); *McGlinn's Public House* at 111 Orondo Street (509–663–9073) for pastas, gourmet pizza, homemade desserts, and live jazz; *Mission Street Bistro,* 202 North Mission (509–665–2406); and *The Windmill* at 1501 North Wenatchee Avenue (509–665–9529) for legendary steaks and freshly baked pies to die for. Then enjoy walking off the calories on a scenic section of the 11-mile *Apple Capital Recreation Loop Trail* that skirts the Columbia River. Find parking and trail access at Riverfront Park at the end of Fifth Street in downtown Wenatchee or at Walla Walla Park off Walla Walla Avenue at the north end of town. The path is wheelchair accessible.

As you head west on US 2 from Wenatchee toward Leavenworth, detour first at the small town of *Cashmere* to tour the Liberty Orchards *Aplet & Cotlet Candy Factory,* located at 117 Mission Avenue (509–782–4088, extension 1). The tour includes samples of the delicious fruit and nut confections. If time allows plan an hour or so to tour Cashmere's *Pioneer Village and Museum,* located at 600 Cottage Avenue (509–782–3230; www.cashmeremuseum.com; there is a nominal admission fee). Volunteers in pioneer dress encourage you and the kids to snoop into some twenty pioneer structures dating from the 1800s that are outfitted with vintage furniture, linens, dishes, kitchenware, clothing, and accessories of those earlier times. Browse the well-stocked wine and gift shop, which offers a selection of wines from Wenatchee Valley wineries. For a bite to eat in Cashmere, try **Walnut Cafe,** 106 Cottage Avenue (509–782–2022), open Wednesday to Sunday.

Once upon a time the town of **Leavenworth** was dying. But that was back in the 1960s, when it was a tired and worn-out 1920s-style railroad and lumber town. Now, with years of revitalization by enthusiastic townsfolk, Leavenworth is a vibrant Bavarian-style village with a bit of Austria and Switzerland thrown in for good measure. And it sits smack in the middle of the central Washington Cascades, in the Icicle River Valley, where the towering mountains look very much like the Alps. The village is a good place for walking because it is small and compact. Carved window boxes and hanging baskets spill over with bright flowers and greenery; shop signs are hand-painted in old Germanic script; building exteriors show gingerbread detailing and rich carving; and tiers of second- and third-floor exterior decks and dormers are also done in the carved and richly appointed Bavarian style.

Enjoy strolling and poking into shops like **Die Musik Box** at 933 Front Street (509–548–6142), where you'll find more than 3,000 music boxes from around the world; **Der Sportsmann** at 837 Front Street (509–548–5623) for clothing related to hiking, biking, fishing, climbing, and skiing as well as bike rental and ski rental/repair; **Rocky Mountain Chocolate Factory** at 636 Front Street (509–548–6525) for fine chocolates, fudge, and caramel apples; the **Cuckoo Clock** at 725 Front Street for a large selection of cuckoo and other kinds of clocks; **Cheesemonger's Shop** at 633 Front Street (509–548–9011); and **Sweet Dreams** at 220 Ninth Street (509–548–5144) for Teuscher fine chocolates from Switzerland and Howard Miller grandfather clocks. You could also visit **Leavenworth Nutcracker Museum,** 735 Front Street, 2B (509–548–4708), to see a variety of nutcrackers, some dating from the fifteenth century.

After all this ogling and shopping, you'll be ready to enjoy coffee and a great meal. Your alpine-influenced choices include **Home Fires Bakery,** 13013 Bayne Road (509–548–7362) in a rustic log cabin; **Cafe Verona & Bakery,** 820 Commercial Street (509–548–1677); **Andreas Keller,** downstairs at 829 Front Street (509–548–6000), for rotisserie-cooked chicken, German potato salad, sausages, sauerkraut, beer, and wine; and **Black Bear Cafe & Coffee House** (509–548–3225) at Best Western Icicle Inn.

For a comfortable overnight stay in the Leavenworth area, consider these hospitable inns: **Enzian Inn,** 590 Highway 2 (800–223–8511), offers European-style Old World ambience. **Bosch Garten Bed & Breakfast,** located at 9846 Dye Road (800–535–0069), offers three guest rooms, a well-stocked library, and a hot tub in an enclosed Japanese teahouse in the garden. **Run of the River**

Bed & Breakfast, a log cabin–style inn located at 9308 East Leavenworth Road (800–288–6491), offers mountain hospitality and elegant amenities in six guest rooms with fireplaces, sitting areas, whirlpool tubs, decks overlooking the Icicle River, and heavenly breakfasts in the great room. *Pine River Ranch,* located at 19668 Highway 207 (509–763–3959 or 800–699–3877; www.prranch .com) and close to *Lake Wenatchee,* offers suites with river-rock fireplaces, whirlpool tubs, and gourmet breakfasts—French toast stuffed with chocolate and nuts and topped with brandied cherries is one of their tasty entrees.

Golf buffs can find the locals' longtime favorite, the ca. 1927 *Leavenworth Golf Course,* 9101 Icicle Road (509–548–7267; www.leavenworthgolfclub .com), where its eighteen scenic holes ramble along the Wenatchee River. You're into fine wines? If so, you can tour several new wineries and tasting rooms: *Eagle Creek Winery,* 10037 Eagle Creek Road (509–548–7668; www.eaglecreekwinery.com); *La Toscana Winery* located 6 miles east of Leavenworth and open by appointment (509–548–5448); and *Icicle Ridge Winery,* 8977 North Road in nearby Peshatin (509–548–7851; www.icicle ridgewinery.com), open daily noon to 5:00 P.M.

Bird-watching aficionados can take in *Leavenworth Spring Bird Fest* in early May. Join a flock of other bird lovers and participate in guided activities along the Wenatchee River and Icicle Creek areas that include Owl Prowl, Wood Duck Walk, Birding by Ear, Birding by Pontoon Boat, Birding Photography, Bird Banding, and Bird Photography Art Show. Find Bird Fest Central and copies of the event guide downtown near the gazebo at Front Street (509–548–5807; www.leavenworthspringbirdfest.com).

For additional information about the area, contact the Leavenworth Visitor Information Center at (509) 548–5807; www.leavenworth.org. Other annual events and activities include *Bavarian Cross-Country Ski Pursuit* in early February, *International Folk Dance Performance* in late May, *Bavarian Bike & Brew Mountain Bike Race* in early June, *International Accordion Celebration* in late June, Icicle Creek Music Center's *Chamber Music Festival* on weekends in July, and the splendid *Leavenworth Outdoor Summer Theater* (509–548–2000) from July through Labor Day. See www.leavenworth summertheater.org for the current schedule, which usually includes the musical *The Sound of Music.*

US 2 west up to Stevens Pass is spectacular, but not nearly as dramatic as it must have been for travelers in the late nineteenth century, when the first railroad line crossed the Cascade Mountains here. The original route included 13 miles of switchbacks cut into the mountainside that required the train to stop on spur tracks, change the track switch, then reverse up the next leg. Folks now drive the mountainous route with ease, including a trip through the 8-mile

Cascade Tunnel, currently the longest railroad tunnel in use in North America. For another Cascades summertime adventure, this one on the ***Iron Goat Trail*** (www.irongoat.org and www.fs.fed.us/r6/mbs), built by volunteers on the old Great Northern Railroad bed, detour from US 2 at milepost 55, which is 9 miles west of Stevens Pass summit, and follow the signs to Martin Creek trailhead and parking area. For great mountain views, waves of blooming wildflowers, and interpretive signs, do the 2⅗-mile round-trip hike along the lower grade to the Twin Tunnels and back. The trail is wheelchair accessible. From here continue west on US 2 through the small towns of Skykomish (there's a Forest Service ranger station here), Index, Gold Bar, and Startup toward Snohomish and Everett to the west. Or you can veer southward toward Edmonds, Bellevue, Seattle, and the greater King County and Puget Sound environs.

Heading south from Leavenworth, US 97 takes you through the southeastern section of the Wenatchee National Forest and toward Cle Elum, Roslyn, Thorp, and Ellensburg. The current route over Swauk Pass is scenic enough, but for a special treat take the old winding highway over ***Blewett Pass.*** Except for occasional logging trucks, you're likely to have the road to yourself. It's also a popular route with bicyclists. For an alternate adventure take Liberty Road 2 miles east from US 97 to the town of ***Liberty,*** the oldest mining town site in Washington State.

The Kittitas Valley pushes into the eastern slope of the Cascade Mountains in the center of the state, and here you'll find the old coal-mining town of ***Roslyn,*** settling back into relative quiet after its starring role in the mid-1980s as Cicely, Alaska, on the *Northern Exposure* television series. The entire town is on the National Register of Historic Places.

Nearby, in the small community of ***South Cle Elum,*** railroad buffs will enjoy a pilgrimage to ***Iron Horse Inn Bed and Breakfast*** at 526 Marie Avenue (509–674–5939). The renovated railroad workers' bunkhouse offers cozy rooms, and on the grounds three comfortable cabooses can accommodate up

> **trivia**
>
> The town of Roslyn was so fiercely proud of its mining prowess that it shipped a twenty-two-ton lump of coal to the 1893 Chicago World's Fair as an exhibit.

to five guests each. Ask about the newest acquisition, a 1928 wood-sided caboose that sleeps two in a cozy love nest. Railroad memorabilia at this pleasant inn include tools, switch lights, toy trains, and conductors' uniforms. Ask the innkeepers about progress on the renovation of the Milwaukee Rail Depot and grounds located behind the inn (see www.milwelectric.org for updates and details about the community effort).

Iron Horse Inn Bed and Breakfast

Iron Horse Trail State Park, a 25-mile section of the John Wayne Pioneer Trail system, runs adjacent to the inn. Here you can ride mountain bikes, enjoy pleasant riverside walks, or try cross-country skiing. In Cle Elum itself you can visit the ca. 1914 Craftsman-style *Carpenter House Museum* and *High Country Artists* on the corner of Third and Billings (509–674–9766; www.upperkittitashistoricalmuseum.com), open weekends from noon to 4:00 P.M. Ask about the *Telephone Museum,* complete with a large vintage switchboard, located at 221 East First Street (509–674–5702), and the *Roslyn Historic Mining Museum* at 203 Pennsylvania Avenue in nearby Roslyn (509–964–9640). Find good Italian fare at *Mama Vallone's Pasta & Steak House* (509–674–5174) and an extensive specialty menu at *Spacone's* (509–674–9609), both located in Cle Elum's small downtown area. Two new eateries to check out include *Diamondback's Restaurant* at 200 East First Street (509–674–9669) and *Pioneer Coffee Roasting Company and Cafe,* 121 Pennsylvania Street (509–674–3864).

For a bit of history restored, turn off Interstate 90 at the Thorp exit (milepost 101), then travel west 3 miles through the village of Thorp, past the schools, to reach the *Thorp Gristmill.* The mill operated from 1883 until 1946, initially powered by a waterwheel. Local citizens have worked to preserve all three stories of the sprawling structure and its fifteen well-crafted antique machines. The mill is open for tours on weekends from the end of May to the end of September and by appointment the rest of the year. Call (509) 964–9640 or (509) 674–5958 before you go.

The city of *Ellensburg* has a unique downtown historic district that is ideal for strolling. Contact the Ellensburg Visitor Information Center (509–925–3137; www.ellensburg-chamber.com) for a walking-tour guide. Along the walk you'll discover more than two dozen ornate brick buildings constructed between the

1880s and 1910, most of which have been renovated and now house small businesses and shops. The *Clymer Museum and Gallery,* in the 1901 Ramsey Building at 416 North Pearl Street, highlights western art, especially the work of local historical painter John Clymer. You'll also see fanciful public art along the streets, including a life-size bronze bull relaxing on a downtown bench.

Central Washington University's Chimpanzee and Human Communication Institute offers unique seminars called *Chimposiums* at its pleasant downtown campus. These one-hour, educational workshops explore scientists' personal observations of world-renowned chimps that communicate using American sign language, as well as present discussions of chimpanzee culture and conversations. Tuition is $10.00 for adults and $7.50 for students. The workshops are offered Saturday morning and Sunday afternoon. Call (509) 963–2244 for reservations (which are recommended) and more information.

Within walking distance of historic downtown areas and the Central Washington University campus, travelers can enjoy warm and hospitable accommodations at *Wren's Nest Bed & Breakfast,* at 300 East Manitoba Avenue; (509) 925–9061; www.wrensnest.com. Innkeeper Marcia Williams offers guest rooms with antique beds, sumptuous coverlets, and fresh flowers from her perennial gardens. She also kept the rich wood floors and woodwork in the ca. 1912 Craftsman-style home. Other welcoming inns in the Ellensburg area include *Pure West Guest House* (7626 Manastash Road; 509–962–2125), where innkeeper Missy Montana likes to give her guests a western welcome; *Westside Loft* (4500 Hanson Road; 888–543–6777) with skylights and cozy built-in beds; and *4W Ranch & Guest Cabins* (11670 Manastash Road; 866–497–2624). Good eats in Ellensburg can be found at the *Dakota Cafe* (319 North Pearl Street; 509–925–4783), at *Pearl's on Pearl* (311 North Pearl Street; 509–962–8899), at *Valley Cafe* (104 West Third Street; 509–925–3050), and at *Yellow Church Cafe* (111 South Pearl Street; 509–933–2233). For pastries, coffee, espresso, and fresh-roasted beans, stop at *D&M Coffee Cafe,* 301 North Pine Street (509–962–6333). For classic hamburgers and vintage gasoline-pump memorabilia, stop by *Red Horse Drive-In,* 1518 Cascade Way (509–925–1956). Then plan a brisk walk or bike ride on a section of the *John Wayne Pioneer Trail* (www.parks.wa.gov/activities), which follows the former roadbed of the Chicago–Milwaukee–St. Paul Pacific Railroad two-thirds of the way across the state. From downtown Ellensburg you can access the lightly graveled trail on North Water Street or just off Chestnut Street near the Kittitas County Fairgrounds complex.

The old road between Ellensburg and Yakima, Highway 821, follows the scenic *Lower Yakima River Canyon* for approximately 25 miles. The drive offers outstanding views of the wide valley nestled between sheer basalt cliffs and the river. A variety of raptors and songbirds live in the canyon, as well as herds of bighorn sheep. The river is famous among anglers as a catch-and-release trout stream.

The Vantage Highway from Ellensburg east to the Columbia River is a great alternative route that misses the traffic of I–90 and offers views of rich farmlands that give way to rolling sagebrush meadows. The highway passes by the ***Quilomene Wildlife Area,*** a 45,000-acre preserve popular with hunters. Watch for the Wanapum Recreational Area and the ***Ginkgo Petrified Forest State Park*** (509–856–2700; www.parks.wa.gov) to your left as you descend to the Columbia River. The park has two short trails highlighting exposed "trees of stone." This area is rich with wildlife, including mammals, reptiles, and songbirds. Fifteen to twenty million years ago this land was moist and lush, covered with tropical swamps and thick forests. When layers of lava from volcanic eruptions covered the area, many logs that had sunk to the bottom of shallow lakes were entombed and eventually turned to stone, after minerals replaced organic materials.

Brochures along the trailhead will help you identify the petrified ginkgo, spruce, and fir logs scattered along the path. The park also has rock carvings of early peoples dated from 200 to 10,000 years old. You'll find drinking fountains, picnic tables, restrooms, and ample parking here. The ***Ginkgo Petrified Forest Interpretive Center*** (509–856–2700) is open from 10:00 A.M. to 6:00 P.M. daily from May through Labor Day and is well worth a visit. It's best to call ahead for hours if you're visiting September through April. The center features more than 200 petrified wood displays as well as a twelve-minute film that tells the petrification story.

The highway ends at ***Vantage,*** where you'll cross the wide Columbia River. Take the 5-mile detour south on Highway 243 to the ***Wanapum Dam Visitors Center,*** open April through October, where you can visit a museum describing the area's history. The museum offers a detailed description of the Native people who inhabited the region for thousands of years and explains the impact of white culture on this tribe. Although the dam itself flooded the tribe's historic village site and ended their traditional livelihood of salmon fishing, the Wanapum people have continued to exist and are working to create a viable future for their community.

From here you can head south on US 97 to explore Yakima and the Yakima Valley, then continue south to the scenic Columbia River Gorge. Or, you could head east on I–90 toward Spokane and the Palouse region.

Places to Stay in North Central Washington

CHELAN

Best Western Lakeside Motor Lodge
2312 West Woodin Avenue
(800) 468–2781

Chelan House Bed & Breakfast
311 South First Street
(509) 888–4000

Wild Rose Bed & Breakfast
427 South Third Street
(509) 682–2974

CLE ELUM

Iron Horse Inn Bed and Breakfast
526 Marie Street
(800) 228–9246
or (509) 674–5939

CONCONULLY

Shady Pines Cabins, RV Park
125 West Fort Salmon Creek Road
(800) 552–2287

CONCRETE

North Cascade Motor Inn
44618 Route 20
(360) 853–8870

Ovenell's Heritage Inn Bed & Breakfast and Log Cabins
46276 Concrete–Sauk Valley Road
(360) 853–8494

ELLENSBURG

Wren's Nest Bed & Breakfast
300 East Manitoba Avenue
(509) 925–9061

LEAVENWORTH

Icicle River RV Resort
7305 Icicle Road
(509) 548–5420

Pine River Ranch Bed and Breakfast
19668 Highway 207
(509) 763–3959 or
(800) 669–3877

Run of the River Bed and Breakfast Retreat
9308 East Leavenworth Road
(800) 288–6491

LOOMIS

Sun Cove Resort
Wannocut Lake
(509) 476–2223

SELECTED VISITOR INFORMATION CENTERS

Ellensburg
(509) 925–3137 or (888) 925–2204
www.ellensburg-chamber.com

Chelan and Lake Chelan
(800) 424–3526
www.lakechelan.com

Leavenworth
(509) 548–5807
www.leavenworth.org

North Cascades National Park
810 Highway 20, Sedro-Woolley
(360) 856–5700
www.nps.gov/noca

Outdoor Recreation Information at REI, Seattle
(206) 470–4060

Winthrop
(800) 463–8469
www.winthropwashington.com

MAZAMA

Mazama Country Inn
42 Lost River Road
(509) 996–2681

OROVILLE

Sun Cove Resort
Wannacut Lake
(509) 476–2223

PATEROS

Lake Pateros Motor Inn
115 Lake Shore Drive
(800) 444–1985

ROCKPORT

Ross Lake Floating Resort
(206) 386–4437

Skagit River Resort &
RV Park
58468 Clark Cabin Road
(360) 873–2250

ROSLYN

Huckleberry House
Bed & Breakfast
301 Pennsylvania Avenue E
(509) 649–2900

STEHEKIN

North Cascades
Stehekin Lodge
(509) 682–4494

TONASKET

Bonaparte Lake Resort
695 Bonaparte Lake Road
(509) 486–2828

TWISP

Riverbend RV Park
19961 Highway 20
(800) 686–4498

Whitetail Crossing
Bed & Breakfast
147 Twisp–Winthrop
Eastside Road
(509) 997–9422

WATERVILLE

Waterville Historic Hotel
102 East Park Street
(509) 745–8695 or
(888) 509–8180

WENATCHEE

Apple Country
Bed & Breakfast
524 Okanogan Avenue
(509) 664–0400

La Quinta Inn
1905 North
Wenatchee Avenue
(800) 531–5900

Rimrock Inn Bed &
Breakfast
1354 Pitcher Canyon Road
(888) 664–5113

WINTHROP

River Run Inn & Cabins
27 Rader Road
(800) 757–2709

WolfRidge Resort &
Cabins
412 Wolf Creek Road
(800) 237–2388

HELPFUL WEB SITES IN NORTH CENTRAL WASHINGTON

Cascade Loop Association
www.cascadeloop.com

Lake Chelan
www.lakechelan.com/

**Mount Baker–Snoqualmie
National Forest**
www.fs.fed.us/r6/mbs

Road Reports, Washington State
Department of Transportation
www.wsdot.wa.gov

Welcome to Okanogan Country
www.visitokanogancountry.com
www.fs.fed.us/r6/oka

Wenatchee Valley
www.wenatcheevalley.org

Winthrop–Twisp Area
www.winthropwashington.com

ALSO WORTH SEEING

Audubon Center and Upper Valley
Museum at Leavenworth
(509) 548–5807

Chelan Valley Players
Chelan
(509) 687–0818

Lake Chelan area wineries
Chelan
(800) 424–3526

Olmstead Place State Park
Heritage Area and Gardens
Ellensburg

Wenatchee Valley Museum
& Cultural Center
Wenatchee
(509) 664–3340

Places to Eat in North Central Washington

CHELAN

Apple Cup Cafe
804 East Woodin
(509) 682–2933

Campbell House Restaurant
104 West Woodin
(509) 682–2561

Latte Da Coffee Stop Cafe
303 East Wapato Avenue
(509) 682–4196

Riverwalk Books & Open Book Espresso
116 East Woodin
(509) 682–8901

CLE ELUM

Cle Elum Bakery
501 East First Street
(509) 674–2233

Pioneer Coffee Roasting Company Cafe
121 Pennsylvania Street
(509) 674–3864

CONCRETE

Perks Espresso
Highway 20
(360) 853–9006

The Cajun Bar & Grill
Highway 20
(360) 853–8518

ELLENSBURG

D&M Coffee Cafe
301 North Pine Street
(509) 962–6333

Dakota Cafe
319 North Pearl Street
(509) 925–4783

Red Horse Drive-In
1518 Cascade Way
(509) 925–1956

LEAVENWORTH

Black Bear Cafe & Coffee House
Best Western Icicle Inn
535 Highway 2
(509) 548–8225

Cafe Verona and Bakery
820 Commercial Street
(509) 548–1677

Home Fires Bakery
13013 Bayne Road
(509) 548–7362

O'Grady's Pantry
Sleeping Lady
Conference Center
7375 Icicle Road
(509) 548–6344

Sandy's Waffle and Dinner Haus
894 Highway 2,
Clocktower Building
(509) 548–6300

MARBLEMOUNT

Buffalo Run Cafe
60084 Highway 20
(360) 873–2461

MAZAMA

Mazama Country Store & Deli
Highway 20
(509) 996–2855

NEWHALEM

Skagit General Store
Highway 20
(206) 386–4489

OMAK

The Breadline Cafe
102 South Ash Street
(509) 826–5836

OROVILLE

Fat Boy's Diner
1518 Main Street
(509) 476–4100

Trino's Mexican Cafe
1918 Main Street
(509) 476–9151

ROSLYN

Roslyn Cafe
201 Pennsylvania Avenue
(509) 649–2763

TONASKET

All Perked Up Espresso
Main Street
(509) 486–8325

**Shannon's Cafe & Ice
Cream Parlor**
626 South Whitcomb
(509) 486–2259

TWISP

**BJ's Branding Iron
Restaurant & Saloon**
123 Glover Street
(509) 997–3576

Cinnamon Twisp Bakery
116 Glover Street
(509) 997–5030

Twisp River Brew Pub
Highway 20
(509) 997–6822

WAUCONDA

**The Wauconda Store
and Cafe**
2432 Highway 20
(509) 486–4010

WENATCHEE

Cottage Inn Cafe
134 Easy Street
(509) 663–4435

Jeepers It's Bagels Cafe
619 South Mission Street
(509) 663–4594

McGlinn's Public House
111 Orondo Street
(509) 663–9073

**The Owl Soda Fountain
& Gifts**
25 North Wenatchee Avenue
(509) 664–7221

WINTHROP

Boulder Creek Deli
Riverside Avenue
(Highway 20)
(509) 996–3990

**Heenan's Burnt Finger
Bar-B-Q Steakhouse and
Rattlesnake Saloon**
716 Highway 20 South
(509) 996–8221

Sheri's Sweet Shop
Riverside Avenue
(509) 996–3834

**Three Fingered Jack's
Saloon**
Riverside Avenue
(509) 996–2411

**Winthrop Brewing
Company & Pub**
155 Riverside Avenue
(509) 996–3183

South Central Washington

The south central section of Washington State sports impressive statistics and offers everything from apples to windsurfing, from two snowcapped mountains each over 8,000 feet high, to waterfalls that drop from basalt ledges with one narrow ribbon of water falling over 600 feet. On the high plateau above the river that stretches north to Yakima, farmers tend vast orchards of apples, apricots, peaches, and cherries. Vintners tend hundreds of acres of grapes including pinot noir, chardonnay, and Riesling. Washington State shares the awesome scenery of the **Columbia River Gorge** with its neighbor Oregon. The wide river forms a natural boundary with Washington to the north and the Beaver State to the south. Snowy Mount St. Helens, now some 8,000 feet high (it was 9,677 feet prior to the eruption of May 18, 1980), and **Mount Adams,** at 12,307 feet high, guard the Washington side. Snowy **Mount Hood,** at 11,235 feet high, overlooks the Oregon side. The watery border extends roughly 300 miles from the eastern end of the gorge at the Tri-Cities (Kennewick, Pasco, and Richland) to the Pacific Ocean at Astoria and the Long Beach Peninsula. Travelers can trek back and forth across the Columbia River on substantial bridges that span the waters at Long Beach/Astoria, Longview/Rainier, Vancouver/ Portland, Stevenson/Cascade Locks, White Salmon/Hood River, Goldendale/The Dalles, and Tri-Cities/Umatilla.

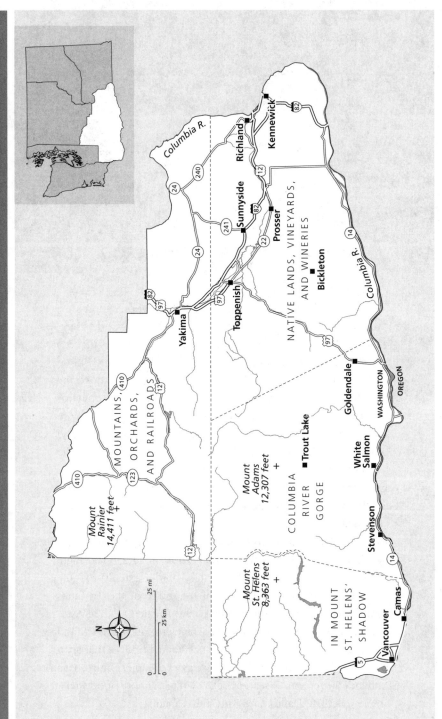

The native Indian tribes who lived in the region weren't so lucky; they had to use canoes or rafts to cross the swift-flowing river, as did the first French and American trappers, British Hudson's Bay Company explorers, American explorers and road surveyors, and the folks who traveled from the east on the Oregon Trail. One of those early groups of explorers sent by the U.S. government, the Lewis and Clark Corps of Discovery, trekked along the north side of the Columbia River in the fall of 1805, reaching the Pacific Ocean around November 15. The party numbered thirty-three and included Captain Clark's slave, York, and Captain Lewis's Newfoundland dog, Seaman.

Where it may take today's travelers a day or so by automobile to complete the same journey from the Tri-Cities of Kennewick, Pasco, and Richland to the Pacific Ocean, it took Lewis and Clark and their corps about one month to

SOUTH CENTRAL WASHINGTON'S TOP HITS

Beacon Rock Golf Course
North Bonneville

Central Washington Agricultural Museum
Union Gap

Columbia Gorge Interpretive Center
Stevenson

Conboy Lake National Wildlife Refuge
Glenwood

Eco Park Resort & Cabins
Mount St. Helens

Fort Simcoe State Park Heritage Site
White Swan

Fort Vancouver National Historic Site
Vancouver

Goldendale Observatory State Park
Goldendale

Hulda Klager Lilac Gardens
Woodland

Liberty Theatre
Toppenish

Maryhill Museum
Goldendale

Mount St. Helens National Volcanic Monument
Castle Rock

North Front Street Historic District
Yakima

Sacajawea State Park
Kennewick

Sandhill Cottages and #7 Coffee Roasting Co. Coffee Bar
Carson

Whistle Punk Forest Heritage Trail
Carson

Yakama Nation Cultural Heritage Center
Toppenish

Yakama Nation Mount Adams Recreation Area
Trout Lake

Yakima Valley Rail and Steam Museum
Toppenish

cover this leg of their journey, mainly by water. At *Sacajawea State Park,* near Kennewick, you can visit an interpretive center devoted to the expedition and the role of Sacajawea, the Shoshoni Indian woman who served as the corps' guide and interpreter. Designed and installed during the 200th anniversary of the *Lewis and Clark expedition,* from 2003 through 2006, exhibits, pictorial displays, and interpretive material (along with panoramic views of the gorge and river) can be seen at these sites: *Hat Rock State Park* near Umatilla; *Horsethief Lake State Park* near The Dalles; the *Columbia Gorge Interpretive Center* near Stevenson; *Beacon Rock State Park,* west of Stevenson and the Bridge of the Gods; *Lewis and Clark State Park* near

Lewis and Clark Expedition
Bicentennial 2003–2006

Early in the nation's history, from 1803 through 1806, Thomas Jefferson undertook planning, recruiting, and dispatching a corps of men for a discovery expedition to the Pacific Ocean. It is said that Jefferson made the right choice in selecting Meriwether Lewis and William Clark to lead the expedition. Jefferson felt the two men, although different in their personalities, possessed qualities important for exploring uncharted wilderness: youth, intelligence, resourcefulness, courage, and a sense of adventure. Both men were experienced woodsmen and frontiersmen as well as seasoned army officers. From 1804 to 1806 the party of thirty-three folks traveled more than 8,000 miles on foot, horseback, and dugout canoe. The record shows the precise time frame as two years, four months, and ten days. Their route encompassed sections of Illinois, Missouri, Kansas, Nebraska, Iowa, South Dakota, North Dakota, Montana, Idaho, Washington, and Oregon. To plan your own travels over the route, check these sites for ongoing events and activities:

Lewis and Clark Bicentennial
www.lewisandclark200.org

Discovering Lewis and Clark
www.lewis-clark.org
A multimedia site incorporating the entire route from east to west

Lewis and Clark Trail Heritage Foundation
www.lewisandclark.org
Information, preservation efforts, and maps of the trail

Fort Clatsop National Memorial
www.nps.gov/focl
Living-history programs mid-June through Labor Day at the 1805–6 winter headquarters site near Astoria, Oregon

Troutdale and Portland; and **Cape Disappointment State Park** and the **Lewis and Clark Interpretive Center** near Long Beach. You can also visit the living-history program at **Fort Clatsop National Memorial,** the expedition's 1805–6 winter headquarters near Astoria, Oregon.

In Mount St. Helens' Shadow

When the British came to Oregon Country in the early 1800s, among the many trading forts they established was Fort Vancouver. This fort was situated near the Columbia River and what is now the city of **Vancouver.** The Interstate Bridge links Vancouver to both Hayden Island and to Portland on the Oregon side of the river. On the island travelers find several service stations, two large, well-stocked grocery stores, two large motor inns that overlook the water, a number of good restaurants, and dozens of large chain stores and shops, along with condominiums, houseboats, marinas, and pleasure boats of all kinds. The island is a good place to pause and stock up on groceries and beverages for a trip north from Vancouver toward Seattle or for a trip east on Highway 14 heading into the Columbia River Gorge area. In earlier days, during the 1940s and 1950s, **Hayden Island** was home to a larger, and much-loved, amusement park, Jantzen Beach, which featured an enormous roller coaster, park, and picnic areas, a large indoor dance pavilion, and two outdoor Olympic-size swimming pools. Linger on Hayden Island on a warm day, head east on Tomahawk Island Drive, passing by the two large grocery stores, and turn down into the shore-side parking area at **Island Café on the River** (503–283–0362), located near McCuddy's Marina at 250 Northeast Tomahawk Island Drive. Walk down the steep ramp, find a table at the floating cafe, enjoy tasty fish-and-chips or juicy burgers and ales, and meet other sun lovers while watching small boats cruise past and ducks quacking for scraps.

Located across the Interstate Bridge from Hayden Island and just east of Vancouver's downtown area, **Fort Vancouver National Historic Site** is well worth a stop. The National Park Service operates the 366-acre complex. First stroll through the informative museum and visitor information area at the upper section of the complex, then walk down the grassy lawn area, or drive down to the large parking area, to find the fort and the fully restored **Fort Vancouver British Gardens.** In the 1840s grapevines trailed over greenhouses for shade and the garden yielded such produce as Thomas Laxton peas, English broad beans, and yellow pear tomatoes. The flower garden section contains a walk-through arbor of hop vines, large clumps of scented lavender, old-fashioned climbing roses, and vintage perennials in large beds. You can also see the remnants of the extensive fruit orchard on the grounds.

Then pay a small admission fee and gain entrance to the restored fort inside the re-created stockade walls. Watch living-history vignettes in the trading house, the blacksmith shop, the bakery cabin, and the kitchen—staff and volunteers in period dress offer youngsters and oldsters alike an authentic look at life in the early 1800s. You learn that both early settlers and members of local native Indian tribes often visited the fort to socialize and trade for tobacco, candles, beads, blankets, and cotton cloth as well as vegetables, grains, and other supplies. Dr. John McLoughlin, the fort's chief factor for many years, lived in the large house that stands next to the kitchen. Visitors can tour the house, which contains furnishings and memorabilia from the McLoughlin family's time here. Fort Vancouver is located at 612 East Revere Street; (360) 816–6200. Visit the fort and its living history programs daily from 9:00 A.M. to 4:00 P.M. during winter and 9:00 A.M. to 5:00 P.M. during summer. You could also tour the historic *McLoughlin House,* 713 Center Street (503–656–5146) in Oregon City just south of Portland to see where Dr. McLoughlin and his family lived after 1845, when he retired from the Hudson's Bay Company and became an American citizen.

You'll notice *Officer's Row,* the stately Victorian-style homes that sit in a tidy row along the boulevard just north of Fort Vancouver. These functioned as housing for military officers during World War II. The lovely houses are now preserved and open to the public during part of the year. Watch Vancouver's Heritage Players reenact tales from the past, including ghost stories around Halloween, in several of the parlors and on several of the wide verandahs. If time allows, call for lunch or dinner reservations at the *Restaurant at the Historic*

Ghosts Galore

It is said that ghosts and spirits hang around at times other than Halloween, perhaps to startle and amuse visitors. Folks claim they've heard or seen them in old theaters and hotels, vintage bed-and-breakfast inns, Victorian houses, ghost towns, and other places appropriate for denizens of the otherworld. Here are a few places to look for friendly ghosts on your travels in Washington state:

Blackman House Museum
(ca. 1878) and also at one of
the town's taverns (the ghost's
name is Henry)
Snohomish

Capitol Theatre
Yakima

Marshall House
Officer's Row National Historic District
Vancouver

Monaghan Hall
(ca. 1898) at Gonzaga University
Spokane

FAVORITE ATTRACTIONS

Beacon Rock Golf Course
North Bonneville

Fort Vancouver National Historic Site
Vancouver

Pomeroy Living History Farm
Yacolt

Mount St. Helens National Volcanic Monument

Reserve (360–906–1101) located in the ca. 1849 Grant House. For more information about the theatrical events and other public events on Officer's Row during the year, call (360) 992–1800, or check www.vnhrt.org.

Vintage-airplane buffs can also visit the ***Pearson Air Museum,*** just east of Fort Vancouver at 1115 East Fifth Street (360–694–7026, www.pearsonair museum.org). Located at the ca. 1905 Pearson Field, the oldest continuously operating airfield on the West Coast, the museum is housed in the Jack Murdock Aviation Center. The center includes two aircraft hangars, a theater, a hands-on activity center for the kids, and a vintage airplane restoration section. Pearson Field offers a fascinating history that dates to World War II. The grounds are open from 10:00 A.M. to 5:00 P.M. Tuesday through Sunday. There is a nominal admission fee.

Visit nearby ***Esther Short Park,*** located off Washington Street between Sixth and Eighth Streets, which offers colorful plantings of roses, azaleas, and rhododendrons. At the park's southeast corner the handsome ***Salmon Run Bell Tower*** displays a historic salmon diorama and its glockenspiel's thirty-six melodious bells play several times each day. Friendly cafes, delis, and coffee shops are located nearby as well. In the park next to the tower and rose gardens is the historic Slocum House, where you might ask what the local theater group is offering at the intimate ***Slocum House Theater*** (360–696–2427; wwwslocumhouse.com). Recent plays included *They're Playing Our Song* by Neil Simon, *The Unexpected Guest* by Agatha Christie, and the popular Broadway musical *Sweeney Todd.* You and the kids can also take in the bustling ***Vancouver Farmers' Market*** (360–737–8298; www.vancouverfarmersmarket.com) at the park on Saturday and Sunday April through October. Also browse up Main Street to find a gaggle of friendly cafes, boutiques, and specialty shops such as ***Ice Cream Renaissance*** at 2108 Main Street and ***Carnelian Rose Tea Company*** at 1803 Main Street (www.carnelianrosetea.com), which offers a fine selection of teas including scrumptious loose-leaf varieties as well as boxed teas imported from England.

Travelers can head north from Vancouver for about 20 miles to Woodland to visit an early garden, the ***Hulda Klager Lilac Gardens,*** at 115 South Pekin Road (360–225–8996; www.lilacgardens.com). It may seem old-fashioned to like lilacs, but thanks to Hulda's work during most of the ninety-six years of her life, garden lovers can enjoy some 250 different hybrid varieties and colors of lilacs and their frothy blooms. Hulda's family settled in this area in 1877, after immigrating from Germany first to Wisconsin in 1865. Hulda received many honors throughout the years, including one from an arboretum in Cambridge, Massachusetts, for her work as a leading hybridizer of lilacs. To the rear of the small Victorian house, garden volunteers have restored the old woodshed, water tower, picturesque windmill, and carriage house. Included in the arboretum section are sixty-four lilacs listed in the national registry. The house is open selected times in April and May, when members of the Hulda Klager Lilac Garden Society don period dresses and greet visitors during the annual open house; lilac starts and plants are offered for sale during this time as well. The arboretum is open daily and is wheelchair accessible.

The ***Cedar Creek Grist Mill National Historic Site*** is located 9 miles east and north of Woodland (360–225–5832). Although rough-hewn and unpretentious, the mill, which dates from 1876, was for generations the center of local industry and also the site of dances, parties, and musical shows. The mill was restored in the early 1980s and is now a working museum, with a water-powered stone flour mill and machine shop on the ground floor. On the second floor you can visit the small museum with photos and artifacts from the mill's history.

The mill is open Saturday from 1:00 to 4:00 P.M. and Sunday from 2:00 to 4:00 P.M. Admission is free, and you may even be able to take home a small bag of fresh-milled flour, but donations are always appreciated. To reach the mill, take Interstate 5 exit 21 at Woodland, turn right at the first stoplight, and proceed east across the Lewis River toward Amboy. Bear left onto Northeast Hayes Road, which becomes Cedar Creek Road. Turn left after 9 miles onto Grist Mill Road and continue 1 mile to the covered bridge that spans Cedar Creek. The mill is on the far bank.

Continue on to Amboy, then turn south on Highway 503 through green fields and forests. In 7 miles turn left (east) on Northeast Lucia Falls Road and go 4½ miles to visit the ***Pomeroy House Living History Farm*** at 20902 Northeast Lucia Falls Road, Yacolt (360–686–3537). You can browse in the British specialty shop to find items such as Dewar's Scotch whiskey marmalade, Cadbury chocolates, and English teas. You can enjoy a spot of tea with scones, tea sandwiches, jellies, and desserts on Wednesday through Saturday from 11:30 A.M. to 3:00 P.M. Sign the reservation list when you arrive. On the first full weekend of

Up Close and Personal: Mount St. Helens National Volcanic Monument

The 52-mile drive from I–5 at Castle Rock (exit 49) east toward Mount St. Helens offers a number of ogling possibilities, with Johnston Ridge the most spectacular at just 5½ miles from the crater. Here are a few of the highlights:

Mount St. Helens Visitor Center, milepost 5, (Washington State)

Hoffstadt Bluffs, milepost 27, food service (Cowlitz County)

Charles W. Bingham Forest Learning Center, milepost 33 (Weyerhaeuser Lumber Company)

Coldwater Ridge Visitor Center, milepost 43 (U.S. Forest Service)

Hummocks Trail, 2⅖-mile trail around colorful rock formations deposited during the 1980 eruption, just east of Coldwater Ridge

Johnston Ridge Observation Center, milepost 52 (U.S. Forest Service)

For more information contact Gifford Pinchot National Forest, Vancouver (360–891–5001; www.fs.fed.us/gpnf/mshnvm). Ask about Ape Cave, Harmony Trail, and Windy Ridge for yet more awesome views of the 1980 volcanic devastation. To linger overnight in the shadow of the mountain, check out **Eco-Park Resort, Cabins, RV Park, and Backwoods Restaurant,** 24 miles east of Castle Rock (360–274–7007; www.ecoparkresort.com).

each month from June through September, you and the kids can see the activities of a homestead farm during the days of candles and kerosene lamps.

Your perspective of the natural world may change after visiting Mount St. Helens, accessible by driving east from Castle Rock. At 8:32 A.M. on Sunday, May 18, 1980, St. Helens exploded in a massive outpouring of lava and dust. The eruption measured 5.1 on the Richter scale. Since then, a total of 110,000 acres has been preserved for research, education, and recreation.

For bedding down easy distances from both Mount Rainier and Mount St. Helens, contact **Cowlitz River Lodge,** 13069 Highway 12 (888–305–2185), and **Mountain View Lodge,** 13163 Highway 12 (360–494–5555 or 877–277–7192); both lodges are located near Packwood. Good eats in the Packwood area can be gotten at the **Blue Spruce Saloon & Diner** on Highway 12 at Willame Street (360–494–5605) and **Peters Inn** on Highway 12 near Skate Creek Road (360–494–4000). Also check the Web site www.destinationpackwood.com for helpful mountain recreation information.

Continuing east on U.S. Highway 12 takes you from Randle to Packwood, then over the high mountain wilderness areas of White Pass, past the fishing resorts along Rimrock Lake, and down the Tieton River Canyon toward Yakima.

Columbia River Gorge

Heading east on Highway 14 from Vancouver, Washington, you'll pass the small mill towns of Camas and Washougal. Take the highway's business loop to explore the Camas downtown area. Fourth Avenue is a pleasant walking street through the main commercial district. From here the highway climbs 1,000 feet up the Columbia plateau at Cape Horn. From the top you'll enjoy an expansive view of the Columbia River Gorge. After descending back to river level, pause in the small community of **Skamania** and snoop in the **Skamania General Store & Deli** (509–427–4820), an old-style rural grocery, then continue east to Beacon Rock State Park (509–427–8265). **Beacon Rock** is an 840-foot basalt tower, the remains of a volcano core, that served as a sign to early river travelers that they had passed the difficult Cascade Rapids and faced no further obstructions to the Pacific Ocean 150 miles west. You can hike 1$\frac{3}{10}$ miles through the forest to Hardy or Rodney Falls. Or for a breathtaking challenge, climb the steep and narrow trail, including a series of wood stairways with railings, to the top of Beacon Rock for panoramic views of the wide Columbia River and forested hills on both the Oregon and the Washington sides of the river. For a scenic round of golf call the folks at **Beacon Rock Golf Course** (509–427–5730 or 800–428–5730) to arrange a tee time.

Just past Beacon Rock and near the town of North Bonneville, you can visit the **Fort Cascades Historic Site,** which includes a 1½-mile self-guided tour. Along the way you'll see prehistoric Indian petroglyphs, the original site of Fort Cascades (which burned during an attack in 1856), and artifacts from the territorial period, when wagons were needed to portage around the rough river waters.

Water travel is easier now, even for the long grain and produce barges that ply the Columbia River, due to the network of dams and locks that begin with the **Bonneville Dam.** Visitors can tour the dam (541–374–8820 for current info) to see the huge electrical generators and the fish-ladder system that allows salmon and steelhead trout to migrate over the dam and continue up the river to spawn. You can view fish through huge underwater windows as they leap and swim upriver. On the Oregon side of the river, accessed by the **Bridge of the Gods** just east of here, you can also see the locks in action, raising and lowering pleasure boats, fishing boats, and grain barges.

Be sure to visit the **Columbia Gorge Interpretive Center** at 990 Southwest Rock Creek Drive near Stevenson; 509–427–8211; www.columbiagorge

.com). The center is located off Highway 14 a couple of miles east of the Bridge of the Gods. This expansive, glass-walled museum highlights the river's colorful history. Witness the geological and climatic forces that formed the gorge at the Creation Theater's twelve-minute multimedia show. Learn about the region's native Indian tribes through oral histories, an interpreted pit house, and dip-net fishing displays. Examine the environmental impact of dams on the river. Other highlights include a 37-foot-tall replica of a nineteenth-century fishwheel, one of many that once harvested millions of pounds of fish each year. The center is open daily (except holidays) from 10:00 A.M. to 5:00 P.M. There is a nominal admission fee.

You can also visit nearby **Skamania Lodge** (509–427–7700 or 800–221–7117; www.skamania.com), a large resort and conference center located on a bluff just above the interpretive center. The resort offers golf, swimming, mountain-bike rentals, guided horseback rides, and tennis. On the main level at the lodge, you will find a well-stocked Forest Service information center (509–427–2528) and Forest Service staff who provide helpful maps and information about hiking trails, wildflower areas, and scenic drives in the gorge. Also on the main level is a lounge for comfortable seating with wide-angle views of the Columbia River and tasty entrees from the bar menu. Nearby **Stevenson** is a

theoregonside

If you have time to spare, take a trip across the Columbia to the Oregon side of the gorge for some beautiful scenery and one of the the highest concentrations of waterfalls in the United States. The best route is along the Columbia Gorge Scenic Highway (Highway 30). Considered a feat of engineering when it was completed in 1910, it is now a lovely, meandering drive along which you can watch the scenery go by from the car or venture out to one of the many trailheads for a hike. Multnomah Falls is the grandest of the waterfalls; at 620 feet it is the second-highest in the United States. At Hood River, just off I-84, stop by the historic Columbia Gorge Hotel (4000 Westcliff Drive; 541–386–5566) for more eye-popping views of the Columbia River.

historic waterfront town and a bustling county seat for Skamania County. Many of its buildings date to the early 1900s, with new businesses sprouting amid the old. The **River House Art Gallery and Studio,** at 115 Southwest Second Street (509–427–5930), features Columbia Gorge images and historic East Coast homes, original watercolors, local pottery, baskets, and pastels. Call to make sure the gallery is open.

There are a number of pleasant eateries in Stevenson, with most of them easy to find along Northwest Second Street, which is Highway 14. Try **It's a Wrap** (509–427–7725), open daily to 3:00 P.M. for healthy wraps and salads; or

Gorge Lovers Sneak Over to Oregon

You won't be chided for taking time to visit the Oregon side of the Columbia River, crossing the bridge from White Salmon and Bingen to the bustling small town of Hood River. You could plan a couple of pleasant day trips:

Drive the 45-mile **Hood River Fruit Loop** into the blooming pear and apple orchards—canopies of white blooms peak around the middle of April. Take in the **Hood River Valley Blossom Festival;** visit wineries and taste local wines, see arts and crafts exhibits, find delicious baked goods and huge apple pies, sip huckleberry milkshakes, buy hardy perennials and herbs, and visit an alpaca farm and browse its country store. Pick up a Fruit Loop map at the Hood River Visitor Information Center (800–366–3530; www.hoodriverfruitloop.com and www.hoodriver.org).

For a second day trip and more awesome close-up views of 11,235-foot Mount Hood, take Highway 35 from Hood River about 25 miles south and west to U.S. Highway 26. Continue about 10 miles west on Highway 26 to Government Camp and take the 6-mile winding road up to the ca. 1937 **Timberline Lodge** and its ski area at 6,000-feet elevation. A Norse king should live in these splendid digs. Tour the second-floor lounge area with its towering fireplaces and huge windows that frame snowy Mount Hood, see the dining areas and lodge rooms, and visit the ground-floor exhibit area that details the lodge's construction during WPA days, including a vintage recording of FDR speaking at the dedication ceremony. For informal eats try the nearby Wy'East Day Lodge Deli. Retrace your route to Hood River and stay overnight there or cross the Columbia River back to the Washington side.

Other spring blossom festivals on the Washington side of the Columbia River:

Apple Blossom Festival in Wenatchee, April to early May (509–662–3616; www.appleblossom.org).

Skagit Valley Tulip Festival in Mount Vernon and La Conner, the month of April (360–428–5959; www/tulipfestival.org).

Big River Grill (509–427–4888) at 192 Southwest Second Street for Northwest pub fare and microbrews. At 240 Southwest First Street, *Walking Man Brewery & Public House* (509–427–5520) offers handcrafted ales and tasty fare such as Caesar salads and clam strips on Wednesday through Saturday. In addition to ten beers on tap, the brewery makes delicious root beer, gingerale, and cream soda. Other pleasant eateries in Stevenson include *Bahma Coffee Bar & Bistro* (509–427–8700) at 256 Second Street for espresso, croissant breakfast sandwiches, lunch specials, and great desserts; and the *Crab Shack* (509–427–4400) at 130 Southwest Cascade Street for seafood and an outside deck for casual dining with a distant view of the Columbia River.

About 20 miles north of Stevenson and Carson, plan to walk the **Whistle Punk Forest Heritage Trail,** a self-guided interpretive trail in the Gifford Pinchot National Forest. Along the wheelchair-accessible trail through the second-growth Wind River Experimental Forest, you and the kids can learn Northwest logging history as well as see old logging equipment used in the area in the 1930s. The Wind River Work Center (509–427–3200), about 10 miles north of Carson via the Wind River Highway, can provide maps and other information about summer wildflower meadows, hiking trails, and winter cross-country ski areas in the Gifford Pinchot National Forest. For resources and information about the ancient art of animal tracking, browse www.bear-tracker.com. You could linger overnight in the Stevenson-Carson area by calling **Sandhill Cottages** (932 Hot Springs Avenue; 800–914–2178; www.sandhillcottages.com), or you could stop for a friendly chat with the owners over a cup of coffee or espresso made from their freshly roasted coffee beans at **#7 Coffee Roasting Company Coffee Bar,** located at the entry.

Farther east along the Columbia is the town of **Bingen,** and just up the hill is **White Salmon.** Until recently these were quiet riverside communities of hardworking old-timers, but they have become recreation meccas, especially for windsurfers. On summer weekends the beaches along this stretch of the Columbia are crowded with wind-surfing enthusiasts of all ages, and the water is alive with colorful sails. The **Inn of the White Salmon** (172 West Jewett Boulevard; 509–493–2335), built in 1937, offers cozy, antiques-decorated rooms and delicious breakfasts featuring European-style pastries, breads, and egg dishes. Just for fun, ask about the Hungarian *flauf,* the artichoke frittata, or the tasty chile relleno—so much for plain toast and cereal; you're on vacation, so enjoy.

Catching the Wind

You're adventurous, you're hardy, and you're in excellent physical shape? The ultimate test may be learning to maneuver a windsurfing board and learning to ply the deep waves on a windy day on the mighty Columbia River near White Salmon and Hood River. To learn about the popular sport of windsurfing, contact the Columbia Gorge Windsurfing Association at 202 Oak Street in Hood River directly south of Bingen on the Oregon side of the river (541–386–9225; www.cgwa.net). A couple of good spots to watch and photograph the sailors are at **Port Marina Park** just west of the bridge in Hood River and farther east at **Maryhill State Park,** south of Goldendale on the Washington side of the river. Maryhill also offers picnic shelters, grassy areas, and riverfront campsites.

Down the street, ***Klickitat Pottery Shop*** (264 East Jewett Boulevard; 509–493–4456) is a fun place to browse and observe an ancient craft in action. The potter often works in a wide-windowed studio on one side of the shop, creating high-quality earthenware pieces for sale in the shop.

For good dining in White Salmon, check out ***The Creamery Cafe*** at 121 East Jewett (509–493–4007) for coffee, bagels, and desserts, open daily to 8:00 P.M. In nearby Bingen try ***Los Reyes*** (509–493–1017) at 120 East Steuben for delicious Mexican fare and ***Big River Diner*** (509–493–1414) for tasty American-style eats and a great salad bar.

There is lots to see and do in the scenic White Salmon River Valley, which stretches from the Columbia River north to 12,307-foot-high Mount Adams. ***Zoller's Outdoor Odysseys*** at BZ Corner, 1248 Highway 141, just north of White Salmon (509–493–2641; www.zooraft.com and www.snakeraft.com), will raft you down the White Salmon River. It's an exhilarating experience and is suitable for families and beginners. The standard trip lasts about three hours, including the return by road to your starting point. Call Mark and Sherrie Zoller for the current river-rafting schedule. The Zollers also offer rafting trips on the Snake River in the Hells Canyon Recreation Area.

In Husum plan to stay overnight in the shadows of Mount Hood and Mount Adams by calling the innkeeper at ***Husum's Riverside Bed & Breakfast*** (509–493–8900; www.gorge-rooms.com). You could also arrange for cozy rooms that come with a hearty farm breakfast at ***Husum Highlands Bed & Breakfast*** (800–808–9812; www.husumhighlands.com). At nearby ***Husum***

Extreme Sports, Columbia Gorge

Kicking it up a notch in terms of all-season outdoor sports in the Columbia River Gorge entails a passion for the extreme. Hardy types of all ages can learn how to

Fly stunt kites	Skateboard
Inline skate	Ski
Kiteboard	Snowboard
Motocross	Surf
Mountain bike	Wakeboard
Parachute	Water-ski
Paraglide	Windsurf

For training and equipment resources, get a current copy of the *Gorge Guide* from the Hood River Visitor Information Center (541–386–2000 or 800–366–3530; www.hoodriver.org).

Hills Golf Course (509–493–1211), you could enjoy a scenic round on the nine-hole course, but you may want to rent a golf cart—the course is *very* hilly.

You and the kids could arrange to go horseback riding on gentle steeds at *Northwestern Lake Riding Stables,* at 126 Little Buck Creek Road (509–493–4965) near White Salmon and Trout Lake. Hours for riding are 8:00 A.M. to sunset daily, and there are horses here for beginners as well as more experienced riders. Children under the age of six are also welcome. Riding lessons as well as day trips and overnight pack trips can be arranged.

For lunch or dinner in the shadow of Mount Adams, locals suggest a favorite, the *Logs Family Restaurant* (509–493–1402), located at BZ Corner on Highway 141 about halfway between White Salmon and Trout Lake. They've been serving up great fried chicken since the early 1930s.

Farther up Highway 141 at the base of Mount Adams, you can enjoy mountain views from the chalet cabins at *Serenity's,* located at 2291 Highway 141 (509–395–2500; www.serenitys.com) 1 mile south of Trout Lake. Each cabin has walls of glass highlighting forested scenery and comes equipped with a kitchenette, a queen-size bed, and a large bathroom. A few have whirlpool tubs and lofts, and one chalet is wheelchair accessible. The chef provides delicious dinners for guests featuring such delicacies as fresh salmon, halibut, or barbecued ribs. The public is welcome for casual patio dining beginning at 5:00 P.M.

Folks say one of the best places to hunker down for a fresh cup of coffee, a sandwich, a slice of apple pie, and a dose of local gossip is *KJ Bear Creek Cafe,* located at 2376 State Highway 141 (509–395–2525), next to the service station in Trout Lake. If you travel by recreational vehicle, check with *Elk Meadows RV Park,* 78 Trout Lake Creek Road (509) 395–2400. The RV sites come with outrageous views of Mount Adams.

For other cozy places to spend the night close to Trout Lake and snowy Mount Adams, check out several bed-and-breakfasts in the area. At *The Farm Bed & Breakfast* (490 Sunnyside Road; 509–395–2488; www.thefarmbnb.com), innkeepers Dean and Rosie Hostetter offer two comfortable guest rooms decorated with antiques and quilts in their large ca. 1890 farmhouse; the two rooms share a bath. When guests head outdoors they find a fine collection of scented roses and colorful perennials like delphinium, iris, snapdragons, coneflowers, cosmos, black-eyed Susans, and sunflowers. On the expansive grounds grow four varieties of maples, along with graceful willows and tall spruce. At *Kelly's Trout Creek Inn Bed & Breakfast* (25 Mount Adams Road; 509–395–2769; www.kellysbnb.com), innkeepers Kelly and Marilyn Enochs offer travelers a comfortable mix of old-fashioned quilts and rustic decor in three cozy guest rooms. During warm weather you can eat outdoors on the deck next to bubbling Trout Creek, where its waters rush over large rocks and low basalt ledges.

In the Mount Adams area, ancient volcanoes produced numerous lava flows, caves, lava tubes, and other natural structures. Many caves in the area were used by farmers in the days before refrigeration to store butter and cheese until they could be transported to market. These caves make the region popular with serious spelunkers (cave explorers), who approach the caverns with the same sense of challenge and caution that mountain climbers have for major peaks.

The *Ice Caves,* a series of lava tubes, are the easiest of the public caves to explore. Their name refers to columns of ice that develop naturally in the lowest chamber during the winter. A century ago the giant icicles were harvested and sold in the Oregon towns of The Dalles and Hood River. The Forest Service has constructed a ladder leading down from the main entrance. A 120-foot tube that slopes southeastward is the most accessible part of the cave. In all there are about 650 feet of passages to explore. Be sure to bring warm clothes, boots, head protection, and dependable lights. Stop at the Mount Adams Ranger Station (509–395–3400; www.fs.fed.us/gpnf), just north of Trout Lake, for more information and directions to the Ice Caves.

Another side of the mountain worth exploring is the Yakama Nation Mount Adams Recreation Area. Brilliant wildflowers cover the area in spring and peak by mid-August. Tribal rangers stock lakes in the area with trout twice during the fishing season. Road conditions can be rough at any time, so trailers more than 24 feet long and compact cars are not recommended. Camping, firewood, drinking water, and restrooms are available at Bench, Bird, and Mirror Lakes on a first-come, first-served basis. Sunrise Camp provides campsites only. Camping and fishing permits are issued at the site.

The road east to Glenwood offers outrageous views of Mount Adams (called *Pahto* by Native people) as you pass through the rich farmlands and climb hills above the White Salmon River Valley. Watch for the turnoff on your right to **Conboy Lake National Wildlife Refuge.** A 1-mile road takes you to the entrance, where you'll find brochures describing this wetland habitat. The Willard Springs Foot Trail, a 2½-mile loop with interpretive signs, is a pleasant way to see carpets of spring wildflowers and learn more about the refuge's wildlife, including porcupines and wood ducks. The refuge is a nesting area for greater sandhill cranes.

Just outside the small community of Glenwood, travelers find the *Flying L Ranch* at 25 Flying L Lane (509) 364–3488; www.mt-adams.com. The Lloyd family built the house in the mid-1940s, and the Lloyd sons, Darvel and Dean, further developed the property in the 1970s and 1980s. Current owners Jacquie Perry and Jeff Berend have continued to update the facilities that include, in addition to six ranch house guest rooms, five rooms in a separate two-story guest house and three cabins tucked into the pines. Guests enjoy a full breakfast served in the ranch cookhouse. You can also bring your own steaks for a cook-out. The area around the ranch is perfect for hiking and biking as well as for cross-country skiing during winter. The place is also a good option for family reunions. Also nearby, travelers can stay at **Ann's Place Bed & Breakfast** (164 Mount Adams Highway; 509–364–3580; www.annsplacebnb.com). Ann and Bob Beveridge offer two cozy rooms with private baths in their home, formerly one of the mountain retreats of avid outdoorsman Supreme Court Justice William O. Douglas. If you arrive late in the day and are a bit hungry, Ann also offers guests steaming bowls of homemade soup, homemade bread, and hot teas or coffee. "I have about twenty soup recipes that I like to use," she says with a grin. Her cookie jar is always filled with scrumptious homebaked cookies. Her breakfasts are simply delicious—for example, baked French toast with apples and cinnamon served with slices of ham.

Returning to Highway 14 and heading east alongside the Columbia River, consider stopping in the small community of Lyle to have brunch or dinner at the **Lyle Hotel Restaurant** (100 Seventh Street; 509–365–5953; www.lylehotel .com). Call ahead for current dinner hours. The menu changes regularly and is upscale for such an out-of-the-way location, with such tasty fare as fresh Pacific oysters, bouillabaisse, salmon and sturgeon medley, moussaka, and spanakopita. The hotel was built in 1905 to serve the town when Lyle was a railroad center linking major towns in the region. The boom ended, the railroad tracks were moved elsewhere, and folks moved on. But the hotel remains a nostalgic reminder of earlier times. The ten small guest rooms feature early American furnishings, some have sitting areas, and some offer views of the Columbia River.

Native Lands, Vineyards, and Wineries

Some of the Columbia River Gorge's greatest wonders are now, unfortunately, flooded under the huge reservoirs behind the Bonneville and The Dalles Dams. Until 1957 the Oregon side of the Columbia River cascaded over Celilo Falls. Native people had camped on this stretch of river for thousands of years, enjoying the area's abundant resources. Indians from throughout the region practiced traditional dip-net fishing from pole platforms jutting close to the swirling torrents. The area was also an important gathering place where tribes met to trade goods, enjoy festivities, and conduct peace councils. In 1805 explorer Meriwether Lewis described the Celilo Falls area as a "great emporium where all the neighboring nations assembled." Hundreds of the ancient pictographs (rock paintings) and petroglyphs (rock carvings) that once commemorated this life are now lost beneath the waters of the river.

She-Who-Watches (Tsagaglalal) is one of the most intriguing petroglyphs still visible. Legend has it that Tsagaglalal, a female chief, told Coyote, the trickster, that she wanted to guide her people to "live well and build good houses" forever. Coyote explained that the time for female chiefs would soon be over, then turned her to stone so she could watch over the river and its people unimpeded into eternity. The original petroglyph is located amid several others at Horsethief Lake State Park, on the Columbia River. Due to vandalism, however, the only way to see the petroglyphs is by guided tour. The tours run from the beginning of April to the end of October on Friday and Saturday at 10:00 A.M. Tours last about one and a half hours and must be booked at least two weeks ahead. For information about costs and reservations, contact Horsethief Lake State Park (509) 767–1159. The park also has a sheltered bay with beaches that are great for swimming and fishing.

Fifteen miles east of Horsethief Lake via Highway 14 and near the junction with U.S. Highway 97 is ***Maryhill Museum*** and a reproduction of England's Stonehenge monument, two legacies of eccentric millionaire and road builder Sam Hill. ***Maryhill,*** open daily from 9:00 A.M. to 5:00 P.M. from mid-March through mid-November, is situated with a fine view of the Columbia River and is filled with an eclectic collection that includes Rodin sculptures and watercolors, nineteenth-century French artwork, Russian icons, regional Indian art, the Queen of Romania's royal memorabilia, and a collection of chess sets. Ask

She-Who-Watches petroglyph

On the Trail in the Columbia River Gorge with Lewis and Clark

Walking by foot, paddling dugout canoes, and sometimes riding horses, thirty-three folks including Meriwether Lewis and William Clark trekked along the north side of the Columbia River in early fall of 1805. The party included Clark's Newfoundland dog, Seaman. In mid-November they would reach their goal, the Pacific Ocean near the Long Beach Peninsula. But in October 1805 they camped at Rock Fort near The Dalles on the Oregon side of the river, a site you can visit. During your travels, you can see interpretive exhibits, pictorial displays, and great views of the gorge at sites where the party stopped on the Washington side of the Columbia River in this eastern section of the gorge.

Horsethief Lake State Park
Located east of Bingen and White Salmon, the site also contains rare Indian rock paintings.

Maryhill Museum
Located west of Goldendale, the museum displays fine Indian baskets, carvings, and other native crafts (www.maryhillmuseum.org).

Hat Rock State Park
Located near Umatilla.

Sacajawea State Park
Located near Kennewick, an interpretive center explores the expedition and the role of Sacajawea, the Shoshoni Indian woman who served as guide and interpreter.

too about the ca. 1946 collection of French fashion miniatures, *Theatre de la Mode. Cafe Maryhill,* in the museum, serves deli-style lunches and snacks, with outdoor seating available overlooking the river. The impressive chateaulike structure, 400 feet long, is located at 35 Maryhill Museum Drive (509) 773–3733; www.maryhillmuseum.org. The *Maryhill Winery* and the *Gorge Amphitheatre* (877–627–9445), located just west of Maryhill Museum, offer outdoor entertainment events and an elegant tasting room and samples of the current wines produced here, including pinot noir, merlot, zinfandel, and chardonnay. The intricately carved antique bar fashioned in the early 1900s of tiger oak reaches some 12 feet high, with mirrors inset along its 12-foot length. It's open daily from 10:00 A.M. to 6:00 P.M. with an outside patio that offers wide-angle views of the gorge.

The town of *Goldendale,* 10 miles north via US 97, has been a commercial center for farmers since its inception. The town's well-kept homes and active downtown continue to emanate a friendly, self-sufficient atmosphere. For a historical perspective on the town, visit the *Klickitat County Historical Museum* (509–773–4303), housed in the stately Presby Mansion at 127 West Broadway Street (Highway 142) and Grant Avenue. Turn-of-the-twentieth-century dolls left on the antique furniture give the impression that a child has just finished playing in the parlor, the kitchen looks as if someone is cooking dinner, the dining room table is set, and period clothing is laid out in the bedrooms. The museum is open from 9:00 A.M. to 5:00 P.M. daily, April to October, or by appointment during the off-season. There is a small admission fee.

For an exhilarating look skyward, continue down Broadway Street and turn north on Columbus, past some of Goldendale's fine old homes. Follow signs uphill to **Goldendale Observatory State Park** (1602 Observatory Drive; 509–773–3141), where volunteer amateur astronomers share their enthusiasm for the stars. During the day, you can view the sun using a special telescope and perhaps catch sight of a solar prominence—arcs of light and energy thousands of miles high. At night, the main 26-inch telescope brings a gaggle of galaxies and nebulae into view. The observatory is open from 2:00 to 5:00 P.M. and 8:00 to 11:00 P.M., Wednesday through Sunday, from April 1 through September 30. Call ahead for winter hours. For more information browse www .perr.com/gosp.html, which contains the evening star-watching schedule and links to Northwest astronomy clubs, NASA sites, and "This Week's Sky at a Glance."

Since you've traveled this far off the beaten path, plan to have a cup of coffee and eats with local folks in Goldendale at **Don's Old Homestead Restaurant** (509–773–6006), at the Far View Motel, 808 East Simere Drive. Other pleasant eateries in the Goldendale area that serve lunch or dinner include **Goldendale Country Kitchen** at 120 West Main Street and **Angelo's Pizza** (111 North Columbus Avenue; 509–773–6939).

At the corner of Broadway and Bickleton Highway, pull into line at **Cornerstone Coffee Drive-thru,** order up, and then take a side trip east onto Goldendale-Bickleton Road 35 miles to the bucolic town of **Bickleton,** population 90. From mid-February to October thousands of mountain bluebirds flock to the area, earning the small town its nickname of "Bluebird Capital of the World." You can see the small handmade blue and white birdhouses everywhere as you drive the back roads of Bickleton; they serve as nesting boxes for the feathered couples and their chicks, gracing residential yards, farms, and roadsides.

Eateries to check out in Bickleton include **Bickleton Market Street Cafe** (106 East Market Street; 509–896–2671) and **Bluebird Inn Tavern** (121 Market Street; 509–896–2273).

Prosser, located on the high Columbia plateau about 40 miles northeast of Bickleton, has more to offer than you might expect for a quiet farm town. **Hinzerling Winery and the Vintner's Inn Restaurant** (509–786–2163 or 800–727–6702; www.hinzerling.com) is located in town at the corner of Wine

Country Road and Sheridan Street. Founded in 1976 by the Wallace family, this is the oldest family-owned and -operated winery in the Yakima Valley. Family members share their knowledge of wine production and samples of wines, including sweet dessert wines and dry gewürztraminer.

Hogue Cellars (509–786–4557), across Wine Country Road from Chinook Wines, offers gourmet pickled vegetables in addition to a wide selection of award-winning wines, including dry, sweet, and sparkling varieties. **Pontin Del Roza** (35502 North Hinzerling Road; 509–786–4449) is located at the corner of Hinzerling and McCreadie Roads in the scenic hill district north of Prosser. You can taste the Pontin family's special Roza sunset blush and pinot gris.

Gourmet cherries, preserves, toppings, and savories are other specialties you'll find near Prosser. The **Chukar Cherry Company** produces these along with Chocolate Chukars, a pitted, ripe, partly dried cherry dipped in dark chocolate. This is, indeed, a royal taste treat. Visit the Chukar Cherry Company gift shop, just west of town at 320 Wine Country Road (800–624–9544; www.chukar.com).

The **Benton County Historical Museum** (509–786–3842), at the Prosser City Park, is open Tuesday through Saturday from 10:00 A.M. to 4:00 P.M. and Sunday from 1:00 to 5:00 P.M. There's a little of everything here including natural history displays, an old-time general store counter, and a selection of women's clothing styles of yesteryear. One of the exhibits contains hand-carved and hand-painted wooden automobiles, foot-long replicas of the real thing.

For a bite to eat in Prosser, try the **Blue Goose Restaurant** (306 Seventh Street; 509–786–1774), the **Barn Restaurant** (490 Wine Country Road; 509–786–1131), or the nearby **El Caporal Mexican Restaurant** (503–786–4910).

The Bluebird Inn Tavern, ca. 1882, Elevation 3,000 Feet

It's said the tavern has gone through more than fifteen owners since it opened in Bickleton in 1882. It used to double as a barbershop, and once it was a social club where hats were forbidden. For a long time the place had no telephone so the womenfolk weren't able to call and check up on their card-playing menfolk. Now, the tavern sells candy to the kids and serves good food including a giant Bluebird Burger. It's closed Monday, open on Tuesday at 3:00 P.M., and other days at 10:00 A.M. It also serves breakfast on Sunday beginning at 8:00 A.M. Pull up to the small western-style structure that looks as though it should have several horses tied up out front, just like a John Wayne movie.

Tour Columbia Gorge and Yakima Valley Vineyards and Wineries

Throw a corkscrew into the picnic basket and visit a flotilla of fine vineyards, wineries, and tasting rooms in the fertile regions of the Yakima Valley and Columbia River Valley.

Alexandria Nicole Cellars
(509) 786–3497
www.alexandrianicolecellars.com
Open Wednesday to Sunday,
11:00 A.M. to 5:00 P.M.

Bookwalter Winery
(877) 667–8300
www.bookwalterwines.com
Tasting room and wine lounge open
daily 10:00 A.M. to 6:00 P.M.

Chinook Wines
(509) 786–2725
www.chinookwines.com
Open Saturday and Sunday,
noon to 5:00 P.M.

Hedges Cellars at Red Mountain
(509) 588–3155
www.hedgescellars.com
Open Friday to Sunday,
11:00 A.M. to 5:00 P.M.

Piety Flats Winery & Mercantile
(509) 877–3115
www.pietyflatswinery.com/winery
Open daily 10:00 A.M. to 6:00 P.M.

Sagelands Winery
(800) 967–8115
www.sagelandsvineyard.com
Open daily 10:00 A.M. to 5:00 P.M.

Yakima River Winery
(509) 786–2805
www.yakimariverwinery.com
Open daily 10:00 A.M. to 5:00 P.M.

For additional information and maps
Yakima Valley Wineries
www.wineyakimavalley.org

Columbia Valley Winery Association
www.columbiavalleywine.com

Prosser Visitor Information
www.prosserchamber.org

Tri-Cities Visitor Information
visittri-cities.com

Yakima Visitor Information
www.visityakima.com

www.winecountrywashington.com

For great espresso drinks and browsing local art, stop by the *Sixth Street Gift Shop & Cafe* (509–786–7657) at 713 Sixth Street.

For a sampling of this rich farming area's home-grown bounty, stop by the *Prosser Farmer's Market* next to Prosser City Park. There you'll find fresh Yakima Valley fruits and vegetables, delectable homemade baked goods, and crafts from local artisans. The market is open Saturday from 8:00 A.M. to 1:00 P.M. from June through October.

You can reach the town of *Grandview* by heading northwest from Prosser on Wine Country Road. The *Dykstra House Restaurant* (114 Birch Avenue), a National Historic Site built in the 1920s, offers delicious meals. The desserts are delicious, the produce is fresh, and the regional wines and ales are plentiful. The restaurant is open for lunch Tuesday through Saturday and serves dinner Friday and Saturday evenings from 6:00 to 9:00 P.M. Call (509) 882–2082 for reservations, which are required on Saturday evening.

For a pleasant spot to stay the night in this rich wine country, call the innkeepers at *Sunnyside Inn Bed and Breakfast* at (800 East Edison Street in Sunnyside; 509–839–5557; www.sunnysideinn.com). They offer thirteen comfortable guest rooms in their large ca. 1919 home with all the usual comforts including restful colors, lovely window treatments, and country accessories. Some rooms come with four-poster beds, cozy sitting areas, fireplaces, and whirlpool tubs. Families are especially welcome here. In the morning a sumptuous country breakfast is served family-style in the large dining area on the main floor.

For pleasant eateries in the Sunnyside area try *Cactus Juice Café* at 632 East Decatur Avenue (509–839–4480), *La Victoria Mexican Café* at 301 South Thirteenth Street (509–839–4772), and for great ales and tasty pub dishes try *Snipes Mountain Microbrewery* at 905 Yakima Valley Highway 12 (509–837–2739).

TOP ANNUAL EVENTS IN SOUTH CENTRAL WASHINGTON

Country Christmas Lighted Farm Implement Parade
Sunnyside, first weekend in December
(800) 457–8089

Festival of the Arts/Volkssport Bike and Walk
Trout Lake, mid-July
(509) 493–3630

Granger Cherry Festival
first weekend in May
(509) 854–7304

The Great Hot Air Balloon Rally
Prosser, late September
(800) 408–1517

Mural-in-a-Day
Toppenish, first weekend in June
(509) 865–3262

Prosser Wine & Food Fair
August
(800) 408–1517

Red Wine and Chocolate Festival
Yakima Valley
President's Day Weekend, February
(800) 258–7270

SausageFest
Vancouver, mid-September
(360) 696–4407

Thanksgiving in Wine Country
Yakima Valley, Thanksgiving weekend
(800) 258–7270

For more off-the-beaten-path adventures, continue west on Emerald-Granger Road, a scenic route that circles south of Snipes Mountain. Nearby, ***Granger Berry Patch Farm*** at 1731 Beam Road (800–346–1417 or 509–854–1413) offers more than twenty varieties of U-pick berries, pumpkins, and Christmas trees in season.

Pause in the small town of ***Granger,*** population about 2,000, to visit ***Worden's Lamp House*** at 112 Main Street (509–854–1557). Inside, you can browse through a display of nearly a hundred different Tiffany-style stained-glass lampshades and learn about the stained-glass process. For good Mexican food stop by ***La Morelense*** at 302 Main Street. If the kids are along they'll want to ogle and play on the real-life replicas of ancient dinosaurs identified and placed around town. Then, if golf is your passion, check for tee times at nearby

One Hundred Years, 1850 to 1950: the Toppenish Murals

Since 1989 folks in the Toppenish Mural Society have funded more than sixty gigantic murals painted outdoors on buildings all over the downtown area, from the Western Auto building and the Reid Building to Providence Toppenish Hospital, Pow Wow Emporium, and Old Timers Plaza Park. We are not talking crayon and stick figures here. The historically accurate scenes represent the life and times of the Toppenish area from 1850 to 1950. Folks visit throughout the year and stroll downtown streets, but on the first Saturday of June you also can watch the Mural-in-a-Day come to life and join the yearly celebration. Stop by the Visitor Welcome Center at 5–A South Toppenish Avenue (509–856–3262; www.toppenish.org); pick up a mural map, and enjoy. Here are a few of the giant-size oil paintings of bygone days you'll see:

Hop Museum Murals (#32), a trio of painted archways open to scenes of harvesting hops, painted by artist Eric Allen Grohe on two walls of the American Hop Museum

Lou Shattuck (#34), an original booster of the Toppenish Pow Wow Rodeo, painted by artist Don Gray of Flagstaff, Arizona

Maud Bolin (#27), rodeo rider and early female pilot, painted by artist Larry Kangas of Portland, Oregon, on the southwest wall of the *Toppenish Review* newspaper building

Rodeo Days (#13), by artist Newman Myrah of Portland, Oregon, painted on the west wall of Ferguson's Saddlery

Ruth Parton (#22), cowgirl and trick-rider, painted by Lesa Delisi of Cashmere on the United Telephone Company building

Western Hospitality (#36), bordello ladies of the night, painted by Betty Billups of Sandpoint, Idaho, on the second-floor windows of the Logan Building

Cherry Hill Golf Course (509–854–1800). Take the Cherry Hill exit off Highway 223 and follow the signs to the nine-hole executive-style golf course, which also offers a pleasant eatery, *Doc's on the Green* (509–854–2294).

About 5 miles north of Granger via Highway 22 is the small community of *Toppenish,* located on the Yakama Confederated Tribes Reservation. Park near the historic railroad depot and enjoy a walking tour of the downtown area and its giant-size murals depicting scenes from early days in the West.

Pause for a look at the grand old *Liberty Theatre,* at 211 South Toppenish Avenue. Built in 1915, the theater boasted the largest stage at the time between Seattle and Spokane and hosted stars such as Lillian Gish, Raymond Navarro, and even Tex Ritter and his horse. Murals painted on the outside show wild horses running free as they did in early times.

When it's time to stop for a bite to eat in Toppenish, locals suggest *Pioneer Kitchen* at 227 South Toppenish Avenue (509–865–3201) for all-day breakfasts, cinnamon rolls, homemade soups, salad bar, hefty Rodeo Burgers, and great pies and cobblers. Try *VillaSeñor* at 225 South Toppenish Avenue (509–865–4707) for good Mexican fare including piping hot appetizers, fajitas, and freshly made tortillas, along with such tasty desserts as flan, sopapillas, and deep-fried ice cream. At *Gibbon's Pharmacy* (117 South Toppenish Avenue; 509–865–2722), you can order juicy burgers and something cool and tasty at the old-fashioned soda fountain. Then, visit the *Amish Connection* at 105 South Toppenish Avenue for authentic Amish foods and handcrafted items and, nearby, *Kraff's Clothing* (509–865–3000), which specializes in colorful Pendleton blankets.

Allow time to visit the country's only museum dedicated to the growing of hops, the *American Hop Museum,* located at 22 South B Street (509–865–4677; www.americanhopmuseum.org). The museum is open from 11:00 A.M. to 4:00 P.M. daily from May through October. You'll see the splendid murals on the front of the large building, a series of arched windows painted on either side of the entrance. The museum focuses on the hop industry that started around 1805 in New York State. In the 1850s hop growers took their perennial hop vines westward where the climate was sunnier and where there was less mildew. The sunny Yakima Valley is a prime area for growing hops, which climb on tall expanses of twine strung in long rows in the fields. In the museum you and the kids can see artifacts, memorabilia, and old photographs collected from all over the United States, including antique hop presses, tools for cultivating hops, a horse-drawn hop duster, old picking baskets, and an early picking machine. Browse in the gift shop and also learn how the hop cones are used to flavor and preserve beers and ales.

The *Yakima Valley Rail and Steam Museum* (509–865–1911), located on South A Street in a restored railway depot built in 1911, contains interesting rail and steam artifacts, a completely restored telegraph office, and a gift shop. In mid-August folks can attend the **Yakima Valley Rail & Transportation Show** at the depot museum held in conjunction with the **Toppenish Western Art Show** in nearby Railroad Park. Great art, railroad memorabilia, food booths, and live country music along with tours of the museum, engine house, and grounds make for a lively day. If you travel through the area over the Fourth of July you can take in the colorful **Toppenish Pow Wow and Rodeo.**

You can picnic in Railroad Park, or head off to Harrah, 8 miles northwest of Toppenish, for more railroad fun. There you can catch the **Toppenish, Simcoe and Western Railroad** for a leisurely 18-mile round-trip to White Swan and back through the Simcoe Valley, with views of snowy Mount Adams. Excursions are offered on Saturday in September and October, and there are special holiday trips. Call the Yakima Valley Rail and Steam Museum at (509) 865–1911 for current schedules and fares.

To learn more about Native American culture, visit the splendid **Yakama Nation Cultural Heritage Center,** on US 97 (280 Buster Road, Toppenish; 509–865–2800). From a distance you'll spot the colorful peaked roof of the center's Winter Lodge, modeled after the ancestral A-shaped homes of the Yakama tribes. Museum exhibits and dioramas show the tribe's history and traditions. A large, angular tule (reed) lodge at the center of the museum shows how extended families lived during the winter. Sweat lodges made from earth, branches, and animal skins illustrate sacred places of physical and spiritual purification. The museum is open Monday through Saturday from 9:00 A.M. to 5:00 P.M. and Sunday from 10:00 A.M. to 5:00 P.M. There is a nominal admission fee.

At the center's gift shop adjacent to the museum, you can purchase fine beadwork and other Native American art and cultural items. The center also maintains an extensive library for children and adults on First Nations history and culture. The library is open to the public Monday to Friday 8:30 A.M. to 5:00 P.M. and Saturday 10:30 A.M. to 5:00 P.M. The **Heritage Inn Restaurant** (509–865–2800), also part of the tribal center, offers delicious meals, including Yakama and other First Nations favorites such as *waykaanish* (salmon), buffalo stew, fry bread, and huckleberry pie. The restaurant is open for Sunday brunch from 8:00 A.M. to 2:00 P.M., Monday to Wednesday from 8:00 A.M. to 3:00 P.M., and Thursday to Saturday from 8:00 A.M. to 9:00 P.M.

Next door to the Heritage Center, the **Yakama Nation RV Resort** (280 Buster Road; 800–874–3087 or 509–865–2000) offers a luxury campground with ninety-five RV spaces with full hookups, a tent site, and a recreation center featuring a basketball court, hot tub, laundry room, and swimming pool. You can also rent a tepee with room for a whole family.

Twenty-five miles west of the Yakama Indian Tribal Center in the heart of the reservation is **Fort Simcoe State Park Heritage Site,** a lovely park with large oak trees, a lush green lawn, and a dozen restored buildings filled with period furnishings. The former military fort is located at 5150 Fort Simcoe Road (509–874–2372; www.parks.wa.gov) near the community of White Swan and on a traditional Native village site. The ancient Mool Mool bubbling springs here have created a shady oasis of reed-filled wetlands surrounded by woods. In summer,

Yakama Nation RV Resort

you may catch sight of green and pink Lewis's woodpeckers, which breed in abundance in the Garry oaks. The park, a popular picnic spot for local residents, features plenty of shade trees, running water, and an adventure playground. The historical buildings and interpretive center are open Wednesday through Sunday from 9:00 A.M. to 4:30 P.M. from April through September.

The **Toppenish National Wildlife Refuge** is located off US 97 south of Toppenish. The refuge's marshlands and thick riverside forests are excellent places to view the fall and spring migrations of Canada geese, grebes, and ducks such as teals, scaups, and pintails. There are bald eagles, prairie falcons, and other wildlife that once populated the entire Yakima Valley area.

Mountains, Orchards, and Railroads

A 10-mile, signed "Fruit Loop" route that circles the orchard-covered hills above the town of **Zillah** is an ideal way to discover the valley's agricultural opulence. To visit Zillah take Interstate 82, exit 52 or 54, or follow the Yakima Valley Highway from Sunnyside through Granger and turn left onto Zillah's First Avenue. The loop starts from the downtown tourist information office at the corner of First Avenue and Fifth Street, where you can pick up a route map during office hours; or just follow the colorful signs from downtown north on Roza Drive and left onto the Yakima Valley Highway. Along the way you'll enjoy grand views of the lower valley's patchwork quilt of farms, and you'll pass by at least seven wineries.

Of course, every winery claims to offer the best product, so it's up to you to determine your favorites. Each has a tasting room where visitors are offered a small sample of the many vintages available. Winery staff are glad to share their knowledge and offer suggestions for the best wine for various occasions. Most tasting rooms also sell nonalcoholic drinks, snacks, and gifts.

If wine tasting has given you an appetite and you forgot the picnic basket, you'll want to eat at *El Ranchito* (509–829–5880), the most authentic Mexican restaurant, bakery, and specialty store you are likely to find in this region. The much-loved restaurant is located at 1319 East First Avenue in Zillah, the last stop on the Fruit Loop tour. It offers an informal atmosphere where farmworker families, local professionals, and tourists all enjoy fresh tamales, burritos, tostadas, and tempting specialty dishes. In warm weather the shaded patio offers a pleasant place to eat.

Worth a stop just a half mile from downtown is *Claar Cellars Winery* (1001 Vintage Valley Parkway; 509–829–6810). The tasting room is open from 10:00 A.M. to 5:00 P.M. daily.

For a nostalgic visit to an old-fashioned country store, winery, and orchard, stop by *Piety Flats Winery & Mercantile* (509–877–3115), just east of I–82 at exit 44 on Donald-Wapato Road. The tasting room is in a fruit and mercantile store dating to 1911 and still has an old wooden floor and most of the original store fixtures. Adjacent to the store is an orchard of antique variety apple trees, which visitors are welcome to explore. In the fall months you can taste the unique flavors of these old-style fruits.

Near Wapato you'll find *Sagelands Winery* (509–877–2112), where the vintner uses innovative techniques to grow premium grapes and produce excellent wines. The impressive French country–style winery, built of local stone and cedar, has a wine-tasting room and gift shop. To reach the winery take I–82 exit 40, follow the road as it curves left toward the hill, then turn right onto Gangl Road.

Just south of Yakima is the town of *Union Gap,* the single gap in the line of hills that divides the upper and lower Yakima Valley. Next to the gap is the *Central Washington Agricultural Museum,* at 4508 Main Street in Fulbright Park (509–457–8735). The large collection of farm equipment is arranged inside a number of display buildings and also outdoors on spiral terraces around a windmill tower. You'll see horse-drawn plows and mowers, huge old steam tractors, antique threshers, and hop harvesters. In the fifteen-acre park you and the kids can also see such things as a blacksmith shop, furnished log cabin, fruit-packing line equipment, and the Museum Grange Library. You might even see working horse teams plowing the museum fields or an old steam harvester in use. To get to the museum from Union Gap, follow Main Street south 2 miles and

across the US 97 overpass to the Fulbright Park turnoff. If you want to picnic, there are shaded tables on the
grounds at Fulbright Park, or for a bite
to eat in Union Gap, check out **Old
Town Station Restaurant** at 2530
Main Street (509–453–8485) and *Jean's
Cottage Inn* at 3211 Main Street (509–
575–9709). For a jolt of java or
espresso, try **Godfrey's Espresso** or
J.D.'s Coffee, both drive-through locations in Union Gap's downtown area.

The city of **Yakima** offers many
activities little-known to outsiders.
For one, walking or bicycling along
the 10-mile **Yakima Greenway Trail**

teapotgas

Just east of Zillah is an unmistakable
landmark, a true vintage roadside
attraction just off I–82 exit 54. The
15-foot-tall white teapot with its red
handle and spout is a gas station,
dating from the early 1920s. The joke
here, which only old-timers or history
buffs are likely to catch without
explanation, is the name: the Teapot
Dome Service Station. The reference
is to the Wyoming oil-lease scandal of
the same name, big news in the early
twenties, as it sent Secretary of the
Interior Albert Fall to prison.

is the perfect way to enjoy the Yakima and Naches Rivers. The path stretches
from the quiet town of Selah at the north, past several riverfront parks, to the
seventy-acre **Yakima Arboretum** at the south end. The arboretum includes
hiking trails, a Japanese garden, and the new Jewett Interpretive Center. You
can also access the Yakima Greenway Trail and a river landing for launching
kayaks and canoes at **Sarg Hubbard Park** (509–453–8280) off I–82 or off
South Eighteenth Street. At the park on Tuesday evenings in July and August,
you can bring a picnic supper and take in free outdoor concerts at 7:00 P.M. that
feature local performers and jazz, blues, country western, and bluegrass musicians and singers. Folks find bleacher seating and lawn areas for blankets and
folding chairs.

Railroad themes permeate Yakima. Along the old railroad line through
downtown, find the renovated North Front Street and browse its eclectic
shops, cafes, and pubs. Check out the **Barrel House** at 22 North First Street
(509–453–3769), which offers fine food, wines, and microbrews. On North
Second Street stop by **Yakima Cellars Winery** (509–577–0461; www.yakima
cellars.com), which offers an elegant tasting room. On Yakima Avenue
between Fifth and Sixth Streets as well as on Second Street and A Avenue, you
can browse a collection of delightful antiques shops. For a quick snack, stop
by a local favorite, **Poochie's Gourmet Hot Dogs,** at 301 South Third Avenue
(509–452–3268), and choose from some thirty types of specialty hot dogs and
sandwiches.

The ca. 1885 Fire Station and Yakima City Hall building at 27 North Front
Street now house **Bob's Keg & Cork** (509–573–3691), serving a variety of

microbrews and Yakima Valley wines Tuesday through Saturday from 11:30 A.M. The *White House Cafe* out near Forty-eighth Avenue at 3602 Kern Street (509–469–2644) offers tasty breakfast and lunch fare.

In 1889 the Switzer Opera House was built at 5 North Front Street and housed Yakima's first performing arts and vaudeville theater. This structure also has been renovated and now houses a variety of shops. For awesome baked goods find *Essencia Artisan Bakery & Chocolatiere* at 4 North Third Street (509–575–5570).

In 1898 the Lund Building was constructed on the corner of North Front Street and Yakima Avenue. In those days it housed such colorful establishments as Sam's Cafe, the Alfalfa Saloon, the Chicago Clothing Company, and the Longbranch Saloon. All those early establishments are gone; nowadays, in place of Sam's Cafe, locals and travelers call ahead for reservations at the splendid *Greystone Restaurant* (5 North Front Street; 509–248–9801). The dining room is open Tuesday through Sunday evening from 6:00 P.M.

The *Capitol Theatre,* at 19 South Third Street (509–853–2787; www.capitol theatre.org), is another historic structure restored to its 1920s splendor. A resident ghost, Sparky, reportedly decided to stay on after the renovation. The theater is now home to the Yakima Symphony Orchestra and offers other concerts and road shows throughout the year. For lively local theater call *Warehouse Theatre Company* in the Allied Arts Center in Gilbert Park at 5000 West Lincoln Avenue (509–966–0951 or 509–966–0930; www.alliedartsyakima.org) for the current schedule produced by avid Yakima area thespians. Recent offerings included old favorites such as *Barefoot in the Park, Forever Plaid, On Golden Pond,* and the popular musical *Godspell.*

Be sure to plan a stop at the *Yakima Valley Museum* (2105 Tieton Drive; 509–248–0747; www.yakimavalleymuseum.org) for a soda, thick milkshakes, and a hot dog ordered at the old-fashioned soda fountain. A bright neon sign greets visitors at the entry to the soda fountain, the floor sports black-and-white square-tiled linoleum, and at the counter folks sit on round stools covered with bright red vinyl. In other sections of the museum you can browse a fine Native American collection, see a collection of wagons and carriages (from stagecoach to hearse), and turn the kids loose in the children's interactive center.

Located in a renovated fruit warehouse, *Glenwood Square* at 5001 Tieton Drive offers old, polished-wood floors and fun shops like *Inklings Books* and the *Little Soapmaker.*

For those who get hungry not just for customary but for fine gourmet Mexican cooking, try the well-known *Santiago's Restaurant* (509–453–1644) at 111 East Yakima Avenue, 5 blocks west of the convention center. The eatery is open for lunch Monday through Friday from 11:00 A.M. until 2:00 P.M. and for dinner beginning at 5:00 P.M. daily; its closed on Sunday. You could also call for dinner reservations at the **Apple Tree Restaurant,** located at the **Apple Tree Golf Course,** 8804 Occidental Road (509–966–7140; www.appletreegolf.com), in the southwest section of Yakima. The chef cooks up apple-wood-smoked prime rib to die for, and the best time to go is evening for sunset views of the golf course and surrounding hills. The course's signature hole is number 17, a large apple-shaped island green connected to the fairway by a footbridge "stem" and with an adjacent sand trap shaped like a large leaf.

Also plan to stay a day or two to further explore this interesting city of railroad memorabilia and this large region of fruit orchards, vineyards, wineries, and tasting rooms. To stay at a cozy bed-and-breakfast inn located in a scenic cherry orchard just west of downtown Yakima, check with the innkeepers at **Orchard Inn Bed & Breakfast** (1207 Pecks Canyon Road; 888–966–1283; www.orchardinnbb.com). You'll find comfortable guest rooms with queen-size beds and whirlpool tubs along with a cozy common area and delicious breakfasts. Nearby, visit **Barrett Orchard Fruit & Gift Shop** (www.treeripened .com), where you will find for sale fresh cherries and other juicy fruits of the season, plus a gift shop, all in a big red barn located on Pecks Canyon Road. You are also invited to walk and browse an interpretive pathway in the cherry orchard. At **A Touch of Europe Inn Bed and Breakfast** (220 North Sixteenth Avenue; 509–454–9775), the innkeepers offer elegant Victorian- and European-style decor in their three guest rooms on the second floor. Gourmet breakfasts are served in the morning room on the main floor.

Two miles east of Yakima, **Birchfield Manor Restaurant and Bed & Breakfast,** at 2018 Birchfield Road (509–452–1960), offers elegant meals and overnight accommodations in a twenty-three-room Victorian-style mansion, complete with crystal chandeliers, a winding staircase, and flower garden. You'll find an abundance of genteel comforts (hot tub, pool, private baths) and a choice of eleven charming, antiques-filled guest rooms. If the notion of a sumptuous thirteen-course gourmet dinner including decadent desserts sounds appealing, call the Birchfield staff to inquire about reservations Thursday through Saturday.

US 12 west of Yakima passes through the orchard-filled Naches Valley on its way to 14,411-foot snowy Mount Rainier and the central Cascades Mountain area. At the entrance to this valley, you can visit the ancient **Indian Painted Rocks** petroglyphs. A short hike up the hillside trail takes you to sheer rock walls where images created by the valley's original inhabitants are still visible. You'll also enjoy wide views of the two fertile valleys stretching below. To reach the site, take US 12 west toward White Pass. At milepost 199 turn left on Ackley Road, then take an immediate right and park on the shoulder of the road near the large historical marker sign.

Just past the Naches Valley, 2 miles west of the Highway 410 turnoff, is the **Oak Creek Wildlife Area,** a feeding station for elk, deer, and mountain goats in winter and a popular spot for hunting and bird-watching. Continuing west, you'll ascend the Tieton River and climb through sagebrush-covered hills and the Gifford Pinchot National Forest up to White Pass at an elevation of 4,500 feet. Along the way you'll pass numerous lakes, fishing resorts, and campgrounds. This scenic route comes with dramatic geological formations and mountain areas covered with Douglas fir, western red cedar, and alpine fir. White Pass has relatively light traffic and long stretches of undeveloped forest, making it a favorite route for bicyclists and a popular destination for all-season outdoor recreation.

To find a good place to eat and bed down for the night that's substantially farther off the beaten path, head northwest from Naches onto Highway 410 toward Mount Rainier National Park. You'll find **Whistlin' Jack Lodge** on the Naches River at 20800 State Route 410 (www.whistlinjacklodge.com). In the restaurant the chef features fresh mountain trout, prime rib, and select seafood served, if you wish, with Washington's best wines. During warm summer months, folks can eat a pleasant lunch outside on the deck. Accommodations include a lodge, guest rooms, a riverfront motel, and streamside cottages with private hot tubs. For further information, reservations, and road conditions and closures during snowy winter months, call the staff at (800) 827–2299 or (509) 658–2433.

If you're traveling RV-style, you could check for RV sites at **Squaw Rock Resort,** located on the Naches River at 15070 Highway 410; (509) 658–2926. Both the RV resort and Whistlin' Jack Lodge are about 40 miles northwest of Yakima and not far from 14,411-foot Mount Rainier. You can access scenic drives and campgrounds on Mount Rainier by crossing over 5,430-foot Chinook Pass. From Naches you could also travel southwest of the mountain on US 12, which winds over 4,500-foot White Pass and down toward Packwood and Randle, then connects with I–5 south of Chehalis and just north of Mount St. Helens. At Randle you could inquire at the Cowlitz Valley Ranger Station (360–497–1100) for back-road directions to see sections of trees blown down when Mount St. Helens erupted in May 1980 and again in 2004.

Places to Stay in South Central Washington

GLENWOOD

Ann's Place Bed & Breakfast
164 Mount Adams Highway
(509) 364–3580

GRANDVIEW

Apple Valley Motel
903 West Wine Country Road
(509) 882–3003

STEVENSON/CARSON

Columbia Gorge Riverside Lodge
200 Southwest Cascade Street
(866) 427–5650

Sandhill Cottages
932 Hot Springs Avenue
Carson
(800) 914–2178

SUNNYSIDE

Sunnyside Inn Bed and Breakfast
804 East Edison Avenue
(800) 221–4195

TOPPENISH

Toppenish Inn
515 Elm Street
(800) 222–3161

Yakama Nation RV Resort
280 Buster Road
(800) 874–3087

TOUTLE/PACKWOOD

Cowlitz River Lodge
13069 U.S. Highway 12
(888) 305–2185

Eco Park Resort Cabins and RV Park
14000 Spirit Lake Highway
(360) 274–6542

TROUT LAKE/HUSUM

The Farm Bed & Breakfast
490 Sunnyside Road
Trout Lake
(509) 395–2488

Husum's Riverside Bed & Breakfast
866 Highway 141
Husum
(509) 493–8900

Kelly's Trout Creek Inn Bed & Breakfast
25 Mount Adams Road
Trout Lake
(509) 395–2769

VANCOUVER

Red Lion at the Quay
on the Columbia River
100 Columbia Street
(360) 694–8341

WHITE SALMON

Inn of the White Salmon
172 West Jewett Boulevard
(800) 972–5226

YAKIMA

Birchfield Manor Inn
2018 Birchfield Road
(509) 452–1960

Orchard Inn Bed & Breakfast
1207 Pecks Canyon Road
(888) 858–8284

HELPFUL WEB SITES IN SOUTH CENTRAL WASHINGTON

Hood River–White Salmon Area
www.hoodriver.org

Klickitat County
www.klickitatcounty.org

Mount Adams Area
www.skamania.org

Vancouver
www.southwestwashington.com

Visit Yakima
www.visityakima.com

Yakima Valley Wineries
www.wineyakimavalley.com

Washington Road Conditions
(800) 695–7623
www.wsdot.wa.gov/traffic

Places to Eat in South Central Washington

BICKLETON

Bluebird Inn Tavern
121 Market Street
(509) 896–2273

BINGEN

La Reyes
740 East Steuben Street
(509) 493–1017

CARSON

#7 Coffee Roasting Company at Sandhill Cottages
932 Hot Springs Avenue
(800) 914–2178

GOLDENDALE

Cafe Maryhill
35 Maryhill Museum Drive
(509) 773–3733

Sodbusters Cafe
1040 East Broadway
(509) 773–6160

GRANDVIEW

Dykstra House Restaurant
114 Birch Avenue
(509) 882–2082

PROSSER

The Blue Goose Restaurant
306 Seventh Street
(509) 786–1774

STEVENSON

Bahma Coffee Bar & Bistro
256 Second Street
(509) 427–8700

Walking Man Brewery & Public House
240 Southwest First Street
(509) 427–5520

SUNNYSIDE

Cactus Juice Cafe
632 East Decatur Avenue
(509) 839–4480

Snipes Mountain Microbrewery
905 Yakima Valley Highway
(509) 837–2739

TOPPENISH

Cattlemen's Restaurant
2 Division Street
(509) 865–5885

TROUT LAKE

KJ's Bear Creek Cafe
2376 Highway 141
Trout Lake
(509) 395–2525

VANCOUVER

Dulin's Cafe
1708 Main Street
(360) 737–9907

Ice Cream Renaissance
2108 Main Street
(360) 694–3892

Island Cafe on the River
250 NE Tomahawk
Island Drive
Hayden Island
Portland, OR
(503) 283–0362

SELECTED VISITOR INFORMATION CENTERS

Hood River Visitor Information Center
405 Portway Avenue
Hood River, OR
(800) 366–3530

Kelso Visitor & Volcano Information Center
(360) 577–8058

Prosser Visitor Information Center
1230 Bennett Avenue
(800) 408–1517
www.prosserchamber.org

Stevenson/Carson
(800) 989–9178
www.skamania.org

Toppenish Visitor Information Center
(800) 569–3982
www.toppenish.com

Yakima Valley Visitors and Convention Bureau
(800) 221–0751
www.visityakima.com

The Restaurant at the Historic Reserve
Officer's Row, Grant House
(360) 906–1101

WHITE SALMON

The Creamery Cafe
121 East Jewett
(509) 493–4007

YAKIMA

Ballesteri's Coffee House
4001 Summitview
(509) 965–8592

El Porton Restaurant
420 South 48th Avenue
(509) 965–5422

The White House Cafe
3602 Kern Street
(509) 469–2644

ZILLAH

El Ranchito Restaurant
1319 East First Avenue
(509) 829–5880

Squeeze Inn Restaurant
611 First Street
(509) 829–6226

ALSO WORTH SEEING

Cove B Estate Winery, Cove B Inn at Sagecliff, and Tendrils Restaurant
Vantage area
www.cavebdirect.com

Columbia Gorge Scenic Highway 30
Oregon

The Gorge Outdoor Amphitheater
Ellensburg
(206) 285–1970

Mount Hood Railroad
Hood River, Oregon

The Seasons Performance Hall
Yakima
www.seasonsmusicfestival.com

Washington's Fruit Place & Gift Shop
Yakima
(509) 966–1275

Northeast Washington

Washington's northeast corner is a high desert and farming region of stark contrasts. In a few hours you can travel through steep basalt canyons thick with the spicy smell of sagebrush, over hills covered with wheat fields and dotted with farms, and through thick pine forests. The region's geological history is dynamic and readily visible in the layered walls of coulees and steep canyons cut deep by ancient glaciers and rivers.

You meet local residents at cafe lunch counters, at small restaurants, or at bistros and brewpubs. The people of this region are close to the earth and its seasonal changes, aware of their relationship to the farms, ranches, forests, and rivers upon which so much of the local economy depends. These hardy folks take pride in their Native American, farmer, rancher, and forestry heritages, which are very much alive in the current culture.

Northeast Washington also offers a variety of all-season outdoor activities, including hiking, bicycling, fishing, hunting, boating, snowmobiling, ice fishing, and skiing. On the shores of many rivers and lakes, secluded retreats and fishing resorts beckon local sportsmen and -women to rub shoulders with visitors from around the world.

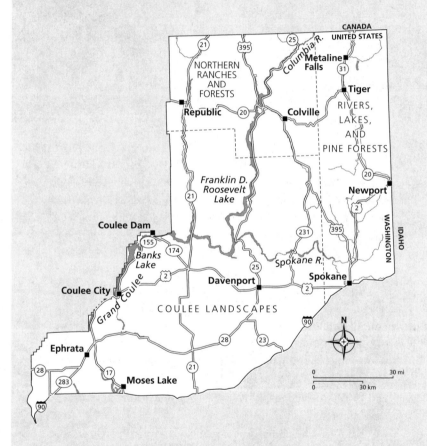

Coulee Landscapes

A good place to start your tour of the region is the town of *Ephrata.* From Interstate 90 take Highway 283 northeast from George or Highway 17 northwest from Moses Lake. You'll pass enormous circular fields of corn, wheat, potatoes, and legumes kept green by massive central-pivot irrigation systems. This high plain is so wide you can glimpse hills to the north but only a hint of a southern ridge. Like many northeast Washington counties, Grant County preserves its past

NORTHEAST WASHINGTON'S TOP HITS

Bing Crosby Memorabilia Room Gonzaga University
Spokane

Colville Tribal Cultural Museum
Coulee Dam

Dry Falls Interpretive Center
Coulee City

Gehrke Windmills
Grand Coulee

Grand Coulee Dam and Franklin Roosevelt Lake
Coulee Dam

Grant County Museum and Village
Ephrata

Fort Spokane
Creston

Kettle Falls Historical Center

Keller Ferry

Lake Lenore Caves
Soap Lake

Lake Roosevelt Vacation Houseboats
Kettle Falls

Lazy Bee Wilderness Retreat
Colville

Lincoln County Historical Museum
Davenport

Manito Park Gardens
Spokane

North Pend Oreille Scenic Byway and Selkirk International Loop
Ione

Northwest Museum of Arts and Culture and Historic Campbell House
Spokane

Pend Oreille County Historical Museum
Pend Oreille

Pioneer Park
Newport

Sherman Pass Scenic Byway
Sherman Pass

Spokane River Centennial Trail
Spokane

Steamboat Rock
Electric City

Stevens County Historical Museum
Colville

Stonerose Interpretive Center
Republic

Washington Hotel
Metaline Falls

in a local historical museum. ***Grant County Historical Museum and Village*** (742 Basin Street Northwest; 509–754–3334), located at the far end of Ephrata, offers some thirty-five buildings and shops that show the region's past. Visitors walk through carefully re-created print, camera, and blacksmith shops, saloons, a one-room schoolhouse, and homesteads arranged on some four acres. You can also see the newest acquisition, a 1971 Burlington Northern caboose, and a collection of the big farm machines that made Grant County a major agricultural producer. The museum is open from early May to the end of September, 10:00 A.M. to 5:00 P.M. Monday through Saturday, 1:00 to 4:00 P.M. on Sunday, and closed on Wednesday. For another glimpse of local history, stop by the ca. 1917 ***Grant County Courthouse,*** west of the highway at the corner of First NW and C Streets. The courthouse is heated geothermally from a nearby hot spring.

Follow Highway 28 north to ***Soap Lake.*** Cherished by local tribes and early settlers for its healing properties, Soap Lake continues to draw people seeking rejuvenation from its buoyant waters. Seventeen minerals, with sodium bicarbonate the most common, give the water its soapy texture, although the frothy piles of suds that once accumulated on the lakeshore have disappeared due to dilution from irrigation. The popularity of this resort town is nothing like its heyday at the turn of the twentieth century, but the crowds still come. You can experience the water's effects with daily soaks at one of the town's two beaches or in baths piped from mineral waters deep in the lake to several of the town's motels. Both public beaches are crowded in summer when water temperatures can reach as high as one hundred degrees Fahrenheit. East Beach, located near the highway and motels, is the most popular with tourists. West Beach, separated by a small, rocky peninsula, is preferred by local residents. It also has public showers, helpful for removing the water's alkaline residue.

If you'd like to linger a day or two to soak in the soft mineral waters, you could ask about accommodations at ***Notaras Lodge,*** in the town of Soap Lake at 13 Canna Street (509–246–0462; www.notaraslodge.com). Folks choose from fifteen different rooms in four large log structures that offer outside entrances and small sitting decks. Your cozy room comes with handcrafted log walls, a comfortable sitting area with upholstered and oversize easy-chairs, and a small kitchenette. Several rooms offer handcrafted log beds and whirlpool tubs, and all rooms come with double plumbing that allows you to choose either the warm Soap Lake mineral water or freshwater for baths. One of the rooms, Eagles Nest, offers a balcony that frames morning sunrises. Another room, The Cabin, offers two queen-size beds, a lovely stained-glass window, and French doors that open to a balcony framing views of Soap Lake. All rooms are decorated with western and antique memorabilia such as cattle brands, saddles, bridles, sombreros, old shotguns, railroad lanterns, and rodeo photographs. Several wood species were used in the construction of the impressive log lodges, including Tennessee red cedar, black walnut, and cherry. The handcrafted and scribed logs range in sizes from 12 to 24 inches or more in diameter.

Don's Restaurant (509–246–1217), just across the street from Notaras Lodge, is a local favorite for steak, pasta, and seafood; it's open daily for lunch and dinner from 11:00 A.M. except for Saturday when it opens at 4:00 P.M. The large mural on the outside wall of cowboys around a campfire was painted by local artist Bill Robinson. For breakfast try *Tumblewood Cafe* in nearby Lakeview, *Mad Hatter's Cafe* on Daisy Street (Highway 17) in Soap Lake, and for good burgers stop at *B&B* (509–246–1231) on Daisy and First.

Soap Lake is the southernmost of the Grand Coulee's chain of mineral-rich lakes. The Grand Coulee was formed by glacial action that cut through layers of thick volcanic basalt. Highway 17, from Soap Lake to *Coulee City,* provides a scenic route through the lower end of the coulee. You'll follow secluded lake beds, cut deep into reddish brown cliffs, their shorelines often crusted white with minerals. Lake Lenore has public access, with several spots to launch a boat or to stop and watch the varied waterfowl in grassy lakeside wetlands.

Off the highway opposite Lake Lenore is the turnoff to *Lake Lenore Caves.* A gravel road, open 10:00 A.M. to 6:00 P.M. daily, takes you to the trailhead for a short hike through fragrant sagebrush, up the cliff sides to the ancient caves. There, like ancient hunter-gatherers, you can find shelter from the heat in these cool, rocky overhangs. Watch graceful cliff swallows, listen to crickets, hear the dry scrub rustling in the breeze, and absorb the stark beauty of the wide coulee landscape.

Between Alkali and Blue Lakes, you may catch sight of the *Caribou Cattle Trail.* A roadside sign marks the point where the trail crosses the road. Originally a Native path, the 500-mile trail was used in the late nineteenth century as a supply route by miners and Blue Lake homesteaders. A few miles north on Blue Lake, *Coulee Lodge Resort,* at 33017 Park Lake Road (509–632–5565), offers six cabins, nine well-equipped 40-foot mobile homes with tip-outs, and a number of campsites. Folks can rent 14-foot aluminum fishing boats for cruising the lake and fishing for rainbow and brown trout and for

FAVORITE ATTRACTIONS

Grand Coulee Dam	Steamboat Rock State Park and Banks Lake
Lake Roosevelt	

Donaldsons, a chubby trout-salmon mix with pinkish meat. "It's absolutely delicious," says Connie Bertsch, who co-owns and manages the resort with her husband, Larry. Visitors can rent Jet Skis and also find a nice swimming beach area for the kids. The resort is located 15 miles north of Ephrata. Nearby, off Highway 17, **Sun Lakes/Dry Falls State Park** (509–632–5583, www.parks .wa.gov) offers lakeside camping with 180 tent and RV sites, plus horseback riding, golf, mountain biking, and wildlife viewing.

The **Dry Falls Interpretive Center** (509–632–5214), open daily April to September and located near Coulee City at the south end of **Banks Lake,** offers spectacular views of what was once a gigantic waterfall—possibly the largest that has ever existed on Earth. Exhibits explain the geological forces that created this massive precipice and why it is now without water. You'll learn of the lush environment that covered this area twenty million years ago during the Miocene epoch and how the largest basaltic lava flows on Earth, up to a mile thick, eventually engulfed 200,000 square miles of the Pacific Northwest. Powerful forces buckled and warped the cooled lava plateau, followed by glaciation and massive flooding, creating the dramatic landscape before you.

U.S. Highway 2 and Highway 17 intersect near **Dry Falls Cafe** (509–632–5634), then US 2 crosses the Dry Falls Dam at the south end of Banks Lake. Turn right off US 2 at **Coulee City** to explore this windblown western town, originally a watering hole along the Caribou Trail. Huge grain elevators now dominate downtown. For information on the town's history, pick up a walking-tour brochure at the **Country Mall Store** on Main Street. If you happen into Coulee City on Tuesday or Saturday between 10:00 A.M. and 3:00 P.M., you can learn about art and local history from members of the **Highlighters Art Club,** who meet at their gallery on Main between Fifth and Sixth (509–632–5373). The group encourages local artists and collects their work. The gallery, in a building constructed in 1905, features art produced by members, such as oil paintings, woodcarvings, and dried-flower arrangements. After all this browsing and perusing local artwork of Coulee City folks, you can pop into **Just Another Espresso** (509–632–5581) on Main Street for soups, sandwiches, and hot or cold beverages. Or just a mile north of Coulee City, you could hunker down for juicy hamburgers at **Big Wally's Gas Station** (509–632–5504) as well as find fishing tackle and information about local walleye fishing. In Coulee City you could also try **Steamboat Rock Restaurant** (509–632–5452), on Main Street near the corner of Fifth Street, open daily, except Monday, from 11:00 A.M., and the **New Crossing Restaurant** at 502 West Main Street (509–632–5677), open daily except Sunday from 7:00 A.M.

If you continue east, US 2 passes through a series of small farm towns at 10-mile intervals. The pleasant farm town of **Wilbur,** at the junction of US 2 and Highway 21, is worth a stop. The town's main park, located south of Main Street, is a shady oasis of mature trees and green lawns. If you're still hot, cross over Goose Creek on the rustic footbridge to swim with local families at the Wilbur outdoor pool. The facility is open throughout the summer and charges a small fee. The town displays its history at the **Big Bend Historical Society Museum** (509–647–5863), housed in a 1915-era Lutheran church 1 block north of Main Street, on Wilbur's west side. The museum is open June through August on Saturday from 2:00 to 4:00 P.M., as well as during "Wild Goose Bill Days," named for the town's infamous founder and held the third weekend in May. The town of Wilbur has but one thoroughfare, Main Street, and there are several good eateries here. Try **Billy Burger, Doxie's Drive-In,** or the **Alibi Tavern.** The Alibi opens daily from 6:30 A.M. to at least 9:00 P.M. "You really can't get lost in Wilbur," points out a longtime resident, who recently moved back to this, her hometown. You could also drive 8 miles east to **Creston** and try **Patty Mac's Cafe** or **Corner Cafe,** both on Main Street. You can't get lost in Creston, either.

For another taste of Washington's varied topography, head north from Wilbur on Highway 21. You'll travel past trees and farms in distant clumps like islands in a sea of grain before the road winds abruptly down through layered coulee cliffs to the Columbia River and the **Lake Roosevelt National Recreation Area.** If you're traveling RV-style, plan to spend at least one night at Keller Ferry at the splendid **River Rue RV Campground** (509–647–2647; www.river rue.com). Folks will find full hookups, clean restrooms, and a full-service deli here. You can also walk about, exercise Fido or Bowser, meet other travelers, and enjoy the bustling activity at the marina and at the ferry landing. At Keller Ferry Marina the Colville Confederated Tribes rent out thirty houseboats from 46 to 59 feet in length that sleep up to thirteen people. For information and current rates, call the Colville Tribe's Roosevelt Recreation Enterprise at (800) 648–5253 (www.rrehouseboats.com). This is a popular Coulee Country vacation option; reservations are accepted in June for the following year. If you are hardy and adventurous, you could bring your own canoe or kayak to reach the isolated campsites along Lake Roosevelt's pristine shoreline. For houseboat rentals

The Gehrke Windmills

Erected in North Dam Park overlooking Banks Lake and near the city of Grand Coulee, more than 650 windmills have been built by local resident Emil Gehrke. He fashioned the folk-art treasures from old cast-off iron parts and painted them in bright colors. Take cameras for good shots of you and the kids and the fanciful windmills.

at the far north end of Lake Roosevelt, contact *Lake Roosevelt Houseboat Vacations & Marina* in Kettle Falls (509–738–6121; www.lakeroosevelt.com). Lake Roosevelt and the Lake Roosevelt National Recreation Area extend 151 miles north from Grand Coulee Dam to the scenic Colville National Forest and to the U.S.–Canadian border into British Columbia. The lake offers 630 miles of shoreline, coves, and bays and offers year-round fishing for kokanee, walleye, large- and smallmouth bass, rainbow trout, perch, crappie, and sturgeon. Twenty-eight campgrounds on the west and east sides of Lake Roosevelt offer campsites, water, picnic tables, fire pits, and restrooms. These campsites are available on a first-come basis, with no hookups for RVs. For some of the most scenic campgrounds, head north on Highway 25 into the northern section of the recreation area that borders the Colville National Forest. Check out Hunters, Gifford, Bradbury Beach, Kettle Falls, Kettle River, and Evans campgrounds, all of which have fresh drinking water and lakeside sites. For other specific campground information and maps, contact the National Park Service headquarters (509–633–9441; www.nps.gov), located in the town of Grand Coulee, or the district park service office in Kettle Falls (509–738–6266).

The *Keller Ferry* offers a free ten-minute crossing with runs every fifteen minutes between 6:00 A.M. and 11:00 P.M. We're talking very small ferry here; yours may be the only car on the ferry's small deck. Many of the large houseboats are launched nearby. The river is often so placid you can see the dry sage-covered cliffs and hills reflected in the water for a doubly scenic view. From the landing on the north side, you can turn left on Swawilla Basin Road to Grand Coulee Dam or continue north on scenic Highway 21 up the Sanpoil River to the old mining town of Republic. The 24-mile road west toward Grand Coulee Dam is a hilly one, surrounded by ponderosa pine, wild roses, purple lupine, and woolly mullein, with occasional old barns and glacial erratics along the way. You may even spot a bear cub or mule deer exploring the dry roadside. Grand Coulee Dam is located 4 miles south of the junction with Highway 155.

In the community of *Coulee Dam,* visit the *Colville Tribal Cultural Museum,* at 512 Mead Way (509–633–0751), open 10:00 A.M. to 6:00 P.M. daily during summer. The museum recounts the story of tribal life when the salmon swam free, before the Columbia River was dammed. Exhibits feature ancient fishing scenes, tribal lodges, and tepees as well as cedar and beargrass basket displays. The museum's gift shop highlights beadwork, paintings, prints, and ceramics by local Native artists and tribespeople as well as Pendleton, Nez Percé, and Navajo blankets. Staff members are on hand to answer questions, and they can describe how to get to the grave site of the legendary Nez Percé leader Chief Joseph, buried in exile from northeastern Oregon on a hillside northeast of Nespelem, 13 miles north on Highway 155.

The Colville Confederated Tribes

Named for an Englishman who was in the rum and molasses business and who never set foot in America, the Colville Confederated Tribes is made up of eleven different bands: Chelan, Entiat, Lakes, Nez Percé (from Northeast Oregon), Methow, Moses, Nespelem, Palus, San Poil, Sweelpoo, and Wenatchi.

Prior to 1826 these separate nomadic bands fished, hunted, and traded furs and goods with each other in the area of Kettle Falls. When Englishmen and white settlers learned of this, the Fort Colville trading post was established. From 1826 to 1887 the Indians traded the lush pelts and hides of beaver, brown and black bear, grizzly, muskrat, fisher, fox, lynx, martin, mink, otter, raccoon, wolverine, badger, and wolf at the post. St. Paul's Mission near Kettle Falls includes the original site of Fort Colville and a rustic log missionary church. In 1872 the Colville Indian Reservation was formed, comprising today about 1.3 million acres. Travelers are invited to visit the tribal headquarters located near Nespelem about 20 miles north of Grand Coulee Dam. Here you can learn about the enterprises owned and operated by the tribes, including a timber and wood products operation; a tree replanting program; a fish hatchery that provides fish for the lakes and streams in the region; and a fleet of thirty recreational houseboats on Lake Roosevelt launched from marinas at Keller Ferry and at Seven Bays Campground (800–648–5253 for rental information). To enjoy fishing certain lakes on the reservation, contact the Tribal Fish and Wildlife Department in Nespelem (509–634–2110).

For a contrast to the "before" picture glimpsed at the museum in Coulee Dam, you can stop by the ***Grand Coulee Dam Interpretive Center*** (509–633–9265) across the bridge to learn the story of one of the world's largest concrete structures, celebrated in Woody Guthrie's famous song "Roll on, Columbia" and the largest component of the Pacific Northwest's extensive hydroelectric system. Exhibits at the visitor center explain the dam's history and engineering. You can also inquire about the current status of tours of the dam facilities. The forty-minute laser light show of animated graphics projected on the dam's surface runs every night Memorial Day weekend through September.

Visitors to the Grand Coulee area can enjoy the extensive ***Community Trail System*** that connects all four towns (West and East Coulee Dam, Grand Coulee, and Electric City) and that offers exercise and spectacular views. The ***Down River Trail***, a 6½-mile hiking, biking, wheelchair-accessible path, follows the Columbia River north from the dam. With gentle grades and landscaped rest stops, these trails offer relaxing strolls.

For an overnight option that offers expansive views of Grand Coulee Dam, including its grand evening Laser Light Show, call the innkeepers at ***Columbia River Inn*** (800–633–6421; www.columbiariverinn.com) located at 10 Lincoln

Grand Coulee Dam

One of the most popular tourist attractions in Washington, and certainly one of the most impressive feats of engineering in the country, the Grand Coulee Dam just naturally attracts superlatives, comparisons, and illustrative examples to convey its sheer magnitude. Here are a few of its facts and figures:

The dam is one of the largest concrete structures in the world, containing nearly twelve million cubic yards of concrete. There is enough concrete in the dam to build a standard 6-foot-wide sidewalk around the world at the equator.

The dam is 500 feet wide at its base, 4,173 feet across the crest, and stands 550 feet above bedrock—as high as the Washington Monument and dwarfing the Great Pyramid of Egypt.

It is the country's largest hydroelectric producer and the world's third-largest, generating 6,494,000 kilowatts in a single instant—more power than a million locomotives.

Each of the six conventional pumps in Grand Coulee's Pump-Generator Plant is powered by a 65,000-horsepower motor that can pump 1,600 cubic feet of water per second, or 781,128 gallons per minute. In addition, six pump-generators, each having a 67,500-horsepower rating, can pump 1,948 cubic feet of water per second. One of these twelve units can fill the water needs of a city the size of Chicago.

Avenue in Coulee Dam. For information on other lodging, including motor inns and RV resorts, contact the Grand Coulee Dam Area Chamber of Commerce at (509) 633–3074 or (800) 268–5332; www.grandcouleedam.org.

Highway 155 follows the eastern shore of Banks Lake back to Coulee City. It is preferable to drive south on this road so that you can easily pull over at viewpoints and appreciate the awesome geology and the varied wildlife. *Steamboat Rock,* a former island in an ancient riverbed, rises like a solidified wave from the lake's north end. Picturesque ***Northrup Canyon Trail*** begins at the end of a ½-mile road across the highway from the rest stop near Steamboat Rock's north end. This moderately difficult trail stretches from a sheltered canyon, through pine forests, and up a steep path to Northrup Lake atop the gorge. You'll see remnants of early days along the way and perhaps view eagles soaring overhead.

Steamboat Rock State Park (509–633–1304) offers 121 campsites with full hookups and day-use facilities on the shore of Banks Lake, located just south of Grand Coulee and Electric City. Reservations are recommended because this is one of the state's more popular campgrounds (888–226–7688; www.parks .wa.gov). A hiking trail to the rock's 640-acre summit offers excellent views of the surrounding terrain. Bring water for everyone in your group, and wear good walking shoes. Keep your distance from the edge of the cliff, since basalt breaks easily, and though rattlesnakes in the area aren't considered particularly aggressive or lethal, a bite is still painful and dangerous. Also on scenic Banks Lake near Electric City, you can find beach and picnic areas, immaculate grounds, cozy cabins, large villas, and RV spaces with hookups at *Sun Banks Resort* (509–633–3786). The resort hosts a popular jazz festival during the summer.

The town of *Creston,* east of Wilbur on US 2, begins and ends in wheat fields near the crest of the Columbia Plateau. Take the left fork 2 miles east of Creston to reach Seven Bays and Fort Spokane. Bachelor Drive (Miles Creston Road) zigzags through a narrow, wooded valley back to rolling wheat fields before it descends into pine forests near Lake Roosevelt and the Lake Roosevelt National Recreation Area.

Located about 15 miles north of Creston, *Seven Bays Campground* (509–725–1676), owned by the Colville Confederated Tribes, offers a hilltop campground with RV hookup sites as well as a marina and store.

You can also visit and camp at nearby *Fort Spokane* and *Fort Spokane Campground* (509–725–2715). Built in 1880 after the overt wars against Native Americans ceased, Fort Spokane was designed to maintain a truce between settlers and seminomadic tribes. Park volunteers and staff show what life was like back then through living-history programs each Sunday at 11:00 A.M. throughout the summer. The visitor center is located in the former guardhouse, one of the original fort buildings. An interpretive trail guides you through the grounds, and the camping and RV sites are rimmed by forest-covered hills.

You can continue north on scenic Highway 25 to Kettle Falls to access the scenic *Colville National Forest* area and the far north section of Lake Roosevelt (509–684–7000 for campground information). At this point travelers are some 100 miles north of Grand Coulee Dam and 40 miles south of the U.S.–Canadian border, where they can cross into the southeastern section of British Columbia. Near Kettle Falls, you can find another contact for houseboat vacations in this scenic northern lake area. Contact the staff at *Lake Roosevelt Houseboat Vacations* in Kettle Falls (509–738–6121; www.lake roosevelt.com) to explore the costs and particulars on their fleet of luxurious houseboats. The staff provides complete orientation to the houseboats' facilities, safety instructions, and how to operate and handle the 62-foot-long craft. There is a two-way marine radio on board in case of emergencies. For a small extra fee, folks can board their houseboat the night before sailing to save the cost of a motel room. The large craft accommodate up to thirteen people and contain full kitchen facilities, baths, common areas, bedrooms and sleeping areas, and outside and topside decks. You bring your own bedding, bath linens, food, and beverages. What can you do on a floating houseboat with no TV and no telephone? Well, for starters, you relax into nature's time. Then you cruise the upper section of the lake and pull into a secluded cove or small bay and perhaps anchor for a day or two. Folks can fish for walleye or trout; dive and swim from the deck or paddle nearby on an inner tube or float tube; relax in the sun with a novel; enjoy a steak barbecue at sunset; and watch for wildlife such as eagles, osprey, deer, and even bear and wild turkeys. The summer season, late June through Labor Day, fills quickly. The value seasons are post–Labor Day through October 31 and May 1 through late June (excluding Memorial Day weekend). The houseboats are rented by the week, midweek, or weekends. For the most outrageous vacation option, ask about the Super Cruisers, which come with a six-person hot tub located on the topside deck right under the stars.

From Highway 25 you can also head south, away from the Lake Roosevelt National Recreation Area, and plunge back into rolling grain country proceeding to *Davenport.* This larger agricultural town west of Spokane is vibrant with daily farm life. The Davenport City Park, south of the highway, surrounds a natural spring where huge cottonwoods have grown for centuries. The sweet water made this an important campsite for Native tribes and, in the late nineteenth century, for settlers and miners traveling along the White Bluffs Road. The park is a pleasant spot for a picnic, with playground equipment, tables, shade, and a community pool. Nearby, at Seventh and Park, is the Lincoln County Historical Museum and Visitor Information Center (509–725–6711), chock-full of items and images collected over the past century, from photos to farm machinery, and including a general store and a blacksmith shop. The museum is open Monday through Saturday from 9:00 A.M. to 5:00 P.M., May 1 to September 30. For good eats in Davenport, try *Edna's Drive-In* (509–725–1071) on Morgan near Third Street.

The rolling landscape continues east along US 2. At the town of Reardan, you can continue to Spokane or turn north toward Colville on Highway 231 for a scenic 70-mile drive up Spring Creek Canyon. Along this road you'll see a scattering of old farms, many of which still use windmills to pump water for irrigation. By the time you reach the Spokane River at Long Lake Dam, the wheat fields and farms have given way to ponderosa pine forests and meadows. At the tiny village of Ford, you can find a friendly pit stop at the *Ford Trading Post,* a post office, general store, rest stop, and gas station all jumbled together in a log building.

Continue on Highway 231 as the road curves west through Springdale. Nine miles north at the town of Valley, turn left on a 3-mile spur road to reach *Waitts Lake.* Waitts is a spring-fed lake surrounded by wetlands and pine forests. Scattered farms and fields dot its western shore, summer cabins and resorts hug the northeast, and public fishing spots offer recreation at the south end. The resorts are informal, catering to local families as well as visitors. *Silver Beach Resort* (3323 Waitts Lake Road, Valley; 509–937–2811) offers travelers five cabins, a general store, boat rentals, swimming and picnic sites, and a pleasant restaurant with a patio overlooking the lake. It's open for dinner Thursday through Sunday, 5:00 to 9:00 P.M.

Rivers, Lakes, and Pine Forests

Spokane, the largest city in the inland Northwest, is situated along the Spokane River near an ancient Indian campsite, where members of the Spo-kan-ee tribe gathered for centuries to fish at the rapids. Although Spokane has grown into a major urban center, it retains much of its frontier identity. You'll see plenty of cowboy hats and pickup trucks even in downtown, and you don't have to go far past the city's suburban developments to find ranches and farms.

The Spokane River is still a dominant feature in the city. The *Spokane River Centennial Trail,* which follows the river, offers an ideal path for walking, bicycling, running, or skating. The Washington portion of the Centennial Trail runs 37 miles—22 from the Idaho border to Spokane's *Riverfront Park* in the center of downtown, where you can see the churning rapids where the Spokane tribe fished for salmon. Nearby you'll find espresso and hot dog stands as well as many pleasant eateries.

The recently renovated *Northwest Museum of Arts and Culture* and ca. 1898 *Campbell House,* located in the city's historic Browne's addition at 2316 West First Avenue (509–456–3931; www.northwestmuseum.org), display the region's Native American and pioneer past and current culture. Early architect Kirtland Cutter designed the thirty-room English Tudor-revival mansion, which showcased the opulent lifestyle of one of the region's mining barons. Both museum and house are open Tuesday through Sunday.

Across the street from nearby Coeur d'Alene Park is the *Fotheringham House Bed and Breakfast* (2128 West Second Avenue; 509–838–1891; www .fotheringham.net). Spokane's first mayor, David B. Fotheringham, built the house in 1891 as his family home. Innkeepers Irene and Paul Jensen invite guests to relax in one of four guest rooms with shared or private bath, soak in an original claw-foot tub, enjoy evening tea and truffles, have a fireside chat in winter, or spend a quiet summer evening on the curved veranda overlooking the splendid perennial gardens. Travelers who love antique furniture and stained glass, combined with hand-carved woodwork, tin ceilings, and Old World ambience, can make this a comfortable base from which to explore the Spokane area.

honorthyfather

Father's Day was "invented" in Spokane in 1910 by a local house-wife, Mrs. John Bruce Dodd. Mrs. Dodd wanted a special day to honor her father, William Smart, a Civil War veteran who had raised her and her five brothers after his wife's early death. She contacted the local YMCA and the Spokane Ministerial Association, who persuaded the city government to set aside the third Sunday in June to "honor thy father."

At the **Marianna Stoltz House Bed & Breakfast,** located in a shady residential neighborhood at 427 East Indiana Avenue (509–483–4316; www .mariannastoltzhouse.com), innkeepers Phyllis and Jim Maguire offer visitors four comfortable guest rooms on the second floor of their large, ca. 1908 Craftsman-style home. The living room, dining room, and parlor all come with leaded-glass windows, high ceilings, and fine woodwork of polished fir. Roomy sofas and upholstered chairs are arranged in cozy groupings, with antique light fixtures and fringed lampshades mixing well with the other period furnishings. For breakfast you might enjoy such tasty fare as French toast with strawberry and mandarin orange sauce, Stoltz House Strada, or croissants with poached eggs topped with bacon and cheese sauce. The inn is just 5 blocks from Gonzaga University (502 East Boone Avenue), where the **Bing Crosby Memorabilia Room** (509–328–4220), located in Crosby Student Center and open to the public, is filled with photographs, letters, and musical memorabilia from the crooner's life. "He lived in the Spokane area as a boy," explains Phyllis.

Waverly Place Bed & Breakfast is located in the Corbin Park Historic District at 709 West Waverly Place; (509) 328–1856; www.waverlyplace.com. Guests find four guest rooms on the second floor with views of the park and grounds, along with comforts such as dormer window seats or turret sitting areas, stained-glass windows, gleaming fir floors, antique queen beds with down comforters and quilts, cozy common areas, and baths with claw-footed soaking tubs and tiled showers. A hearty and delicious breakfast, prepared by innkeeper Marge Arndt and daughter Tammy, amply prepares you for a fine day of exploring the Spokane area.

In the early 1900s **Corbin Park,** then the regional fairgrounds, housed a ½-mile racing track, and the Gentlemen's Riding Club was soon established nearby. Sulky and harness racing were popular sports, with many prominent gentlemen of Spokane and their ladies attending regularly. Locals as well as visitors especially enjoy the park and its shady walking paths that pass by many vintage homes built in the early 1900s.

Good eateries abound in the Spokane area. In the downtown and near Riverfront Park check out the **Onion Family Restaurant** at 302 West Riverside

(509–747–3852) for pastas, fajitas, chicken, gourmet salads, and a variety of hamburgers; *Rock City Italian Grill* at 505 West Riverside (509–455–4400) for serious Italian food lovers; *Sawtooth Grill* at 801 West Main Street (509–363–1100) near River Park Square downtown for great burgers in a rustic mountain-cabin setting; and *Steam Plant Grill and Brew Pub,* located in historic Steam Plant Square (159 South Lincoln Street; 509–777–3900). Located near Manito Park, *Lindaman's Café* at 1235 South Grand Boulevard (509–838–3000) shouldn't be missed for freshly made entrees, great salads and sandwiches, and tempting desserts (if possible take a picnic along to the park); and *Just Jerry's* at 1228 South Grand Boulevard (509–455–7545) is frequented for its tasty regional fare.

To get acquainted with the natural history of the area, go hiking at *Dishman Hills Natural Resource Conservation Area,* a 518-acre sanctuary with an easy 2½-mile loop walk in the southeast hills. Spokane County Parks staff can provide more information (509–477–4730). Or walk in the splendid *John A. Finch Arboretum,* at 3404 West Woodland Boulevard (509–624–4832) with its stands of rhododendron, azaleas, and lilacs. The arboretum encompasses a mile-long natural area that covers some sixty-five acres along the banks of Garden Springs Creek west of downtown Spokane off Sunset Boulevard. One of the best outdoor experiences awaits travelers at *Manito Park Gardens,* South

TOP ANNUAL EVENTS
IN NORTHEAST WASHINGTON

Laser Light Show on the Grand Coulee Dam
Grand Coulee, May–September
(800) 268–5332

Lilac Festival
Spokane, May
(888) 776–5263

Wild Goose Bill Days
Wilbur, early June
(509) 647–5551

Colville PRCA Rodeo
Colville, mid-June
(509) 684–5973

Curlew Barrel Derby
Curlew, early June
www.ferrycounty.com

Pend Oreille Poker Paddle
Newport, mid-July
(509) 447–5812

Pioneer Days
Davenport, mid-July
(509) 725–6711

North East Washington Fiddle Contest
Republic, early August
(509) 775–3387

City of Lights
Grand Coulee area, all of December
(800) 268–5332

Grand at Eighteenth Avenue (509–625–6600; www.spokaneparks.org). Start your tour at **Rose Hill,** situated on a four-acre slope that overlooks the other garden sections. You'll see formal beds of some 1,500 roses representing over 150 varieties, as well as borders of old-fashioned scented roses. From here walk down to the **Joel E. Ferris Perennial Garden,** a three-acre oasis of lawns and large perennial beds where you'll see colorful hellebores, solidagos, and cosmos as well as salvias, poppies, spiky liatris, and phlox. Next visit the splendid **Duncan Formal Gardens,** just opposite **Gaiser Conservatory.** The conservatory houses collections of colorful begonias, fuchsias, and tropical plantings. Then access a meandering path just beyond the Lilac Garden and below Rose Hill to find the secluded **Nishinomiya Japanese Garden.** The graceful curved bridge over the reflecting pond, called a "ceremony bridge," is borrowed from the Oriental tradition. A small waterfall flows from the rising sun toward the setting sun; the three vertical stones in the central pond suggest cranes or ships at sea. Don't miss this splendid park and its wonderful gardens.

For more information about what to see and do in the area, contact the Spokane Area Visitor Information Center at 201 West Main Avenue (888–776–5263; www.visitspokane.com). Before heading north from Spokane, gas up and fill your picnic cooler with snacks and beverages.

From Spokane you can take US 2 north, but first you may want to detour onto U.S. Highway 395 and visit the **Fire Lookout Museum** (509–466–9171; www.firelookout.com/lomuseum) located just north of downtown Spokane. You and the kids can inspect a replica of the kind of fire lookout used to house fire-lookout volunteers in the high mountain areas of Washington and Oregon during the summer and fall fire seasons. Call ahead for visiting hours. Continue north to the community of **Deer Park** and call ahead to make an appointment to visit the **Red Shed** (509–466–2744), which has a collection of vintage farm machinery and household items dating from the 1890s to the 1950s.

From Deer Park head east a few miles to US 2 and head north on this route through lush farmlands to the gentle Pend Oreille (pond-er-RAY) River Valley. On the banks of the Pend Oreille River, you'll find the town of Newport and its Idaho neighbor, Oldtown. As you enter **Newport** from the southwest, you'll see **Centennial Plaza** to your right with its huge steam-engine wheel and the **Pend Oreille County Historical Museum** (509–447–5388) in the 1908 brick Milwaukee Railroad passenger depot. The museum features antique quilts, kitchen items, books, photographs, tools, and news articles from local sources, as well as a settler's cabin, a one-room schoolhouse, and old farm machinery. It is open daily from 10:00 A.M. to 4:00 P.M. mid-May through September. Located nearby, at 337 Washington Street, is **Owen's Grocery & Deli** (509–447–3525), a great spot for snacks, espresso, and a cool treat at the old-fashioned soda fountain.

Steam-engine wheel in Centennial Plaza

Newport's Centennial Plaza also has a three-level drinking fountain "serving man, beast, and dog" since 1911. Across the street is Newport's oldest building, **Kelly's Tavern** (324 West Fourth Street; 509–447–3267), a watering hole for miners, loggers, settlers, railway workers, and city folk since 1894. The tavern's impressive lead-glass bar was shipped around Cape Horn to San Francisco and then carried by wagon train to Newport.

For a scenic overnight option in Newport, consider **Inn at the Lake,** at 581 South Shore Diamond Lake Road (509–447–5772; www.innatthelake.com). Travelers find four guest rooms in this Italian villa–style home constructed in 1993 and situated above the lake. The rooms offer superb lake views along with decks and gas-log fireplaces. The largest suite comes with an elegant four-poster bed and a couple-size whirlpool tub. For lunch or dinner with lake views, call **Diamond Shores Lodge Restaurant** (509–447–5133), also on South Shore Diamond Lake Road. Newport is 8 miles from the Idaho border and about 40 miles north of Spokane.

You can travel north on either side of the Pend Oreille River, but Le Clerc Road on the east bank is quieter and more scenic. A half mile north from the Newport/Oldtown bridge, you can visit an ancient Indian campsite at **Pioneer Park.** Recent archaeological studies there have uncovered artifacts, earth ovens, and house pits that indicate use by the Kalispel Tribe for at least 800 years and by prehistoric hunter-gatherers for possibly 2,000 to 4,000 years. The park offers quiet, forested camping and picnic spots and views of mergansers, herons, and other waterfowl in nearby wetlands and river islands.

As you continue north, watch for osprey, hawks that catch fish by speed-diving into water and build large nests on river pilings and snags. A bridge crosses the Pend Oreille River at Usk, a tiny mill town named after a Welsh river.

Local Theater Thrives

Regardless of your travels in the Evergreen State or how far off the beaten path you may roam, it's certain that local theater groups are meeting, choosing Broadway plays and musicals, casting parts, poring over scripts, rehearsing, building sets, gathering props and costumes, and getting ready for opening night. Check out these dedicated theater groups, take in a local production, and meet fellow stage lovers from near and far.

Centerstage
1017 West First Avenue
Spokane
509–747–8243
Dinner theater and cabaret-style theater

Cutter Theatre
302 Park Street
Metaline Falls
509–446–4108
www.cuttertheatre.com
Presents musicals, dramas, and dinner mystery theater

Spokane Interplayers Ensemble
174 South Howard Street
Spokane
509–455–7529
www.interplayers.com
Presents comedies and dramas
September through June

Spokane Theatrical Group
509–777–2378
www.spokanetheatrical.org
Performing in various venues in the area since 1977

A few miles north of the Usk bridge on Le Clerc Road, you may spot a herd of buffalo in pastures by the river. This is the ***Kalispel Indian Reservation,*** the smallest reservation in Washington. The Kalispel people once numbered more than a thousand, spread out over the river valley. Now numbering in the hundreds, the tribe has worked to consolidate its small holdings and has developed community buildings, a bison herd raised for meat, and an aluminum plant in Cusick.

At the ***Manresa Grotto,*** located a few miles north, a short climb up a winding dirt pathway takes you to the dome-shaped grotto, formed by the waves of an ancient glacial lake. There you'll find rows of stone pews before an altar of mortared rock, a site of religious ceremonies for more than a century. The view is enchanting—the peaceful river valley surrounded by forested hills, all framed by the gray stone arch of the grotto entrance.

Le Clerc Road ends across the bridge from the town of ***Ione,*** once the site of the most successful lumber mill in northeast Washington. Get a historic walking-tour brochure at the Ione Drug Store at Main and Fourth. Just west of the drugstore is the Old Railroad Depot, built in 1909. You can take in some breathtaking scenery on the historic ***North Pend Oreille Valley Lion's Club Excursion Train*** from Ione to Metaline Falls and back. Two-hour rides through forests, through two tunnels, and over the Box Canyon trestle high above the Pend Oreille River are scheduled during selected summer and fall weekends. Call (509) 442–5466 between noon and 6:00 P.M. for more information and reservations, which must be made at least two weeks before each ride. The current schedule and fees are also posted at www.povn.com/npovlions.

For more scenery, continue northeast on Sullivan Lake Road on the east side of the Pend Oreille River. *Sullivan Lake,* dammed in 1910 to run the cement plant at Metaline Falls, is situated at the foot of snowcapped peaks. There are forested campsites at Noisy Creek at the lake's south end and near the Sullivan Lake Ranger District Office at 12641 Sullivan Lake Road (509–446–7500) at the north end. In winter you can hike to the bighorn sheep observation area from the Noisy Creek Campsite. The 4⅓-mile *Lakeshore Trail* connects the two campsites and offers great views, especially during autumn, as well as lakeshore access. The *Mill Pond Historic Site* includes a barrier-free interpretive trail from the western edge of Mill Pond, a small lake created in 1910 located northwest on Sullivan Lake Road. The path follows a wooden flume that once ran between Sullivan Lake and Metaline Falls.

Continue west on Sullivan Lake Road to reach *Metaline Falls,* a small town nestled on the east bank of the Pend Oreille River that has attracted a lively artist community. The town's block-long main street (Fifth Street) ends at the city park and visitor center, a brightly painted railway car above terraced flower beds. To the left of the park is the *Washington Hotel* (225 East Fifth Avenue, Metaline Falls; 509–446–4415; leave a message). Built in 1910, the hotel has been restored to its earlier elegance as the centerpiece of a bustling turn-of-the-twentieth-century mining town. Owner Lee McGowan, Metaline Falls artist and former mayor, decorated the eighteen rooms, and she maintains a deli and art gallery on the hotel's first floor. Nearby, at 221 East Fifth Avenue, you can meet the locals over breakfast, lunch, or dinner at *Cathy's Cafe* (509–446–2447), open daily from 5:30 A.M. You could also try another good eatery, *Western Star Bar & Grill* (509–446–2105) in nearby Metaline at 202 North Highway 31.

The building that houses the Cutter Theater at 302 Park Street in Metaline Falls (509–446–4108) was built early in the century and named for talented Spokane architect Kirtland Cutter. The historic school, built of locally kilned bricks, has been renovated as a performing arts center. Stop by to browse the permanent history exhibits and the traveling art exhibits in the art gallery. Visit the theater's Web site at www.povn.com/cutter for schedules of plays, performances, and upcoming events in the area.

For a spectacular view, follow Highway 31 north about 12 miles, then turn left on the ¾-mile access road to *Boundary Vista House.* There you'll have excellent views of Boundary Dam in its steep canyon as well as surrounding mountains. Cross back over the river west of Metaline Falls and take the Boundary Road turnoff to Boundary Dam and Gardner Cave. Along the way you'll see beaver dams in the wetlands next to this scenic woodland road.

Boundary Road divides after 11½ miles. Take the left fork to reach the 1,055-foot-long **Gardner Cave** at **Crawford State Park** (509–446–4065; www.parks.wa.gov). The cave's limestone walls were formed from the bodies of ancient sea creatures that settled into ooze on the floor of an ancient ocean 500 million years ago. Groundwater seepage cut away the stone over the past 70 million years, creating the passage with its fantastic patterns. Visitors must be accompanied by a ranger to enter the cave. Tours are conducted Thursday through Monday from Memorial Day through Labor Day; they leave from the parking lot at 10:00 A.M., noon, and 2:00 and 4:00 P.M. and take about an hour. Bring along a light jacket or sweater, since the cave is always cool, and a flashlight.

Northern Ranches and Forests

Three miles south of Ione at **Tiger,** Highway 20 turns west from the riverbank and heads over the Selkirk Mountains. As you drive through the small community of Tiger, stop at the **Tiger Historical Center Museum.** The building, the historic Tiger Store, was recently restored and converted to its present use to serve as a visitor center and gateway to the **North Pend Oreille Scenic Byway and Selkirk International Loop.** The original building, Tiger Store and Post Office, was constructed in 1912 and served the community until 1975, when the post office was moved to Cusick. The center is open June through September, Friday through Monday from 10:00 A.M. to 5:00 P.M. The road climbs and descends through evergreen forests and past a chain of glacial lakes cradled between the peaks. Among the biggest trees you'll see are Douglas fir, spruce, white pine, grand fir, and tamarack, all giant conifers. The aspen, birch, and mountain larch (tamarack) all turn vibrant colors of yellow, orange, and lime green in late September and October. The highway follows the Little Pend Oreille River through the Colville National Forest and past the **Little Pend Oreille Wildlife Area.** Leo, Thomas, Gillette, and Twin Lakes all have campsites with lakeshore access. The **Springboard Trail** from East Gillette Campground offers an easy 2⁄10-mile loop with interpretive highlights on the area's history and ecology as well as a platform with a view of the lakes.

Beaver Lodge Resort (509–684–5657; www.beaverlodgeresort.com), situated on Lake Gillette at the 3,200-foot level 25 miles east of Colville, has miles of hiking, cross-country ski, and snowmobile trails nearby. The lodge features rustic wood cabins at the lake's edge, RV hookups, forested or lakeside campsites, laundry, swimming, boat rentals, a grocery store, and a cozy cafe over-looking the lake.

The pine forest begins to thin as you continue winding west on Highway 20 and descend into the pastoral Colville River Valley. *Colville* is a large, bustling town at the junction of Highway 20 and US 395. In town follow signs from the highway (Fifth Street) leading 2 blocks uphill on Wynne Street to reach the *Keller Heritage Center* and *Stevens County Historical Museum* (509–684–5968). A trail leads up from the museum to the Graves Mountain Fire Lookout at the top of a small hill, where you can enjoy a panoramic view of the valley, town, and mountains. Keller House Museum tells the area's story in chronological order from geological, Native American, and European perspectives. The museum is open June through September from 10:00 A.M. to 4:00 P.M. and on Sunday from 1:00 to 4:00 P.M.

If you've worked up an appetite during your travels, you'll find several pleasant restaurants in Colville. Try *Cafe Italiano* at 153 West Second Avenue (509–684–5957) for tasty Italian dinners; *Rancho Chico* at 151 North Main Street (509–684–4819) for Mexican fare; *Ronnie Dee's Drive-In* at 505 North Lincoln (509–684–2642) for good burgers; and one of the locals' favorites, *Café Al Mundo* at First and Main (509–684–8092) for eclectic Northwest fare.

If you're heading north from Colville toward the Canadian border and southern British Columbia, try *Whitebird Saloon & Eatery* in Northport (509–732–6638) for tasty backcountry-style grub. Wear jeans, even suspenders, and go casual.

For a fun adventure, you can drive 38 miles north of Colville into the Colville National Forest past the hamlets of Aladdin and Spirit, then continue past Northport and Deep Lake for another 8 miles. But first call and arrange to stay with Joann Bender, novelist, and Bud Budinger, geotechnical engineer, at *Lazy Bee Wilderness Retreat,* located at 3651 Deep Lake Boundary Road (509–732–8917). You're deep into the forests of pine, cedar, Douglas fir, larch, and birch and at a crisp elevation of 2,000 feet. And you're also about 4 miles from the U.S.–Canadian border crossing at the town of Boundary. The couple offers two comfy suites with shared bath, a floor-to-ceiling library in the cozy common area, eight log-burning fireplaces, and delicious breakfasts along with quantities of solitude and relaxation. Inquire about meal options and costs.

The original site of Kettle Falls is believed to be one of the oldest continuously occupied spots in the Northwest. As long as 9,000 years ago, an ancient tribe known as the Shonitkwa fished the steep falls. Over the centuries Indians established permanent communities near the falls that existed until European settlement eroded traditional lifestyles. The actual falls and historic sites are now submerged under Lake Roosevelt. During the early spring drawdown in March or April, remnants of flooded islands and historic towns like **Old Marcus** (located about 5 miles north on Highway 25) are revealed.

You can learn more about the "People of the Falls" at the impressive **Kettle Falls Historical Center,** 1188 St. Paul's Mission Road (509–738–6964), on a spur road north of Highway 20 and 3 miles west of Kettle Falls, just before the bridge over Lake Roosevelt. The center features murals and models for each season of the year, telling the ancient story of tribal life near the falls. The exhibit and gift shop of local artwork are open from 11:00 A.M. to 5:00 P.M. Wednesday through Sunday, from May 15 through September 15.

Many family-owned farms and fruit orchards in the area offer berries, cherries, apricots, peaches, pears, apples, and grapes in season from June through September. Look for signs along nearby Peach Crest Road. Contact Kettle Falls Chamber of Commerce (509–738–2300; www.kettlefalls.org) for more information and an orchard directory and map of more than a dozen fruit-picking spots.

In late August you can take in the annual **Garlic Faire** at **China Bend Vineyards & Winery,** located about 23 miles north of Kettle Falls at 3596 Northport Flat Road (800–700–6123; www.chinabend.com). From roasted garlic and garlic corn to garlic soup and pizza, garlic lovers indulge in a festive day of tasting and buying garlic products. The winery produces delicious table and dessert wines that don't contain sulfites and also offers freshly made organic products such as salsa, pickled garlic, dilly beans, and a selection of tasty fruit preserves.

If you are traveling in winter when Lake Roosevelt is at its fullest, you'll find the best bald eagle viewing area around along Highway 25. Take the turnoff south before Kettle Falls Bridge and head toward the Gifford Ferry. The concentration of eagles reaches a peak in mid-February, when the striking white and black adults and mottled brown and white juveniles perch on top of gnarled snags and rocky outcroppings at the water's edge while on the lookout for fresh fish.

If the high desert, rolling hills, and pine forests beckon you to stay another night, you could call ahead to **River Bluff Log House** (509–722–3784; www.theriverbluff.com) near **Inchelium.** Inquire about the self-contained log cabin with wraparound deck and nonstop views of Lake Roosevelt on this northern section of the Columbia River. These breathtaking views fill the soul, and stresses melt away. Take the toll-free ferry at Gifford across the lake to Inchelium. For more stress-reducing scenery, the kind that even the locals don't tire of, from Inchelium take the county road heading west for about 35 miles past Twin Lakes to Highway 21. If you're tent camping, traveling by RV, or want a lakeside cabin, contact **Rainbow Beach Resort,** located on Twin Lakes

Life on a Cattle Ranch, Northeastern Washington Style

It's early morning and you squint at the bright yellow eastern horizon. The leather saddle creaks as you guide your horse along the stream toward the herd. You learn that the seasons come and go in a regular rhythm on a cattle ranch. The list of chores commands attention. Ranch life here is firmly anchored to the high desert, pine and fir forests, mountain ranges, and to the rivers and streams. Times for fun and frivolity come when the chores are done. Although we're not talking a rerun of *City Slickers* here, many ranch families now welcome travelers who seek a hearty dose of western hospitality and who hanker to sit astride a horse for a few days. Squinting at sunrises or gazing at sunsets or riding along a stream or meadow with friendly ranch hands is a good thing. Check out this host of seasonal chores and activities from the K-Diamond-K Guest Ranch located near Republic:

January—Winter feeding, snowmobile rides

February—New calves born

March—More calves, timber harvest

April—Branding calves, fishing

May—Spring roundups, barn dance

June—Rodeo and barn dance, Prospector Days

July—Rodeo and barn dance, draft horse show

August—Hay harvest, fiddle contest

September—County fair

October—Fall roundups, hunting

November—Calves weaned, timber harvest

December—Winter feeding

(509–722–5901). Call well ahead for reservations—it's a popular spot during summer months. For a quiet retreat on Twin Lakes try **Hartman's Log Cabin Resort** (509–722–3543), with cozy lakeshore cabins and a homey family-style restaurant. After crossing the Kettle River Range and intersecting with Highway 21, head north along the picturesque Sanpoil River for about 30 miles to the community of **Republic.** You can also reach Republic from Kettle Falls by continuing west on Highway 20, the **Sherman Pass Scenic Byway,** winding up and over 5,575-foot Sherman Pass.

If you've ever hankered for wide-open spaces, western hospitality, and delicious family-style meals at a guest ranch, contact the Konz family at **K-Diamond-K Guest Ranch,** located just south of Republic on the Sanpoil River at 15661 Highway 21 South (888–345–5355; www.kdiamondk.com). The family offers four spacious guest rooms in the large log-style home and offers a host of activities from horseback riding, mountain biking, and fishing to bird- and wildlife watching, stargazing, hunting, and winter snowmobiling and cross-country skiing. If you like, you could even go along on a seasonal cattle drive astride your steady steed. Autumn is one of the most memorable seasons on the ranch, with vibrant fall colors, warm days, crisp evenings, and night skies jam-packed with glittering stars.

A loop around **Curlew Lake** to the north makes a pleasant bike ride or drive. The 7-mile-long lake is surrounded by mountains and rolling hills. Some early log cabins are still visible in the area. **Curlew Lake State Park** offers lakeside picnic sites, a swimming area, boat launches, and campsites. Several small resorts are scattered along the lakeshore. **Fisherman's Cove Resort** at 1157 Fisherman's Cove Road near Republic (509–775–3641) welcomes families and offers rustic cabins in a quiet, lakeside setting. **Tiffany's Resort** at 1026 Tiffany Road (509–775–3152) on the opposite shore offers comparable amenities.

The Kettle River History Club's **Car and Truck Museum** is located at 1865 North Highway 21 (509–779–4808) between the towns of Malo and Curlew. This is an old-car aficionado's dream: dozens of carefully preserved and restored cars, including vintage Model T Fords, Buicks, actor Walter Brennan's 1928 Phaeton, the only 1917 Chevrolet Royal Mail Roadster still running, and one of the only three 1920 Howard Cooper fire trucks ever made, all in operating condition. The museum is open from 10:00 A.M. to 5:00 P.M. daily in summer.

The quiet town of **Curlew** is nestled between dry hills on the east bank of the Kettle River. Follow signs to the right off the highway, then left and right again into town. Curlew's main street, lined with dark-wood buildings with western false fronts, overlooks the river through tall cottonwoods. The old **Ansorge Hotel Museum** on River Street (509–779–4808) no longer provides food or lodging, but you can tour the building, which is complete with period furnishings and clothing from its heyday in the early 1900s. It's open weekends from mid-May to the end of September, 1:00 to 5:00 P.M. The **Curlew Riverside Cafe** (813 River Street; 509–779–4813) offers Mexican and American food prepared from fresh ingredients. The dining room, with its wood-burning stove, fans, and rustic wood furniture, overlooks the Kettle River. Dinner is served from 4:00 to 9:00 P.M. Wednesday through Sunday and on weekends during the winter and early spring.

On your way back south on Highway 21 toward Republic, take the West Curlew Lake Road turnoff to your right (west) at Curlew Lake's north end for a less-traveled route along the lake's western shore. Klondike Road veers right about a mile south of the lake and then descends past pine trees and houses hugging the steep hillside into Republic.

Clark Avenue, the town's main street, was named for Republic Gold Mining and Milling Company president "Patsy" Clark. While most buildings' false fronts are recent additions to boost the town's already rustic feel, the **Republic Drug Store** (ca. 1906), on the corner of Clark and Fourth Avenues, boasts an original storefront with hand-cranked awnings and pressed tin ceiling. At the north end of town, you'll pass a lovely stone Episcopal church, built in 1909, whose windows shimmer with stained-glass doves.

Kettle River History Club's Car and Truck Museum

To participate in a paleontological treasure hunt, follow Sixth Avenue west a block onto Kean Street across from Patterson Park to the **Stonerose Interpretive Center** at 15 Kean Street (509–775–2295), open May through October, Tuesday through Saturday from 10:00 A.M. to 5:00 P.M.; from June 14 through September 13, it's open Sunday 10:00 A.M. to 4:00 P.M. There, the curator and assistants can introduce you to the fascinating world of fifty million years ago, when an ancient lake covered the town site of Republic. Fossil-hunting tours are permitted during the hours the center is open. Bring along a hammer and chisel, or rent some there, to use at the dig site north of town. The fossils you discover will be identified for you to take home, or, if you are lucky enough to find a new or rare species, you will be applauded as a paleontological hero, and your fossil will be kept for further study.

For tasty eats in the Republic area, try **Hometown Pizza** at 18 North Clark Street (509–775–2557) for good pizza and salad bar; **Esther's Mexican Restaurant** at 90 North Clark Street (509–775–2088) for super burritos, shredded beef taco salads, and homebaked pies; and **Mel's Diner** at 30277 Highway 20 (509–775–0830). For coffees, espresso, and homemade pastries, stop by **Java Joy's Espresso** in Republic at 1015 South Clark Street (509–775–2025) and **River Street Espresso** in Curlew at 9 River Street (509–779–4937).

Places to Stay in Northeast Washington

COLVILLE/KETTLE FALLS

Beaver Lodge Resort
2430 Highway 20 East
Colville
(509) 684–5657

Lake Roosevelt Houseboat Vacations
Kettle Falls
(509) 738–6121
www.lakeroosevelt.com

Lazy Bee Wilderness Retreat
3651 Deep Lake Boundary Road
Colville
(509) 732–8917

COULEE CITY

Coulee Lodge Resort
33017 Park Lake Road NE
(509) 632–5565

COULEE DAM

Columbia River Inn
10 Lincoln Street
(800) 633–6421

ELECTRIC CITY

Sky Deck Motel
South Highway 155,
Cadillac Drive
(509) 633–0290

Sunbanks RV Resort & Marina
Banks Lake,
South Highway 155
(509) 633–3786

INCHELIUM

Hartman's Log Cabin Resort
South Twin Lake
(509) 722–3543

METALINE FALLS

Washington Hotel
225 East Fifth Avenue
(509) 446–4415

REPUBLIC/CURLEW

Fisherman's Cove Resort
1157 Fisherman's Cove Road
Republic
(509) 775–3641

K-Diamond-K Guest Ranch
404 Highway 21 South
Republic
(509) 775–3536

Northern Motor Inn
852 South Clark Street
Republic
(888) 801–1068

Wolfgang's Riverview Inn
2320 Highway 21 North
Curlew
(509) 779–4252

SOAP LAKE

Notaras Lodge
13 Canna Street
(509) 246–0462

SPOKANE

Marianna Stoltz House Bed & Breakfast
427 East Indiana Avenue
(509) 483–4316

Red Lion River Inn
700 North Division
(509) 326–5577

Waverly Place Bed & Breakfast
709 West Waverly Place
(509) 328–1856

HELPFUL WEB SITES IN NORTHEAST WASHINGTON

Experience Spokane
www.visitspokane.com

Grand Coulee Dam area
www.grandcouleedam.org

Kettle Range Conservation Group
www.kettlerange.org

Republic–Curlew area
www.ferrycountry.com

Washington State Parks
www.parks.wa.gov

SELECTED VISITOR INFORMATION CENTERS

Colville Visitor Information Center
(509) 684–5973
www.colville.com

Grand Coulee Dam Area Visitor Information Center
306 Midway
Grand Coulee
(800) 268–5332, (509) 633–3074

Kettle Falls Visitor Information Center
(509) 738–2300
www.kettlefalls.org

Newport Visitor Information Center
(509) 447–5812
www.newportoldtownchamber.com

Republic Area Visitor Information Center
15 North Kean Street
(509) 775–3387
www.ferrycounty.com

Spokane Area Convention & Visitors Bureau
801 West Riverside, Suite 301
(509) 747–3230, (888) 776–5263

VALLEY

Silver Beach Resort
3323 Waitts Lake Road
(509) 937–2811

Places to Eat in Northeast Washington

COLVILLE/KETTLE FALLS

Café al Mundo
100 South Main Street
Colville
(509) 684–8092

Little Gallea Cafe
345 West Third Street
Kettle Falls
(509) 738–6776

Sandy's Drive-In Cafe
1053 Highway 395 North
Kettle Falls
(509) 738–6444

Whitebird Saloon & Eatery
Northport
(509) 732–6638

COULEE CITY

Fuller's Dry Falls Cafe
Junction of Highways 2 and 17
(509) 632–5634

The New Crossing Restaurant
502 West Main Street
(509) 632–5677

Steamboat Rock Restaurant
420 West Main Street
(509) 632–5452

DAVENPORT

Edna's Drive In
302 Morgan
(509) 725–1071

GRAND COULEE

Flo's Cafe
316 Spokane Way
(509) 633–3216

Sandwich Gardens & Pizza
211 Main Street
(509) 633–3367

Melody's Restaurant & Lounge
512 River Drive
Coulee Dam
(509) 633–1151

METALINE FALLS

Cathy's Cafe
221 East Fifth Avenue
(509) 446–2447

Western Star Restaurant
202 North Highway 31
(509) 446–2105

NEWPORT

Diamond Shores Lodge Restaurant
South Shore Diamond Lake Road
(509) 447–5133

REPUBLIC/CURLEW

Curlew Riverside Restaurant
813 River Street
Curlew
(509) 779–4813

Ike's Merchantile Cafe
15 North Clark Street
Republic
(509) 775–2846

Java Joy's Espresso
1015 South Clark Street
Republic
(509) 775–2025

SOAP LAKE

Don's Restaurant
14 Canna Street
(509) 246–1217

SPOKANE

High Noon Gourmet Sandwiches
237 West Riverside
(509) 838–5288

The Onion Family Restaurant
302 West Riverside
(509) 747–3852

The Shop Coffeehouse
924 South Perry Street
(509) 534–1647

Steam Plant Grill
159 South Lincoln Street
(509) 777–3900

VALLEY

Silver Beach Resort Restaurant
3323 Waitts Lake Road
(509) 937–2811

WILBUR

Alibi Tavern
4 Southwest Main Street
(509) 647–2649

ALSO WORTH SEEING

Discovery Loop
Curlew–Republic

Highland Heritage Loop
Curlew

Selkirk International Loop
North Pend Oreille County

Sherman Pass Scenic Byway
Kettle Falls

Southeast Washington

Southeast Washington is a region of rolling hills and wide blue skies. Much of the terrain is covered with waving fields of dryland (unirrigated) wheat, offering endless variations of shapes, textures, and colors. The best way to explore this area is to get off the major highways and drive or bicycle along endless miles of farm roads that connect the area's small communities. Walking, bicycling, or sitting in a grassy park or meadow, you often will hear the melodious trill of a western meadowlark, catch sight of a soaring hawk, and smell the soil warmed in the sun.

Few corners of this fertile region have been left untouched by human enterprise, although the seasonal crops still depend on natural cycles of snow, rain, and sun. Hundreds of acres burst with new green shoots following spring rains or undulate with tall and golden grains in the late summer sun. The lives of farm and ranch families are integrated with their land and the seasons. In early spring, huge eight-wheel-drive tractors comb the terrain for planting, pulling 20-foot-wide plows that raise spires of dust. In late summer, giant combines range in straight or curved rows to harvest wheat, lentils, and peas. Farmhouses and big old barns nestle in valleys surrounded by tall shade trees planted by previous generations.

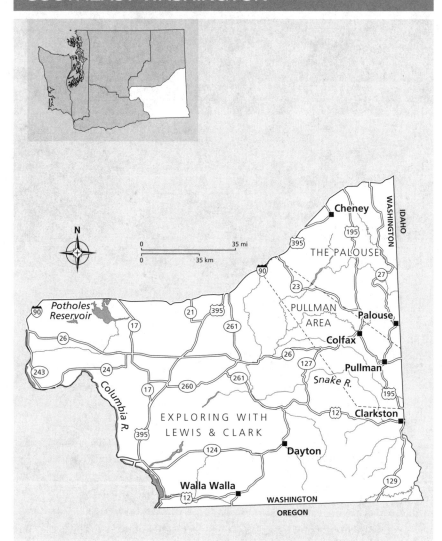

The quiet towns of this region, devoted to serving the hardworking farm families, also welcome travelers. Walking down any main street, you'll see old brick buildings that once housed banks, stores, and fraternal organizations, many now in the process of being renovated for new enterprises such as coffeehouses, bakeries, cafes, and tasting rooms for the many new wineries in the region. Tall grain elevators stand like sentinals next to rail depots. Many deserted rail depots throughout the region and the state have been, or are in the process of being, preserved and are coming to life again as local history museums and vibrant community art centers.

Stop at the local cafe (many towns have only one), where for the price of a cup of coffee and a piece of homemade pie you might hear stories of local history and gossip from fellow patrons eager to swap tales. The town cemetery, usually located on a nearby hilltop, is also a good place to learn about the community's past.

SOUTHEAST WASHINGTON'S TOP HITS

Appaloosa Museum & Heritage Center
Moscow, Idaho

The Bank Left Gallery and Green Frog Cafe
Palouse

Bishop's U-Pick Orchard
Garfield

Dayton Depot
Dayton

Ferdinand's Ice Cream Shoppe
Washington State University
Pullman

Fort Walla Walla Museum Complex
Walla Walla

Heritage Square
Walla Walla

Holland and Terrell Libraries
Washington State University
Pullman

The Little Theatre of Walla Walla
Walla Walla

McCann Manor Bed and Breakfast
Dayton

Perkins House
Pullman

Premier Alpacas Ranch & Guest House
Uniontown

Ray Chatters Newspaper and Printing Museum
Palouse

Three Forks Pioneer Village Museum
Pullman

Turnbull National Wildlife Refuge
Cheney

Weinhard Hotel
Dayton

Whitman Mission National Historic Site
Walla Walla

The Palouse

Palouse is derived from the French word *pelouse,* meaning "green lawn," an appropriate name for one of the most fertile grain-growing regions in the world. The Appaloosa, a breed of horses distinguished by its spotted coat and gentle disposition, is a descendant of early horses used by the Native people of the Palouse.

Although most of this region is now farmed, there are still areas where the original Palouse environment is preserved. Chief of these is the **Turnbull National Wildlife Refuge** located at South 26010 Smith Road (509–235–4723; www.fws.gov/turnbull) south of Spokane on the Cheney–Plaza Road. The 16,000-acre refuge includes miles of lakes and marshes that attract a wide variety of wildlife including elk, deer, coyotes, beaver, and muskrat. More than 50,000 ducks, geese, and other migratory birds cruise in for rest stops along the Pacific Flyway. Generations before pioneers arrived, the Spokane tribe cherished this natural garden for its abundant roots and herbs, such as blue camas, wild onion, and kinnikinnick.

Early farmers tried to drain these marsh areas but found the soil poor. Rescued from development in the 1920s, the area was set aside as a wildlife preserve in 1937. Now visitors to Turnbull can bicycle, walk, or drive on a 5-mile gravel loop road to experience the area's original beauty. Signs along the Pine Creek Trail help acquaint you with the area's background and natural history. A wooden boardwalk over shallow Black Horse Lake allows close-up viewing.

Heading south on Rock Lake Road, watch the landscape change from rocky pine-covered meadows to rolling wheat farms. The terrain changes again around **Rock Lake,** a quiet expanse of water surrounded by basalt outcroppings. This

Appaloosa Horse Museum

For a closer look at the history surrounding the Palouse's namesake horse, head east from Pullman on Highway 270 to the Appaloosa Museum & Heritage Center (2720 West Pullman Road; 208–882–5578; www.appaloosa.com). Straddling the state line but technically in Moscow, Idaho, the museum explores the Nez Percé and Palouse Tribes' connection with the breed with exhibits of Native American artifacts. Other exhibits explore the Appaloosa's Asian and European roots, and there's a saddle collection, western art, and western tack and clothing on display. During the summer, you can see the horses in their fenced pasture. The museum is open Monday through Friday from 10:00 A.M. to 5:00 P.M. year-round, and on summer Saturdays from 10:00 A.M. to 4:00 P.M.

FAVORITE ATTRACTIONS

**Appaloosa Museum & Heritage
Center**
Moscow, Idaho

Dayton Depot
Dayton

Fort Walla Walla Museum Complex

The Little Theatre of Walla Walla
Walla Walla

Palouse Falls
Starbuck

Pullman Civic Theatre
Pullman

Steptoe Butte
Colfax

**Whitman Mission National
Historic Site**
Walla Walla

area was the home of Chief Kamiaken of the Yakama Indian Nation. Along the lake's southeast shore, you can see the *Milwaukee Road Corridor,* a railroad line until 1980, now converted to a public trail. This trail system, known as the *Iron Horse Trail State Park* (www.parks.wa.gov) west of the Columbia River, stretches from King County near Seattle across the Cascade Mountains and east to the Idaho border. The popular trail is used by hikers, bicyclists, equestrians, and even wagon trains.

After traveling through the rolling hills of the Palouse, you can also enjoy seeing the region from two towering buttes that offer panoramic views of the quilted landscape. *Kamiak Butte County Park,* named for Chief Kamiaken, is a 3,360-foot-tall island of pine, fir, and larch surrounded by wheat fields. The butte is 5 miles southeast of the town of Palouse near the Idaho border. The 3½-mile Pine Ridge Trail through the forest takes you on a self-guided nature walk to the top of the butte and back. The park has nine campsites, with campfire pits and cooking grills. Water is available May through October, but there are no RV hookups or showers. Picnic tables and three shelters with electricity, water, and barbecue make this a great spot for an impromptu outdoor feast. There is also an amphitheater for evening programs on local and natural history presented by volunteers from late June through August. For current information contact Whitman County Parks in Colfax, (509) 397–6238; www.whitman county.org.

Steptoe Butte, 15 miles north of Colfax, is, at 3,612 feet, the highest point in the region and a National Natural Landmark. Drive the road that spirals four times around the butte to the top to enjoy panoramic views of the Palouse's rolling fields and low hills as well as the distant Blue Mountains and Bitterroot Mountains. At the base you'll find a pleasant picnic area in an old apple orchard

Palouse fields

planted by one of the area's early homesteaders. In the 1880s another early entrepreneur operated a roadhouse at the bottom of the butte and a hotel at the top, which burned down in 1896.

Oakesdale, located a few miles north of Steptoe Butte, is home to *Barron's Flour Mill,* a huge timber-frame structure, which was moved piece by piece from Illinois in 1889, and which still contains the original milling and sifting equipment. The mill was used to produce flour until 1939 and continued as a grain cleaning and storage facility until the 1960s. You can stop to take a gander at the historic structure by parking off Highway 271 as you enter Oakesdale. *For a Song Cafe* (509–285–4606) offers good eats Tuesday through Friday from 10:00 A.M. to 4:00 P.M.

Travel northeast on Highway 27 from Oakesdale to reach the village of *Tekoa,* population 826. You could pause here for a bite to eat at *The Feeding Station,* 205 North Crosby Street (509–284–3144), which opens most days at 7:00 A.M.

Located south of Tekoa in *Garfield* (population 641), the *R.C. McCroskey House* at 803 North Fourth Street (509–635–1459) is a classical revival–style Victorian mansion constructed in 1898. Owner Donna Gwinn has restored the historic home to its original grandeur. Call ahead to inquire if tours are currently offered.

Bishop's U-Pick Orchard (509–635–1276; www.bishop-orchard.com), in Garfield at Eighth and Adams Streets (follow Spokane Street west past Garfield's city park), offers a wealth of apples from mid-September through the end of October. People come from miles around to make their own fresh juice on Steven Bishop's four handmade oak cider presses, patterned after the ones his great-grandfather used when he homesteaded in Garfield. The Garfield Grocery offers snacks and espresso drinks, and the *Grace Cafe* on California and Second offers gourmet fare Tuesday to Sunday from 6:00 A.M. to 10:00 P.M.

South of Garfield is the town of **Palouse,** once a bustling commercial center supplying gold-mining and logging camps in Idaho. The town's main street is lined with splendid old brick buildings, many now in the process of being renovated. Palouse's Main Street historic district is listed on the National Register of Historic Places. One old storefront now houses **Ray Chatters Newspaper and Printing Museum,** a half block east of the town's only streetlight at 110 East Main Street. The museum features newspapers from the area as well as an impressive collection of old presses and other printing equipment dating from the late 1800s. Call Janet Barstow at (509) 878–1742 or Jack Rupe at (208) 882–3771 for current hours.

Stop in at 110 South Bridge Street in the ca. 1889 Bank Building in Palouse to visit **The Bank Left Gallery** and **Green Frog Cafe** (509–878–1490), a favorite gathering place for locals.

You can browse at **Small Town Quilts** at 124 East Main Street; at **Open Eye Antiques** (509–878–1210) at 119 East Main Street for retro and country antiques and collectibles; at the **Potpourri & Linda's Whimseys** at 100 East Main Street (509–878–1678) for a splendid selection of Victorian gift items; and then pop into nearby **Saint Elmo's Antiques** to see more antiques and collectibles. Cap off your tour of Palouse by stopping at **The Family Cafe,** 124 West Main Street, for a tasty lunch or dinner (breakfast is served all day as well); it's open daily except Monday and Tuesday. *Note:* The best days to visit small

Bagels, English Muffins, Lentil or Split Pea Soup, Anyone?

In the morning I love a toasted bagel or English muffin with crunchy peanut butter topped with sprinkles of cinnamon and sugar. I also love steaming hot lentil or split pea soup for lunch. The ingredients for these tasty foods—wheat, lentils, and peas—are major crops grown in the Palouse region. After harvest they are barged about 200 miles down the Snake River from the Clarkston-Lewiston area to Pasco, passing through the scenic 2,000-foot-deep Snake River Canyon and negotiating through locks at Lower Granite Dam, Little Goose Dam, Lower Monumental Dam, and Ice Harbor Dam. At Pasco the large barges, pushed by fat tugboats, then enter the wide Columbia River and travel another 200 miles downriver, passing The Dalles, Maryhill, Hood River, Cascade Locks, North Bonneville, Washougal, and Camas and detouring onto the Willamette River at Portland-Vancouver. Here the wheat, lentils, and peas are loaded onto huge transport ships at the port of Portland. These vessels travel another 100 miles downriver on the Columbia River to Astoria and then out onto the Pacific Ocean for journeys to ports far and wide. Bagels, English muffins, lentil or split pea soup, anyone?

towns in the Palouse area are Wednesday through Saturday, when most establishments are open.

Pullman Area

Pullman is the Palouse region's largest city and a bustling mixture of agricultural businesses and student life. It is home to Washington State University (WSU, affectionately called *Wazzu*), founded in 1890 and which emphasizes agricultural sciences. Contact the Pullman Visitor Information Center (800–365–6948; www.pullmanchamber.com) for the current football schedule and to inquire about lodgings and about tours of the scenic campus and its historic buildings.

WSU has a splendid ***Museum of Anthropology*** featuring displays on human evolution and on the development of language and culture—and on the Northwest's mysterious Sasquatch. The museum is open weekdays during the school year (Monday to Thursday from 9:00 A.M. to 4:00 P.M., Friday from 9:00 A.M. to 3:00 P.M.). Art lovers can enjoy the University's ***Museum of Art,*** in the Fine Arts Center at the corner of Stadium Way and Farm Way. The gallery offers eleven changing exhibitions a year, featuring past and contemporary international, regional, and student artists working in painting, sculpture, photography, and architecture. The gallery is open daily from 10:00 A.M. to 4:00 P.M. and on Thursday until 9:00 P.M. ***Holland and Terrell Libraries*** (www.wsulibs .wsu.edu) on the campus house a number of historical collections; call instruction librarian Corey Johnson (509–335–8628) to inquire about a tour of the library.

After you've worked up an appetite from museum touring, you'll want to stop at ***Ferdinand's Ice Cream Shoppe*** (509–335–2141), a WSU campus ice-cream parlor named after the friendly, flower-sniffing bull. On the walls are quotations by author Munro Leaf and illustrations by Robert Lawson from the classic book about Ferdinand, which has been beloved by generations of children. Ferdinand's sells WSU's own Cougar brand of high-quality dairy products (such as the award-winning Cougar Gold cheese), produced by the Departments of Food Science and Human Nutrition of the College of Agriculture and Home Economics. Ferdinand's is located at 101 Food Quality Building, east of the Stadium Way tennis courts. Its hours are 9:30 A.M. to 4:30 P.M. weekdays and on football weekends.

For a step back in time to the Old West, visit the ***Three Forks Pioneer Village Museum,*** located about 4 miles north of Pullman. This re-created town, assembled during the past three decades by farmer Roger Rossebo, has a general store, barber shop, blacksmith's shop, jail, and hardware store, displaying

Stay and Play in a College Town

Although it's a busy college town servicing Washington State University and its thousands of Cougar fans, Pullman offers a variety of pleasant reasons for lingering in your travels to the far southeast corner of the state. Take an invigorating walk in a splendid city park or along a rails-to-trails pathway, stroll in a lovely garden, play a round of golf, put together an impromptu picnic, or stop at a friendly cafe.

Reaney Park, off Gray Lane and Lentil Lane, is home of the *Reaney Park Summer Concert Series* (800–365–6948) and also hosts the National Lentil Festival in late August. Find outdoor pools, a gazebo, playground area, picnic tables, and barbecue area. *Sunnyside Park,* located on Cedar Street, is home to Pullman's yearly Fourth of July community celebration. The twenty-five-acre park offers tennis courts, Frisbee, a golf course, walking trails, a baseball diamond, city garden plots, and a picnic and barbecue shelter that overlooks two ponds and a waterfall.

Lawson Gardens, located at Derby Street near Dilke Street, offers thirteen acres of formal gardens including a reflecting pool, gazebo, seasonal annuals and perennials, and splendid rose gardens.

The Bill Chipman Palouse Trail, reclaimed from a former railroad bed near the Pullman-Moscow Highway (State Route 270), offers 7 miles of bicycle- and pedestrian-friendly trails between Pullman and Moscow, Idaho, the home of the University of Idaho.

In downtown Pullman you can find a jolt of java, tasty sandwiches, decadent baked goods, and local conversation at *Swilly's* (200 NE Kamiaken Street; 509–334–3395), *Café Moro Coffee Shop* (100 A East Main Street; 509–338–3892), and *Daily Grind Downtown Coffee House* (230 East Main Street; 509–334–3380). *Caution:* If the notion of enduring pep rallies, marching bands, and being trampled by some 40,000 WSU Cougar sports fans doesn't appeal, plan your trips to the Pullman area on weekends sans football. Also best to avoid Dad's Weekend and Mom's Weekend. Check www.pullmanchamber.com (800–365–6948) and www.football-weekends.wsu.edu for current schedules and information.

thousands of antiques dating from the 1800s, including a piano shipped around Cape Horn, a pioneer kitchen, and a schoolhouse. The museum is open by appointment from May to September. There is a small fee. Call (509) 332–3889 for reservations and directions.

In *Colfax,* the Whitman County seat along the banks of the Palouse River, you could stop to see the splendid *Perkins House* at 623 North Perkins Street. The ca. 1884 mansion listed on the National Register of Historic Places was built by city founder James Perkins, who established his fortune by constructing the region's first sawmill. It is open for tours from 1:00 to 5:00 P.M. Thursday and Sunday, from June to September. An old-fashioned ice-cream social is held at

TOP ANNUAL EVENTS IN SOUTHEAST WASHINGTON

Autumn Harvest Hullabaloo & Arts and Antiques Fair
Colfax, mid-October
(509) 397–3712

Dogwood Festival
Clarkston, throughout April
(800) 933–2128

Balloon Stampede
Walla Walla, early May
(877) 998–4748

Asotin County Fair
Asotin, April
(509) 243–4411

Dayton Days
Dayton, late May
(800) 882–6299

Slippery Gulch Days & Rodeo
Tekoa, late June
(509) 284–3861

Sweet Onion Festival
Walla Walla, mid-July
(509) 525–0850

National Lentil Festival
Pullman, mid-August
(800) 365–6948

The Sun Festival
Clarkston, August
(800) 933–2128

Dayton Depot Festival
Dayton, mid-September
(800) 882–6299

the mansion the last Sunday in June. For current information contact the Colfax Visitor Information Center at (509) 397–3712.

The most unusual attraction in Colfax is the **Codger Pole,** the world's largest chain-saw carving at 65 feet. The pole commemorates a grudge match played between the Colfax football team and its St. John rivals wherein Colfax attained the victory that was snatched from it a quarter of a century earlier. The likenesses of the team members are carved on the pole, which occupies a prominent spot on John Crawford Boulevard, just off Main Street. Meet local folks at **Top Notch Cafe,** 210 North Main Street (509–397–4569).

To bed down in the ponderosa pine and farm country near Colfax, call the Gilchrest family at **Union Creek Guest Ranch,** located a few miles southwest via U.S. Highway 195 at 2501 Upper Union Flat Road (509–397–3292; www .unioncreekranch.com). Guests are welcomed to this 2,200-acre ranch in the pines. Eight guest rooms in the main ranch house share three full baths. You will find a one-acre fishing pond stocked with rainbow trout, a gaggle of small farm animals, and stalls for your horses. The family grows winter and spring wheat and barley, and they also grow the famous peas that come from this section of Washington State. Penny Gilchrest serves a hearty country breakfast of bacon, ham, eggs, and hash browns along with fresh fruit, juices, homemade cinnamon rolls, and often, her delicious apple crisp tortillas.

If you are traveling farther south via US 195 toward Uniontown, you can check with Leslee and Dale Miller at ***Premier Alpacas Ranch & Guest House*** (401 South Railroad Avenue; 509–229–3655; www.premieralpacas.com). The remodeled guest bunkhouse contains sleeping quarters for four, with cozy quilts and comforters, and comes with a spiral staircase to the sleeping loft, a snack kitchen, a sofa bed on the main level, and a cheery woodstove. The couple raises alpacas, smaller cousins to the taller llama. "The alpacas stand about 36 inches in height and come in twenty-two different colors," says Leslee. This is a place to relax into farm and ranch time. An indoor lap pool, located in a sunroom at the main house, is available for guests to use to work out the kinks. Guests are served a generous ranch breakfast of, perhaps, oven-baked French toast with Gran Marnier sauce or a frittata made with fresh farm eggs, spinach, potatoes, roasted red peppers, and Parmesan cheese.

Another splendid option in Uniontown is to contact the innkeepers at the ***Churchyard Inn Bed & Breakfast*** (206 St. Boniface Street; 509–229–3200; www.churchyardinn.com). Guests find comfy bed-and-breakfast accommodations in the European Flemish–style convent (ca. 1905) that once housed a group of Catholic nuns. The house and its interior were completely renovated, including the fine hand-detailed woodwork, moldings, and doors of red fir, the impressive staircases and spacious hallways, and the seven bedrooms and several balconies. The inn is located next to historic Saint Boniface Catholic Church (ca. 1904), one of the first such churches in the region.

Country-Western Music and Eastern Washington Go Together

While driving the highways and byways of the eastern section of the state, you'll most likely hear country-western singers and their tunes when you click on the radio and cruise the stations. It comes with the territory. Here are some favorite titles:

"Easy on the Eyes, Hard on the Heart"

"Let's Take It One Step at a Time"

"My Heart Has a History of Lettin' Go"

"I'm Old Enough to Know Better but Still Too Young to Care"

"All My Exes Live in Texas"

"Love Gets me Every Time"

"Prop Me Up Beside the Juke Box When I Die"

The first Sunday in March brings the annual benefit **Sausage Feed** (since 1948 the men of **Uniontown** have made sausage from a renowned secret recipe). An old-fashioned **Threshing Bee** takes place in early September. Public golf links are located in nearby Lewiston and in Clarkston. Linger and watch local artists at work at **Artisans at the Dahmen Barn** in the nearby historic barn, Thursday through Saturday from 10:00 A.M. to 6:00 P.M. For good eats in Uniontown, ask about **Eleanor's Place,** a local saloon on Main Street (509–229–3389) that offers a good selection of microbrews and is reported to serve the best hamburgers on the Palouse. Also, be sure to stop at the splendid **Sage Baking Company** on Main Street in Uniontown, which offers crusty rustic breads as well as tasty pastries, coffee drinks, and deli fare on Friady and Saturday, 7:00 A.M. to 3:00 P.M. Snoop into several antiques shops on Main Street, including **Spendid Old Stuff, Deluxe Used Goods, Littlefield Antiques,** and **Green Cottage Antiques.**

Exploring with Lewis and Clark

South of Pullman at the confluence of the Snake and Clearwater Rivers, you can visit **Clarkston** and, across the Snake River, **Lewiston,** Idaho. These twin cities are the embarking point for adventures at Hells Gate State Park, the Nez Percé Reservation, and boat or raft tours through Hells Canyon, the deepest river gorge in North America. Contact the Clarkston Visitor Information Center, 502 Bridge Street, (800) 933–2128 or (509) 758–7712 for information on river trips, bike and walking paths, and lodgings.

Captain William Clark, Meriwether Lewis, and their original Corps of Discovery, numbering more than thirty, including Clark's Newfoundland dog, Seaman, camped for nine days on the Snake River at present-day Clarkston, from October 1 to 10, 1805. Plan your own stop here to visit the **Lewis and Clark Expedition Timeline,** etched and painted in the pavement at Hells Canyon Marina, 1550 Port Drive. The nearly blocklong timeline illustrates key events from the Corps of Discovery's journey across the western half of the United States, including canoeing down sections of the nearby Snake River and the Columbia River on their way to the Pacific Ocean. U.S. Highway 12 from Lewiston and Clarkston west toward Pomeroy and Dayton roughly parallels the party's return journey in 1806. For a state-by-state listing of happenings and activities following the Lewis and Clark Bicentennial, browse www.lewisandclark200.org.

After all this busy history browsing you may be ready for some vittles. Check out **Sun Bean Coffeehouse Cafe** at 720 Sixth Street in Clarkston (509–751–8887) for great breads, soups, and sandwiches; find tasty homemade pie and cool libations at the old-fashioned soda fountain at **Wasem's Drug-**

store, 800 Sixth Street (509–758–2565); and for waterside dining with great views call ***Rooster's Waterfront Restaurant*** on the Snake River at 1550 Port Drive (509–751–0155). Travelers with RVs can find a scenic spot to hook up at ***Granite Lake RV Resort,*** 306 Granite Lake Drive (509–751–1635) just east of the port and overlooking the Snake River.

Heading west on US 12, you many want to stop and explore Pomeroy. Park 1 block over on Columbia Street, where you'll see colorful flower beds planted down the center of the street where the train tracks once ran. Browse along Main Street and poke into inviting shops such as ***Three Forks Art Gallery,*** 804 Main Street; ***Victorian Rose & Collectibles,*** 741 Main Street; and ***Pomeroy Pharmacy & Gifts,*** 764 Main Street. Detour into eclectic ***Meyer's Hardware,*** 796 Main Street (509–843–3721), for coffee and espresso drinks.

You can also bed down in Pomeroy in a comfy style by checking on guest rooms at the ***Picket Porch Bed & Breakfast*** at 266 Fourteenth Street (509–843–1150). If you're traveling RV-style and want hookups, call the ***Last Resort RV Park*** at 2005 Tucannon Road (509–843–1556), about 10 miles south of Pomeroy in the scenic Umatilla National Forest. The Forest Service ranger station at 71 West Main Street (509–843–1891) just west of Pomeroy can supply maps and information about forest camping, hiking, and fishing (including flyfishing) along the Tucannon River.

The town of ***Dayton*** is another well-preserved historic community. When Lewis and Clark explored the region on their return trip in 1806, what is now

Poke into History in Pomeroy and Pataha

Off US 12 between Clarkston and Dayton are the small towns of Pomeroy and Pataha, where you can snoop into local history.

In Pataha, pull off at 50 Hutchens Hill Road to see the old **Pataha Flour Mill** (509–843–3799), which now houses a fine restaurant, gift shop, and historical memorabilia of the Garfield County area.

In Pomeroy, you can check out the ca. 1916 **Seeley Building** at 67 Seventh Street, which housed an early vaudeville theater; the **Historic Hotel Revere** at the corner of Main and Seventh Streets, which is under renovation; the **Garfield County Museum** at 708 Columbia Street (509–843–3925), open Friday afternoons and by appointment for groups; and the **Denny Ashby Memorial Library,** 856 Arlington Street (509–843–3710), open Monday, Tuesday, and Thursday afternoons. At the **Pomeroy City Park,** off Fifteenth Street, is a plaque that shows where the Lewis and Clark Corps of Discovery camped on May 3, 1806, on the return trip.

Dayton's main street served as a racetrack for Native tribes who camped in the area. Although this land was first homesteaded by cattle ranchers in 1859, grain farming took over within a few years. Dayton was also a stagecoach stop between Walla Walla and Lewiston. Logs from the Blue Mountains traveled down to the town mill by an 18-mile flume. By 1880 Dayton had become the Columbia County seat.

To see the historic **Dayton Depot** (509–382–2026), the oldest existing railway station in the state, turn west from Main Street onto Commercial. The depot is open from 10:00 A.M. to 5:00 P.M. Tuesday through Saturday. For information about self-guided historic walking tours and the lively **Dayton's Depot Days Festival** in mid-September, contact the Dayton Visitor Information Center at (509) 382–4825; www.historicdayton.com.

The **Purple House Bed and Breakfast** at 415 East Clay Street (509–382–3159), built in 1882 by a pioneer physician and philanthropist, is one of Dayton's finest homes. Travelers find four guest rooms, a guest library, a lovely parlor, and an outdoor pool. To linger a day or two you could also call the friendly innkeepers at the ca. 1893 **McCann Manor Bed & Breakfast** at 212 South Second Street (509–382–8967; www.mccannmanor.com).

Just for fun stop by **Dingles of Dayton,** at 179 East Main Street (509–382–2581). In this old-fashioned general store, you'll find everything from nuts and bolts, nails and screws, and plumbing supplies, to teddy bears, coloring books, crystal glassware, and fishing rods. "If you can't find it at Dingles, you don't need it," proclaims the store motto.

If exploring makes you thirsty, stop at the **Elk Drug Store** at 270 Main Street to order milkshakes and sodas from an old-fashioned soda fountain. Step back in time in grand style at the ca. 1889 **Weinhard Hotel** (235 East Main Street; 509–382–4032; www.weinhard.com), restored in a Victorian motif with 14-foot-high ceilings, elaborate antiques, and a rooftop garden. All fifteen

Patit Creek Campsite: Camping Lewis and Clark Style

On May 2, 1806, the Lewis and Clark Corps of Discovery camped near Dayton for one night on their return trip home. Some eighty life-size metal silhouette sculptures produced and arranged on the site by Dayton artists and community members show the entire party setting up camp. The silhouettes include horses, cooking gear, and even Clark's dog, Seaman. To reach the site, turn off US 12 just north of downtown Dayton and onto Patit Creek Road.

rooms have private baths and antique furniture. Enjoy fine Italian specialties at *Weinhard's Cafe,* at 229 East Main Street (509–382–1681). The cafe is open Tuesday through Saturday for lunch and dinner. For gourmet fare and great desserts in a comfortable setting, try the popular *Patit Creek Restaurant* at 725 East Dayton Avenue, on US 12 at the north end of town (509–382–2625). Another local favorite, *Skye Book & Brew* at 148 East Main Street (509–382–4677), offers good reads along with microbrews, espresso, and casual fare. *Panhandlers Restaurant,* 400 West Main Street (509–382–4160), open daily from 7:00 A.M. to 8:00 P.M., offers good breakfasts as well as steaks, burgers, salads, and tasty desserts. For espresso, cinnamon rolls, soups, and sandwiches, don't miss *Patit Valley Products Cafe* at 232 East Main Street (509–382–1998).

Dayton is the access point for the Blue Mountains in the Umatilla National Forest, which includes the *Wenaha-Tucannon Wilderness,* an area of steep ridges, talus slopes, and tablelands accessible only by backcountry trails. Wildlife includes Rocky Mountain elk, white-tailed and mule deer, bighorn sheep, black bear, cougar, and bobcat. For information about backcountry camping and hiking, call the Pomeroy Ranger Station at (509) 843–1891. During the winter months, ski buffs enjoy *Ski Bluewood* (509–382–4725; www .bluewood.com) in the Blue Mountains, 22 miles southeast of Dayton. Its Skyline Express chair provides a vertical rise of 1,125 feet and more than twenty downhill runs. There are also runs for beginning and intermediate skiers.

Palouse Falls State Park, located 30 miles north of Dayton, offers a glimpse of what the many river canyons in the area looked like before most were dammed. The falls tumble 198 feet over basalt-column cliffs, surrounded by grass- and sage-covered hills. On the way north to the falls via Highway 261, those who love flyfishing may want to pause in the small community of *Starbuck* to visit *Darver Tackle Shop* at 105 McNeil Street (509–399–2015). Flyfishing gurus tie flies, tell stories, and offer fishing tackle for sale in this small shop that draws folks from all over the region. Ease into *Howes Cafe* on Main Street (509–399–2211) for good eats. From here you cross the Snake River via a bridge rather than on the old Lyons Ferry that once carried vehicles across, then proceed about 7 miles to Palouse Falls State Park. Although this park offers only ten primitive campsites, nearby *Lyons Ferry State Park* (www.parks.wa.gov) offers fifty standard campsites with no hookups. *Lyons Ferry Marina* (509–399–8020), on the Snake River just off Highway 261, offers RV sites, boat-launch facilities, and a cozy eatery, *Coffees on Cafe.*

To the south, toward *Walla Walla,* the Walla Walla Valley is known primarily for fertile fields of grain, but since the late 1980s the valley also hosts some twenty wineries and large vineyards with such gourmet grapes as merlot, cabernet sauvignon, and syrah harvested each year. Tasting rooms abound in

Palouse Falls

the valley. For lists and maps check with the Walla Walla Area Visitor Information Center at 29 East Sumach Street, Walla Walla (509–525–0850 or 877–998–4748; www.wallawalla.com). You can also collect self-guided walking tour maps for the nostalgic downtown area and helpful information about the bustling arts scene in this farm and college town. The **Walla Walla Foundry** (509–522–2114) specializes in bronze but also produces works in gold, silver, and aluminum. You can visit more than twenty eclectic art galleries and also see twenty-four historic homes in the area.

Downtown, after browsing the art galleries, gift shops, historic buildings, and antiques shops that range along Main Street, join the locals and relax in **Heritage Square,** nestled in the heart of town. On one side of the square, you'll see a mural of nineteenth-century downtown Walla Walla. On the opposite wall is the 1902 Odd Fellows building facade. The park also has playground equipment, a picnic area, and restrooms. Or, for a pleasant lunch on a sunny day, you can find an outdoor table under the striped awning at **Merchants LTD & French Bakery,** 21 East Main Street (509–525–0900), which also offers espresso, a take-out deli, freshly baked pastries, and regional wines. Locals suggest **Colville Street Patisserie,** 40 South Colville Street (509–301–7289), for desserts, wines, and espresso.

Walla Walla is home to several inviting bed-and-breakfast inns and guest ranches. The ca. 1909 Craftsman-style **Green Gables Inn Bed and Breakfast,** 922 Bonsella Street (509–525–5501; www.greengablesinn.com) has served as a family home, a residence for nurses, and most recently was renovated by Jim and Margaret Buchan with warm colors, handsome woodwork, splendid window treatments, and fine period antiques. Five guest rooms offer elegant and comfortable havens with private baths. Two of the rooms have private outside decks. A separate carriage house cottage sleeps four and comes equipped with a full kitchen.

You could also call the innkeepers at *Inn at Blackberry Creek,* 1126 Pleasant Street (509–520–5732; www.innatblackberrycreek.com), a ca. 1912 Victorian farmhouse offering travelers three guest rooms and tasty breakfasts.

For those who want to get farther away from civilization, call the owners at *Top of the Mountain Cabins* at 9052 Mill Creek Road (509–529–4288; www.mountainretreats.com). You can even bring your horses. Ask about the three secluded cabins located at a crisp fresh-air elevation of 3,800 feet next to the Umatilla National Forest. The cabins come with bed and bath linens, cozy sitting areas, woodstoves, kitchenettes with eating and cooking utensils, and patio furniture. *Note:* Those who have four-wheel-drive vehicles can best negotiate the bumpy mountain road up to the cabins. Bring your own food supplies.

You don't have a horse and you don't relish eating at the top of a mountain? Not to worry—you can find great eateries in Walla Walla. Check out another local favorite, *Clarette's Restaurant,* 15 South Touchet Street (509–529–3430), for all-American-style fare and all-day breakfast; *Cookie Tree Bakery & Cafe*

Live Theater in the Far Southeast Corner

Linger and enjoy getting acquainted with local folks and avid thespians by taking in a live theater production along your travels. Musicals, comedies, and dramas galore are offered in communities large and small throughout the year.

Pullman Civic Theatre (509–332–8406; www.pullmancivictheatre.org) performs five plays yearly, including such favorites as *The King and I* and *The Homecoming.*

Idaho Repertory Theatre (208–885–7212; www.uitheatre.com) in nearby Moscow, Idaho, performs in the 417-seat Hartung Theatre on the University of Idaho campus. Recent offerings included *Lend Me a Tenor* and *The Comedy of Errors.*

Liberty Theater, Dayton (509–382–1380; www.libertytheater.org). Local productions by the **Touchet Valley Art Council** have entertained audiences with musicals such as *Oliver!, The Sound of Music, Oklahoma!,* and *The Music Man.*

The Little Theatre of Walla Walla (509–529–3683; www.ltww.org) has produced plays since 1944. Current offerings include *Harvey, 1940s Radio Hour, The Cemetery Club,* and *Charlotte's Web.*

Summer Outdoor Musical, Fort Walla Walla Park. The Community College Foundation (509–527–4275) offers such Broadway favorites as *South Pacific* and *The Music Man.*

Harper Joy Theatre in Walla Walla (509–527–5180; www.whitman.edu) has presented *The Merchant of Venice* and *Urinetown: The Musical.*

(23 South Spokane Street; 509–522–4826) for homemade sandwiches, espresso, cookies, and pastries; and *Mill Creek Brew Pub & Restaurant* (11 South Palouse Street; 509–522–2440) for good pub food and regional ales.

Southwest of town is the splendid *Fort Walla Walla Museum Complex* (509–525–7703; www.fortwallawallamuseum.org) at 755 Myra Road on the grounds of Fort Walla Walla Park. The museum complex includes a re-created pioneer village with fourteen historic log buildings filled with antique household items and settlers' tools. There are also six large museum buildings with additional displays of pioneer life, equipment from horse-farming days, and railroad equipment. The historical complex is open daily from 10:00 A.M. to 5:00 P.M., from April to October. Nominal admission fees help maintain and support museum development.

Be sure to also visit the *Whitman Mission National Historic Site* 7 miles west of town (509–522–6360; www.nps.gov/whmi), which commemorates the mission established there by Marcus and Narcissa Whitman in the early 1800s. Museum displays and an interpretive trail on the mission grounds describe the history of the region and bring to life activities in the Walla Walla Valley between 1836 and 1847, when waves of settlers stopped at the mission on their arduous trek along the Oregon Trail. For a panoramic view of the grounds, walk through the small grove of trees, past the tepee, and up the path to the nearby hilltop monument. Although the original buildings did not survive the years, their locations are outlined on the grounds. The visitor center is open daily from 8:00 A.M. to 6:00 P.M. in summer and 8:00 A.M. to 4:30 P.M. in winter.

Places to Stay in Southeast Washington

CLARKSTON

Best Western Rivertree Inn
1257 Bridge Street
(800) 597–3621

COLFAX

Union Creek Guest Ranch
2501 Upper Union Flat Road
(509) 397–3292

DAYTON

McCann Manor Bed & Breakfast
212 South Second Street
(509) 382–8967

Mill House Cottage
504 North First Street
(509) 382–2393

The Weinhard Hotel
235 East Main Street
(509) 382–4032

POMEROY

The Picket Porch Bed & Breakfast
266 Fourteenth Street
(509) 843–1150

PULLMAN

Paradise Creek Quality Inn
Southeast 1050 Bishop Boulevard
(509) 332–0500

UNIONTOWN

Premier Alpacas Ranch & Guest House
401 South Railroad Avenue
(509) 229–3655

SELECTED VISITOR INFORMATION CENTERS

Clarkston Visitor Information Center
(509) 758–7712, (800) 933–2128

Colfax Chamber of Commerce
(509) 397–3712

Dayton Visitor Information Center
(509) 382–4825, (800) 882–6299

Pullman Visitor Information Center
(509) 334–3565, (800) 365–6948
www.pullmanchamber.com

Walla Walla Area Visitor Information Center
(509) 525–0850
www.wallawalla.com

WALLA WALLA

Best Western Walla Walla Suites Inn
7 East Oak Street
(509) 525–4700

Green Gables Inn Bed & Breakfast
922 Bonsella Street
(509) 525–5501

Inn at Blackberry Creek Bed & Breakfast
1126 Pleasant Street
(509) 520–7372

Places to Eat in Southeast Washington

CLARKSTON/LEWISTON

Bogey's Restaurant at Quality Inn
700 Port Drive
(509) 758–9500

The Sugar Shack
923 Sixth Street
(509) 758–2090

Sycamore Street Grille
900 Sixth Street
(509) 758–0881

Rooster's Waterfront Restaurant
1550 Port Drive
(509) 751–0155

COLFAX

Top Notch Cafe
210 North Main Street
(509) 397–4569

DAYTON

Country Cupboard Bakery, Deli, & Espresso
330 East Main Street
(509) 382–2215

HELPFUL WEB SITES IN SOUTHEAST WASHINGTON

Historic Dayton
www.historicdayton.com

Walla Walla Area Visitor Information
www.wallawalla.com

Washington Road Conditions
(800) 695–7623
www.wsdot.wa.gov/traffic

Welcome to Pullman-Moscow
www.pullmanchamber.com
www.moscowchamber.com

Patit Valley Products Cafe
232 Main Street
(509) 382–1998

Skye Book & Brew
148 East Main Street
(509) 382–4677

Weinhard's Cafe
229 East Main Street
(509) 382–1681

PALOUSE

The Family Cafe
124 West Main Street
(509) 878–1716

Green Frog Coffee Shop Cafe
110 South Bridge Street
(509) 878–1490

PULLMAN

Café Moro Coffee House
100 East Main Street
(509) 338–3892

Daily Grind Coffee House
230 Main Street
(509) 334–3380

Ferdinand's Ice Cream Shoppe
Food Quality Building
WSU Campus
(509) 335–2141

The Fireside Grille
195 SE Bishop Boulevard
(509) 334–3663

TEKOA

The Feeding Station
205 North Crosby
(509) 284–3141

UNIONTOWN

Eleanor's Place
Main Street (US 195)
(509) 229–3389

WALLA WALLA

Clarette's Restaurant
15 South Touchet Street
(509) 529–3430

Coffee Connection Cafe
57 East Main Street
(509) 529–9999

JP's on the Green
Milton-Freewater Golf Course
299 Catherine Avenue
Milton-Freewater, OR
(541) 938–0911

Stone Soup Cafe
105 East Main Street
(509) 525–5008

ALSO WORTH SEEING

Charles Houston Shattuck Arboretum
(ca. 1910)
Univeristy of Idaho, Moscow
(208) 885–6250

Frazier Farmstead Museum and Gardens
Milton-Freewater, Oregon

Useful Resources

Government Agency Resources

Bicycle Program

Washington State Department of Transportation

310 Maple Park Avenue

Olympia, 98501

(360) 705–7277

Call this "bicycle hotline" for information on bicycling in Washington.

National Park Service, U.S. Forest Service Outdoor Recreation Information Center

222 Yale Avenue North

Seattle, 98109

(206) 470–4060

www.nps.gov and www.fs.fed.us/r6

Information on camping, hiking, and trail conditions for western Washington's National Parks and Forests.

North Cascades National Park Service Complex (U.S. Department of the Interior), Mount Baker Ranger District (U.S.D.A. Forest Service), and North Cascades Institute

810 State Route 20

Sedro-Woolley, 98284

(360) 856–5700, extension 515 (recreation desk)

www.nps.gov/noca and www.fsfed.us/r6/mbs

Information about North Cascades National Park, Mount Baker and Mount Baker Ranger District, Ross Lake, and Lake Chelan. Contact North Cascades Institute for a current catalog of year-round seminars on Washington State's natural and cultural history. The complex, about 5 miles east of I–5, is open daily 8:00 A.M. to 4:30 P.M. from Memorial Day weekend through mid-October and Monday through Friday (same hours) during the rest of the year. Farther east on Highway 20, and 14 miles east of Marblemount, the North Cascades Visitor Center in Newhalem (206–386–4495) is open daily from 9:00 A.M. to 4:30 P.M.

Washington Department of Fish and Wildlife

21961 Wylie Road
Mount Vernon, 98273
(360) 445-4441
www.wdfw.wa.gov/
Ask about the Great Washington State Birding Trail map for the Cascade Loop. The Cascade Loop map details sixty-eight places to visit, hike, and view bird species, from the shores of Puget Sound to the North Cascade Mountains and eastern high desert.

Washington State Department of Natural Resources

111 Washington Street SE
P.O. Box 47016
Olympia, 98504
www.dnr.wa.gov
DNR manages more than 135 primitive recreation sites with hiking trails, 4WD roads, and limited backcountry facilities.

Washington State Ferries

Colman Dock/Pier 52
801 Alaskan Way
Seattle, 98104-1487
For schedule information call (206) 464–6400 in Seattle or in-state only (800) 808–7977
www.wsdot.wa.gov/ferries

Washington State Parks and Recreation Commission

7153 Cleanwater Lane
Olympia, 98504
(360) 902–8844 (Monday to Friday, 8:00 A.M. to 5:00 P.M.)
www.parks.wa.gov
Information on state parks and campgrounds available for day and overnight stays.

Washington Tourist Information

off Capitol Way on the Capital grounds in Olympia
(360) 586–3460
Call (800) 544–1800 to request a Washington Travel Kit that includes the *Washington State Traveler's Guide*.
U.S.–Canadian Border Crossing Information
(206) 553–0770
www.customs.treas.gov

Other Resources

Artguide Northwest

Tipton Publishing Company

13205 Ninth Avenue NW

Seattle, 98177

(206) 367–6831

This semiannual guide lists all galleries, museums, and antiques shops west of the Cascades.

Birds and Birding: Web sites

Audubon Washington: www.wa.audubon.org

Seattle Audubon Society online guide: www.birdweb.org

Tweeters e-mail list on birds and birding in Cascadia, hosted by Burke
    Museum at University of Washington: www.scn.org/earth/tweeters

Washington Ornithological Society: www.wos.org

Exploring Washington's Past: A Road Guide to History

Ruth Kirk and Carmela Alexander

University of Washington Press

Seattle, 1989

This comprehensive handbook describes local history for much of Washington, including fascinating stories and insights about many of the places described in *Washington Off the Beaten Path*.

Olympic Park Institute

111 Barnes Point Road

Port Angeles, 98363

(800) 775–3720 or (360) 928–3720

www.olympicparkinstitute.org

Call for a free catalog of backcountry-related courses in Olympic National Park and courses at the institute located at the historic Rosemary Inn complex on Lake Crescent.

Plants and Animals of the Pacific Northwest

Eugene Kozloff

University of Washington Press

Seattle, 1976

This interesting and informative guide is the ideal companion for amateur naturalists.

Sierra Club, Cascade Chapter
1516 Melrose Avenue
Seattle, 98122
For outings and events information check
www.cascade.sierraclub.org

Sound Experience
2310 Washington Street
Port Townsend, 98368
(360) 379–0438
www.soundexp.org
A nonprofit educational organization specializing in environmental, marine science, and sailing programs for youths and adults aboard the 136-foot-long ca. 1913 tall ship *Adventuress.*

Washington Atlas & Gazeteer
DeLorme Publishing
This atlas provides topographical maps covering all of Washington State at approximately half an inch to the mile, making it ideal for exploring back roads.

Washington Hiking Trails Association
(206) 625–1367
www.wta.org

Washington Water Trails Association
4649 Sunnyside Avenue North
Room 305
Seattle, 98103-6900
(206) 545–9161
www.wwta.org
Promotes preservation of marine shorelines and the creation of the Cascadia Marine Trail, a network of sites accessible to kayaks and canoes throughout Puget Sound. At a cost of $25, membership includes a water trail guidebook and quarterly newsletter.

Indexes

Entries for Lodgings and Museums appear only in the special indexes on pages 220–24.

LODGINGS

MUSEUMS

About the Author

Myrna Oakley has traveled the byways of the Pacific Northwest and western British Columbia since 1970, always with a camera in hand and an inquisitive eye for natural and scenic areas, as well as for small inns, scenic and historic gardens, and places with historical character and significance. In this process she has developed an affinity for goosedown comforters, friendly conversations by the fire, and intriguing people who generally prefer to live somewhat off the beaten path.

In addition to *Washington Off the Beaten Path*, she has written *Oregon Off the Beaten Path, Recommended Bed & Breakfasts: Pacific Northwest, Public and Private Gardens of the Northwest,* and *Bed and Breakfast Northwest.* She teaches about the business of freelance writing, novel writing, and travel writing at local colleges and universities in the Portland environs. She also dreams about writing a mystery novel for young adults and plans to sneak away one of these days to one of the islands with her voluminous files and laptop computer.